Cultural Studies of Law

This edited collection is a cultural analysis of how law is shaped into procedure and principle by the conditions of everyday life. Law is constitutive of culture just as culture and cultural analyses shape, resist and interrogate legal regulation, exception and norms. So too does law have a dual capacity in the field of culture: it enables the formation of subjects and of cultural practices, and it constrains those very formations. This book uses the animating critical concerns of cultural studies over the last 20 years – that is, the symbolic, material, economic, and political practices and power relations that are inscribed in everyday life – to analyse the assembly of practices, procedures, sites, interactions and agents of law. The chapters in this collection accordingly examine the conditions of law's everyday life, in situations ordinary and extraordinary, to show it in the moment of its working.

This book was originally published as a special issue of *Cultural Studies*.

Cristyn Davies is a Research Associate at the University of Sydney, Australia. She has published widely in cultural studies and, gender and sexuality studies.

Sara L. Knox is an Associate Professor in the School of Humanities and Communication Arts, University of Western Sydney, Australia. She is an interdisciplinary scholar researching the representation of violence in a range of cultural sites.

Cultural Studies of Law

Edited by
Cristyn Davies and Sara L. Knox

LONDON AND NEW YORK

First published 2014 by Routledge

2 Park Square, Milton Park, Abingdon, Oxfordshire OX14 4RN
711 Third Avenue, New York, NY 10017

Routledge is an imprint of the Taylor & Francis Group, an informa business

First issued in paperback 2018

Copyright © 2014 Taylor & Francis
Images in Chapter 3 © 1962 Pakula-Mulligan Productions, Inc. and Brentwood Productions, Inc.

All rights reserved. No part of this book may be reprinted or reproduced or utilised in any form or by any electronic, mechanical, or other means, now known or hereafter invented, including photocopying and recording, or in any information storage or retrieval system, without permission in writing from the publishers.

Notice:
Product or corporate names may be trademarks or registered trademarks, and are used only for identification and explanation without intent to infringe.

British Library Cataloguing in Publication Data
A catalogue record for this book is available from the British Library

ISBN 13: 978-1-138-01855-6 (hbk)
ISBN 13: 978-1-138-37919-0 (pbk)

Typeset in Sabon
by Taylor & Francis Books

Publisher's Note
The publisher accepts responsibility for any inconsistencies that may have arisen during the conversion of this book from journal articles to book chapters, namely the possible inclusion of journal terminology.

Disclaimer
Every effort has been made to contact copyright holders for their permission to reprint material in this book. The publishers would be grateful to hear from any copyright holder who is not here acknowledged and will undertake to rectify any errors or omissions in future editions of this book.

Contents

Citation Information   vii
Notes on Contributors   ix

1. The Force of Meaning: Cultural Studies of Law
   Sara L. Knox and Cristyn Davies   1

2. Memory and Echo: Pop cult, hi tech and the irony of tradition
   Desmond Manderson   11

3. Temporal Horizons: On the possibilities of Law and Fatherhood in
   To Kill a Mockingbird
   Austin Sarat and Martha Merrill Umphrey   30

4. Entertaining Torture, Embodying Law
   Peter J. Hutchings   49

5. Instrumental and Gratuitous Violence: The torture and death of
   Gul Rahman in the CIA Salt Pit
   Joseph Pugliese   72

6. Constructing 'Decency': Government subsidized cultural production
   during the culture wars
   Cristyn Davies   92

7. Weapons of Sex, Weapons of War: Feminisms, ethnic conflict and
   the rise of rape and sexual violence in public international law during
   the 1990s
   Rana Jaleel   115

8. Legitimating Transphobia: The legal disavowal of transgender rights
   in prison
   John Nguyet Erni   136

Index   161

Citation Information

The chapters in this book were originally published in *Cultural Studies*, volume 27, issue 1 (January 2013). When citing this material, please use the original page numbering for each article, as follows:

Chapter 1
The Force of Meaning: Cultural Studies of Law
Sara L. Knox and Cristyn Davies
Cultural Studies, volume 27, issue 1 (January 2013) pp. 1–10

Chapter 2
Memory and Echo: Pop cult, hi tech and the irony of tradition
Desmond Manderson
Cultural Studies, volume 27, issue 1 (January 2013) pp. 11–29

Chapter 3
Temporal Horizons: On the possibilities of Law and Fatherhood in To Kill a Mockingbird
Austin Sarat and Martha Merrill Umphrey
Cultural Studies, volume 27, issue 1 (January 2013) pp. 30–48

Chapter 4
Entertaining Torture, Embodying Law
Peter J. Hutchings
Cultural Studies, volume 27, issue 1 (January 2013) pp. 49–71

Chapter 5
Instrumental and Gratuitous Violence: The torture and death of Gul Rahman in the CIA Salt Pit
Joseph Pugliese
Cultural Studies, volume 27, issue 1 (January 2013) pp. 72–91

CITATION INFORMATION

Chapter 6
Constructing 'Decency': Government subsidized cultural production during the culture wars
Cristyn Davies
Cultural Studies, volume 27, issue 1 (January 2013) pp. 92–114

Chapter 7
Weapons of Sex, Weapons of War: Feminisms, ethnic conflict and the rise of rape and sexual violence in public international law during the 1990s
Rana Jaleel
Cultural Studies, volume 27, issue 1 (January 2013) pp. 115–135

Chapter 8
Legitimating Transphobia: The legal disavowal of transgender rights in prison
John Nguyet Erni
Cultural Studies, volume 27, issue 1 (January 2013) pp. 136–159

Please direct any queries you may have about the citations to clsuk.permissions@cengage.com

Notes on Contributors

Cristyn Davies is a Research Associate at the University of Sydney, Australia. She has worked in research across the tertiary and private sectors at the intersections of Cultural Studies, Humanities and the Social Sciences. Her doctoral research investigates the impact of the culture wars in the USA on cultural policy, cultural production and gendered and sexual citizenship. Her areas of expertise include gendered and sexual subjectivities; cultural policy, regulation and moral panic; neoliberalism and governmentality; constructions of childhood and youth and narrative and (heritage and new) media. She has authored and co-authored articles in journals including: *Sexualities, Cultural Studies Review, Contemporary Issues in Early Childhood and Australian Feminist Studies*. She is coeditor of: *Rethinking School Violence: Theory, Gender, Context* (2012), and *Queer and Subjugated Knowledges: Generating Subversive Imaginaries* (2012). She has collaborated with academics, writers, performance artists and digital and new media artists on a range of projects.

John Nguyet Erni is Professor and Head of the Department of Cultural Studies, Lingnan University, Hong Kong. His books include: *Unstable Frontiers: Technomedicine and the Cultural Politics of "Curing" AIDS, Internationalizing Cultural Studies: An Anthology* (with Ackbar Abbas), *Asian Media Studies: The Politics of Subjectivities* (with Siew Keng Chua), and *Cultural Studies of Rights: Critical Articulations* (2011). Over the past few years, since completing a Master of Laws in Human Rights in 2005, he has been focusing his work on the cultural politics of human rights (especially over the questions of gender/sexual rights, human rights documentaries and environmental rights). He is completing a book on rethinking human rights as a cultural studies project, and co-authoring a book on the politics of racial discrimination in Hong Kong.

Peter J. Hutchings is Professor and Dean of the School of Humanities and Communication Arts at the University of Western Sydney, Australia. Previously, he has worked at the University of Sydney, the Boston University Sydney program, the University of Hong Kong, and at the Australian

NOTES ON CONTRIBUTORS

Learning and Teaching Council. He is also the past President and Vice-President of the Law and Literature Association of Australia. His publications have appeared in local and international refereed journals as well as in the mainstream print media, and he is the author of *The Criminal Spectre in Law, Literature and Aesthetics: Incriminating Subjects* (2001). His current research is on sovereignty and cinema after 9/11.

Rana Jaleel is a PhD candidate in the Program in American Studies, Department of Social and Cultural Analysis at New York University, USA. She holds a JD from Yale Law School.

Sara L. Knox is Associate Professor in the School of Humanities and Communication Arts at the University of Western Sydney, Australia, and a member of the Writing and Society Research Group. She is author of *Murder: a Tale of Modern American Life* (1998). Her ongoing scholarly research is divided between concern with death, violence and representation and the altogether more upbeat subject of contemporary cultures of reading. Her most recent work includes a chapter on 'Random School Shootings, Teen Culture and the Representation of Violence', in *Rethinking School Violence: Theory, Gender, Context* (2012) and her contribution to a collection of essays on audiobook culture, *Audiobooks, Literature and Sound Studies* (2011). Her novel, *The Orphan Gunner* (2007), won the 2009 Asher Literary Prize and was shortlisted for the Commonwealth Writer's Prize and for the Age Book of the Year.

Desmond Manderson is an international leader in interdisciplinary scholarship in law and the humanities and the author of several books including *From Mr Sin to Mr Big* (1993); *Songs Without Music: Aesthetic Dimensions of Law and Justice* (2000); *Proximity, Levinas, and the Soul of Law* (2006); and *Kangaroo Courts and the Rule of Law – The Legacy of Modernism*. His work has led to essays, books, and lectures around the world in the fields of English, philosophy, ethics, history, cultural studies, music, and anthropology, as well as in law and legal theory, through which he has articulated a vision in which law's connection to these humanist disciplines is critical to its functioning, its justice, and its social relevance. From 2002 to 2011 he held the Canada Research Chair (Tier 1) in Law and Discourse in the Faculty of Law at McGill University, Montreal, Canada and in 2009, he became Foundation Director of the Institute for the Public Life of Arts and Ideas. In 2012, he returned to Australia in order to take up a prestigious Australian Research Council Future Fellowship at the Australian National University, where he holds a joint professorial appointment in the ANU College of Law and the Research School of Humanities and the Arts.

Joseph Pugliese is an Associate Professor and Discipline Leader of Cultural Studies in the Department of Media, Music, Communication and Cultural Studies, Macquarie University, Australia. He has published widely on state violence, bodies and technologies, refugees and asylum seekers and cultural studies of law. His most recent publications include an edited collection: *Transmediterranean: Diasporas, Histories, Geopolitical Spaces* (2010) and a monograph: *Biometrics: Bodies, Technologies, Biopolitics* (2010). He is currently working on a forthcoming monograph titled *State Violence and Execution of Law: Biopolitical Caesurae of Torture, Black Sites, Drones*.

Austin Sarat is William Nelson Cromwell Professor of Jurisprudence & Political Science and Director of the Mellon Project on Student-Faculty Research at Amherst College, USA. He is the author or editor of more than 70 books. Among his most recent books are *Subjects of Responsibility: Framing Personhood in Modern Bureaucracies* (co-edited with Andrew Parker and Martha Merrill Umphrey) (2011) and *When Governments Break the Law: the Rule of Law and the Prosecution of the Bush Administration* (co-edited with Nasser Hussain) (2010). Among his numerous prizes and awards is the James Boyd White Prize from the Association for the Study of Law, Culture and the Humanities, awarded for distinguished scholarly achievement and outstanding and innovative contributions to the humanistic study of law.

Martha Merrill Umphrey is Professor of Law, Jurisprudence and Social Thought at Amherst College, USA. Among her many publications she is the editor of *TRIALS* and co-editor (with Austin Sarat and Lawrence Douglas) of a series published by Stanford University Press – the *Amherst Series in Law, Jurisprudence & Social Thought*.

Sara L. Knox and Cristyn Davies

THE FORCE OF MEANING

Cultural Studies of Law

Introduction

Law has a dual capacity in the field of culture: it enables the formation of subjects and of cultural practices, and it constrains those very formations. The tensions created by that paradox are instrumental in constituting the political field. Cultural Studies of Law move beyond textual analysis by attending to the networks of social practices through which law is constitutive of culture just as culture and cultural analyses shape, resist and interrogate legal regulation, exception and norms. Law is a cultural product, but its operations, venues and discourses are unique, as is its coercive power. We take it as given that the law must act to efface both its own rhetoricity and its interestedness in order to function as law, and in this way stands in awkward relation to culture, and to history. A Cultural Studies of Law is anodyne, therefore, in seeking not just to make the law accountable but to show that law might be taken as the preeminent object of culture – preeminent precisely because of its claims to neutrality and objectivity.

Law's intersections with disciplines from the Humanities and Social Sciences were well established even before the so-called 'cultural turn'. Legal anthropology, beginning with Malinowski's work on systems of reciprocity and authority in *Crime and Custom in a Savage Society* (1926), established the grounds of legal pluralism and, in examining the tensions between formal and informal systems of law, opened up the study of law (what it is, how it works and upon what) to embrace a wider cultural field. The development of the concerns of legal anthropology with normative systems and their operation in the 1980s was carried forward by feminist and critical legal scholars in increasingly complex theoretical analyses of law's presumptive space 'above' culture, a thinking through of law's relation to culture that proposed the dependences of the former in the concept of *interlegality*: 'the intersubjective or phenomenological dimension of legal pluralism' (de Sousa Santos 2002, p. 97). At the same time, interdisciplinary law and history scholars were unpicking the quite different ways in which the disciplinary practices of law and history understood and 'legislated' the past – differences consequential for peoples figured as incompetent of exercising sovereign rights; whose present claims (for land, cultural independence, language, etc.) continue in the spectral realm of exclusion (e.g. Fitzpatrick (2001) on imperialism and the semantics of 'discovery').

In terms of a discussion of Law and Cultural Studies, and the basis for a Cultural Studies of Law, it is the Critical Legal Studies 'movement' that is of most significance here. As David Saunders suggests, the 'Leftist' reformist ambit of Critical Legal Studies (CLS) was two-fold. It sought to re-invent law from the inside out with an excoriating critique of legal education and its curricula, and from the outside in by re-imagining the precepts and claims of law in socio-political terms: making law account for itself (Saunders 2007, p. 80) by casting light upon its hidden workings and operations of meaning that order, occlude and exclude. In Saunders' view of the movement, this 'critical unblocking' (Saunders 2007, p. 83) produced more sound than fury. The intellectual energy of the movement dispersed over the 20 years following its founding in the Wisconsin–Madison Conference in 1977, partly through a process of the narrowing and migration of its concerns into other fields of scholarship; and partly due to the success of the CLS intervention itself. The critical concerns of the movement have inflected the direction of legal education, even if only modestly, and so too have the attacks of CLS on legal positivism had lasting effect: indeed, effects deducible from the concerns of the work of the scholars collected here.

Following the theoretical turn of CLS, and on the heels of the law and literature movement's initiation of the 'textualist' turn, scholars across both Cultural Studies and Law have focused their attention on mapping or re-orienting the intersections between their disciplines. Thanks to the growth in the scholarly field of law and literature, and the vigour of critical legal theory and feminist legal studies, the relationship of law to culture continues to receive attention, but arguably there is more to be made of those small but instructive words yoking the disciplines. The phrase *Cultural Studies of Law* suggests that the animating critical concerns of Cultural Studies over the last 20 years – that is, the symbolic, material, economic, and political practices and power relations that are inscribed in everyday life – should be brought to bear upon the assembly of practices, procedures, sites, interactions and agents of law. Such inquiry has emerged through special editions of journals such as this one, and also through key monographs and edited collections which include, but are not limited to, Robert Post's (1991) *Law and the order of culture*; Steve Redhead's (1995) *Unpopular Cultures: The Birth of Law and Popular Culture*; Paul W. Kahn's (1999) *The Cultural Study of Law: Reconstructing Legal Scholarship*; Austin Sarat and Thomas R. Kearns' (1998) *Law in the Domains of Culture*; David Theo Goldberg *et al.*'s (2001) *Between Law and Culture: Relocating Legal Studies*; Austin Sarat and Jonathan Simon's (2003) *Cultural Analysis, Cultural Studies, and the Law: Moving Beyond Legal Realism*; Austin Sarat *et al.*'s (2010) edited collection *Law and the Stranger* and Austin Sarat's (2011) edited collection, *Imagining Legality: Where Law Meets Popular Culture*.

At the last century's turning, Austin Sarat and Thomas Kearns (1998, p. 10) identified the cultural lives of law as 'located within the emergent crisis of representation as well as contemporary changes in the organization of symbols and the rhythms of symbolic construction', determining that law and legal studies were late comers to Cultural Studies. From the late 1980s, scholars working in the arena of critical legal studies had turned their attention to the particular significance of law and culture (Chase 1986, 1989, 1994, Macauley 1987, Silbey 1992), and Coombe (2005) issued a prescient warning: 'a Cultural Studies of Law', she wrote, 'will only emerge as a distinctive field of academic inquiry when scholars stop reifying law and start analyzing it as culture' (2005, p. 36). Distinguished by neoliberalism as a dominant mode of governance and marred by the 'culture wars', the last decades of the twentieth century were in the USA (but also in the United Kingdom, Australia and – to a lesser degree – New Zealand) characterized by governmental policies, practices and legal regulation that have shaped everyday living. Neoliberal policies aimed at economic de-regulation, privatization and the reform of tax and labour laws to privilege corporate interests – a process that eroded the capacity to minister once strong welfare states and that weakened the impulse toward, and capacity for, reform in nascent welfare. This disobliging social and economic climate was to provide excellent fodder for the burgeoning Cultural Studies of Law. The shocks of the events of 9/11 altered the socio-cultural and political landscape in marked ways – ushering in an era of American legal exceptionalism, of state sanctioned racism and securitization with broad-ranging impacts on international relations.

This issue revolves around the leakiness of the jurisprudential and the legal in the field of culture. That is, a leakiness that is mirrored in the bleed between national and international law, and the migration of legal cultures, precepts, norms and models between both different – even distinctive – legal systems and cultural venues even more disparate. The contributions are less concerned with what William MacNeil (2007) nattily terms 'pop law', even where the object of critical scrutiny can be considered a popular cultural text. (After all, two of the three popular cultural texts discussed by the contributors have long since been dislodged from their cultural moment; so too have the audiences to which they speak changed, as have the general circumstances of a viewers' likely encounter with the work.)[1] The articles collected in this special issue aim instead at a re-contextualization of law and its effects. While the quotidian ('a-legal' or 'otherwise' [MacNeil, 155; 156]) is not the direct focus of their inquiry, the conditions of what might be termed 'law's everyday life' are nevertheless examined, and at some depth. Our understanding of a 'Cultural Studies of Law' follows Joseph Pugliese's lead (2005). While a study of the unhappy relationship between magistrates and their gowns of office, or of the rite of passage of the getting of chambers would be valuable offerings to one kind of a Cultural Studies of Law, the contributors here mobilize that term differently. This special issue is pre-eminently occupied with questions of doctrine, procedure and principle; with, if you like, the *operability* or inoperability of systems of justice in given cultural conditions.

The two leading papers in this issue come from outstanding interdisciplinary scholars, scholars who have been at the forefront of the 'cultural turn' of critical legal studies. Desmond Manderson considers the vulnerabilities of a dynamic, pluralist vision of law, where the 'memory traces' of past legal forms and conceptualizations of justice haunt contemporary law and culture. Using the long-running primetime television drama *24* as the fulcrum of his analysis, Manderson examines the show's textual demonstration of proofs of the 'efficacy of torture' but, more importantly, the ways in which its screen logic invokes and revivifies earlier forms of 'moral jurisprudence' and 'legal jurisprudence' where true justice, and law's capacity to act, derive from a secret, almost numinous, source, one that cannot be questioned or scrutinized and the lights of which must be taken by faith. It is here worth quoting Manderson as he warns:

> What law 'is' is not a brute fact about the world; it is necessarily a consequence of how we represent it. By presenting an image of law in which communication is depicted as weakness, and trust is synonymous with secrecy, cultural representations themselves constitute justice as unresponsive, non-reciprocal, and external to discourse. Such an approach undermines the relevance and power of a pluralist approach to law itself. (Manderson forthcoming)

Manderson's analysis of the *longue duree* of cultural representations of law provides a sobering cautionary. But the question of the complexity and resilience of cultural representations of law is taken up in quite another way by Austin Sarat and Martha Umphrey in the article following. Legal pluralism assumes the co-existence of different forms of law and justice. The 'memory traces' of earlier forms may lie heavy on the current conscience of law, but so too are cultural representations of law future oriented, not only do they recall the past – they call the future into being. Sarat and Umphrey trace this prospective power of law – its generative possibilities – by unpacking the figuring of fatherhood and the role of father in the classic film version of *To Kill a Mockingbird*. Atticus Finch's vocation as a lawyer is discursively tied to his role as father: his power and agency in both contexts being almost entirely prospective. His principled defense of Robinson – the African-American man accused of raping a white woman – is optimistic and doomed to failure. But Finch's arguments are less pitched at the jury before him – a jury in lockstep with its times, and irretrievably biased – than at a future when all men are treated as equal before the law. Likewise, Atticus's strategies of fathering – many of which are ineffectual – point themselves beyond all present difficulty, in the process enacting that generational contract 'sacrificing the present for a better future'. The idealistic forward lookingness of Atticus Finch is eloquently contrasted with the film's other pivotal representation of fatherhood: that of

Bob Ewell, the dirt-poor farmer who brings the accusation of his daughter's rape. Sarat and Umphrey artfully demonstrate the subtle ways in which Ewell — the walking personification of all that's worst about Southern law and honor — is backward looking. This pointed reading of *To Kill a Mockingbird* models the logic of 'redemptive constitutionalism' (Robert Cover, quoted in Sarat and Umphrey). Here cultural representations of law not only represent a future orientation of law to 'the good' but actually constitute that address. They call the future into being.

It is significant that three of the seven contributors to this issue have chosen to address the use of torture by US military and intelligence personnel, its routinization in a cultural moment where extraordinary measures have become an ordinary mode of operation. What Joseph Pugliese elsewhere describes as the 'twinned strategies of violence and effacement in law' (2005, p. 4) can be seen operating in Manderson's article on the television drama *24* (where the torture of suspects — always efficacious for extracting good and timely intelligence — works strophe/antistrophe with the busywork of investigation); in Peter Hutchings' article on the transformation of John Rambo from tortured vagrant to avenging patriot [torturer] in *First Blood*; and in Pugliese's own investigation of the workings of a torture continuum and 'redaction' as the blacking out of the sensitive sections of documents, but also of those facilities where torture occurs. All three articles deal with a paradoxical situation where the instrumentality of torture is self-evident but where, in actuality, its instruments operate outside of law.

Peter Hutchings treats this paradox through a discussion of the contorted — and compelling — logics of torture, as exemplified by the circumlocutions of the infamous Bybee memo and the strategic evolution of contemporary practices of torture: practices reverse engineered from training programmes designed to train US troops and operatives to *resist* torture into procedures for interrogation that operationalized torture. That evolution is an act of willful invention — misguided and oddly fanciful — given what must necessarily be forgotten in the transmutation of a defense against torture into a manual for its practice: the question of the efficacy of torture as an instrument for extracting reliable intelligence information. Survival, Evasion, Resistance, Escape (SERE) training was originally a response to KGB, The Soviet Committee for State Security interrogation methods that aimed less at intelligence gathering than at the extraction of false confession. What was wanted was *an image of truth, not the truth itself*. An image of truth shaped not for secret advantage over the enemy but for a war of propaganda and moral one-upmanship (during the Korean war, sunken eyed and sleepless US Air force pilots in the hands of their captors publicly confessing to having used 'germ bombs' on civilian targets, confessions not only false but patently florid). As Hutchings goes on to show those discursive antecedents for torture, however, buried beneath a legal logic of necessity, sovereign power and a state of 'permanent exception' keep coming into view: notably in the sudden shocking appearance of torture as entertainment in the Abu Ghraib prison photos.

So too are the conditions by which torture comes into view treated by Joseph Pugliese in his examination of the torture and death of Gul Rahman in a Central Intelligence Agency (CIA) secret prison in Afghanistan. Pugliese traces the relations of legal and governmental power that were instrumental in establishing US regimes of torture and death, elegantly mapping the intersecting modes of instrumental and gratuitous violence that operate across multiple CIA prison sites, the collective effects of what he terms a 'torture continuum'. Linking this US torture continuum to a complex genealogy that precedes the events of 9/11, Pugliese argues that current practices of torture are also inscribed with histories of colonial and racist violence. In his careful reading of the sanctioning of a range of torture practices implemented by US officials, Pugliese examines the juridical and socio-cultural effects when defendants claim impunity from prosecution by claiming to have deployed these practices *without* specific intent to cause severe pain or to kill. He also examines the subsequent physical, ontological and juridical dimensions enabling the dehumanization of Gul Rahman, and examines the medicalized instrumentalization of torture wherein 'the body of the torture victim is kept alive only in order to render it viable for the extortion of information'. Through his reading of redacted legal texts, an analogy is drawn between such texts and the reading of maps, or 'articulating topographies of ruin'.

The contribution of Cristyn Davies here turns the direction of enquiry in the issue toward a focus on gender, sexuality and the law. Pre 9/11 America was defined by a series of regulations aimed at placing limits on what might be culturally produced, disseminated or consumed – a phenomenon that has continued into this century, although now also marked by the contemporary forces of securitization, counterterrorism and nationalism (Puar 2007). History tells us that moral entrepreneurs turn to the law as if to put culture in its place. Davies examines the production of normative subjectivity and the construction of 'appropriate' and exportable knowledge through cultural policy and legal regulation during the culture wars in the USA. Focusing on a 1998 US Supreme Court case, *National Endowment for the Arts v. Finley*, Davies is concerned with the construction and application of decency offered in the case, arguing that cultural policy is a technique of governmentality and a means through which citizenship and national identity is formed and constrained, and self-governance inculcated. For Davies, law is a key technology through which governance and subjectivity is produced, constituted and regulated. She argues that policies such as the 'decency' clause depend on a series of coercive technologies and practices, which ensure that only particular kinds of individuals are understood as embodying norms that are constitutive of citizen-subjects that the state desires. Davies concludes that the introduction of the 'decency' clause may be understood, in part, as a response to a perceived failure in the arts community of individuals to effectively self-regulate and embody standard socio-cultural norms.

The final articles in the issue return to law's capacity to take account of violence, but carry through the emphasis of Davies on contestation around gender and sexuality. Sitting squarely on the indefinite article linking culture and law is the body. The recent vigour of work theorizing the impact of hate speech recognizes this, for instance, by developing a tradition of legal thought that responds to the blunt – and the pointed – force of words. Hate speech presupposes a direct link between the invocation to act and resulting injury, for it conjures the very body it reviles, doing so with the object of the punishment or destruction of that body. Laws to regulate hate speech and bring hate crime into legal and cultural view are the result of hard work of activists and critical race scholars and, more recently, of critical legal studies of the institution of gender. The contributions of Rana Jaleel and John Erni both register that inheritance, but in quite different ways.

Rana Jaleel's article examines a process of cultural and legal borrowing: the impact of the US feminist cultures war of the 1980s on international law, despite the contests of the culture wars being in the first instance bound by time and place, and by institution and jurisdiction. Jaleel demonstrates the evolution of a concept of rape as an instrument of genocide and ethnic cleansing – rape as a collective not an individual injury. While skirmishes in the feminist culture wars around sex work and pornography ultimately failed in asserting the universality of women as a vulnerable class and category, it is precisely that formulation that is the animating logic of the response of international criminal law to war rape. Jaleel's genealogy tracks the progress of a cultural and political intervention that has had significant unforeseen consequences, not only for the workings of international law, but – more significantly – for the ways in which it is now possible to perpetrate, suffer and witness to sexual violence.

John Erni's contribution to this issue looks at the law's failure to rise to the challenge of recent cultural shifts in gender practices and identities by a comparative analysis of the legal response in the USA and Hong Kong to the incarceration of transgendered inmates – a minority population so routinely and systematically exposed to harm in US prisons that redress has been sought on Eighth Amendment grounds. Erni suggests that the blindness of US Federal and State law to the vulnerability of transgendered prisoners is related to the law's refusal to look – or inability to see – the gendering of sexual violence in prisons more generally. Unlike the situation that Jaleel addresses, where activist legal scholars find the discursive wherewithal to reconceptualize rape as a collective injury, there is no possibility – no preconditions, discursively – for the 'sexual terrorism' Erni addresses to come into cultural view and under legal purview. Leveraging off an analysis of the legal response to rape in US prisons, and the failure of arguments about 'cruel and unusual punishment' in respect to sexualized violence against male to female transgendered prisoners assigned to men's prisons, Erni turns to a discussion of the still more profound institutional and cultural blindness to transgendered subjects in Hong Kong, where transgender people 'are almost entirely obscured from social existence'. The inability of law to categorically account for transgendered subjects in Hong Kong is complicated by more thoroughgoing cultural and institutional silences.

Each of the contributions in this issue critically examines sites of legal contestation and the performative workings of law in contemporary culture. In the pages following, the interests of legal scholars and cultural theorists meet to address the 'complex cultural borrowings' and 'importations of new meanings' and 'points of resistance' (Sarat and Kearns 1998, p. 10) that mark the productive relation of law and culture. And so doing, these contributions add to a growing, and significant, interdisciplinary scholarship.

Note

1 'To Kill a Mockingbird' is a case in point here. Both the novel and the film adaptation continue to be influential texts, but the nature of their influence has changed: a change at least partly due to canonization by curricula. But it is precisely this changing of the cultural horizon of a text already idealistically oriented to an imagined legal and cultural future (specifically, the future of race relations in the USA) that is the focus of Austin Sarat and Martha Umphrey's contribution to this issue.

References

Chase, A. (1986) 'Toward a legal theory of popular culture', *Wisconsin Law Review*, vol. 527, pp. 527–570.
Chase, A. (1989) 'Symposium: popular legal culture', *Yale Law Journal*, vol. 98, pp. 1545–1558.
Chase, A. (1994) 'Historical reconstruction in popular legal and political culture', *Seton Hall Law Review*, vol. 24, pp. 1969–2029.
Coombe, R. (2005) 'Is there a Cultural Studies of Law', in *A Companion to Cultural Studies*, ed. T. Miller, London, Blackwell, pp. 36–62.
Fitzpatrick, P. (2001) *Modernism and the Grounds of Law*, Cambridge, UK, Cambridge University Press.
Goldberg, D. T., Musheno, M. & Bower, L. C. eds. (2001), *Between Law and Culture: Relocating Legal Studies*, Minneapolis, University of Minnesota Press.
Kahn, P. (1999) *The Cultural Study of Law: Reconstructing Legal Scholarship*, Chicago, University of Chicago Press.
Macauley, S. (1987) 'Images of law in everyday life: the lessons of school, entertainment and spectator sports', *Law and Society Review*, vol. 12, pp. 185–218.
MacNeil, W. P. (2007) *Lex Populi: The Jurisprudence of Popular Culture*, Palo Alto, CA, Stanford University Press.
Malinowski, B. (1926) *Crime and Custom in a Savage Society*, London, Routledge and Keegan Paul.
Manderson, D. (forthcoming). 'Memory and echo: pop cult, hi tech and the irony of tradition', doi: 10.1080/09502386.2012.722292.
Post, R. (ed.) (1991) *Law and the Order of Culture*, Berkeley, University of California Press.
Puar, J. (2007) *Terrorist Assemblages: Homonationalism in Queer Times*, Durham, NC, Duke University Press.
Pugliese, J. (2005) 'Charged crossing: cultural studies of law - An introduction', *Social Semiotics*, vol. 15, pp. 1–4.
Redhead, S. (1995) *Unpopular Cultures: The Birth of Law and Popular Culture*, Manchester, Manchester University Press.
Sarat, A. (2011) *Imagining Legality: Where Law Meets Popular Culture*, Tuscaloosa, Alabama, The University of Alabama Press.
Sarat, A. & Kearns, T. R. (1998) *Law in the Domains of Culture*, Ann Arbor, University of Michigan Press.
Sarat, A. & Simon, J. eds. (2003) *Cultural Analysis, Cultural Studies, and the Law: Moving Beyond Legal Realism*, Durham, Duke University Press.
Sarat, A., Douglas, L. & Umphrey, M. M. eds. (2010) *Law and the Stranger*, Stanford, Stanford University Press.
Saunders, D. (2007) 'The critical jurist and the moment of theory', *Postcolonial Studies*, vol. 10, pp. 77–92.

Silbey, S. S. (1992) 'Making a place for a cultural analysis of law', *Law and Social Inquiry*, vol. 17, pp. 39–48.
de Sousa Santos, B. (2002) *Toward a New Common Sense: Law, Globalisation, and Emancipation*, London, Butterworths.

Desmond Manderson

MEMORY AND ECHO

Pop cult, hi tech and the irony of tradition

> *Much contemporary writing about law treats popular culture as a creature of modern technology and the phenomenon of mass media. This misunderstands both its continuity with traditional forms, and the precise differences that modern technology creates. Popular cultural representations of law and justice appeal to a longstanding tradition evident in familiar archetypes of cowboys and superheroes. Indeed, such a tradition reaches back to much older Christological models of justice and subjectivity, which modernism has deflected but never destroyed. On the other hand, hi-tech media embeds those traditions in technology's language of passivity and its strange but insistent erasure of the past. Under conditions of the contemporary world, popular culture appears not as the memory of past thinking about law, but as an echo. The irony is that while popular culture's presentations of law appeal to a substantive tradition, their formal hyper-modernity not only negates that past but undermines the pluralist and discursive openness which are its well-spring. In a world shorn of faith in the traditional structures sustaining the 'moral economy' and a moral legality, the appeal to simply trust in an inarticulable justice opens the prospect not of salvation but of legal tyranny.*

The cultural study of law is sometimes in danger of reifying its subjects of inquiry. Research in the field has been significant in expanding the sources of legal analysis to include film, television, art and literature. But at the same time, there is often a sense that what we are learning about is either on the one hand the depiction *of* law in forms of cultural representation, or on the other the other hand, the regulatory force exerted *by* law over those forms. Either way the analysis remains strongly wedded to a conventional distinction between 'culture' and 'law' characterized by very different modes of production,

---

Parts of this essay originally appeared as Manderson, D. (2011) 'Trust us Justice: 24, popular culture and the law', in *Imagining Legality: Where Law Meets Popular Culture*, ed. A. Sarat, Tuscaloosa, University of Alabama Press, pp. 22–52, for which permission is gratefully acknowledged. The current essay has been substantially modified, reframed, and redirected for this special issue.

discourse and circulation. There is a sense in which that is right; a TV series and a Supreme Court judgment are hard to confuse. Nonetheless, this structural-functionalism fails to do justice to the ways in which law exists *only* as representations; and the ways in which the many fields of culture are crucial agents in the iterative and dynamic process by which those representations are made, gain or lose currency, appeal and power. Law is not just a more or less ordered set of rules. It is also a set of ideas, an ideology, a framework that lays down the terms of justice, the nature of authority and the background conditions that structure our identity and our relationships with others, with institutions and with objects – as Robert Cover put it, a 'nomos' (1984). Culture makes law but not just in the weak sense of being a force that helps influence 'it'; in the strong sense that there is no 'it' without it.

Along with the tendency to 'separate out' the spheres of law and culture has come a certain historical amnesia. A lot of recent writing in the field has tended to treat the question of the cultural representation of law as a distinctly modern phenomenon (Moran *et al.* 2004, Sarat *et al.* 2005, MacNeil 2007). In the process two distinct questions are confused. In relation to the content or ideas about law which cultural representations and narratives express, there is I think a crucial continuity across quite long tracts of time. In relationship to the effects which the technological characteristics of modern culture have had on the articulation of those ideas, significant contradictions begin to emerge. In previous eras, the form and content of cultural representations of law were often highly traditional. In the present day, while the content of these representations has not lost its capacity to memorialize much older traditions and discourses about law, the advanced technologies that characterize its form pull in the opposite direction. What is unusual about late modernity is not the dynamic relationship between cultural forces and legal ideas. It is rather that at least to some extent the relationship between these two dimensions, what cultural representations say about law and how they say it, has become strangely dissonant.

Continuities: cultural representations as sites of recollection and resistance

For as long as there has been law (and there has always been law), and for as long as there has been culture (and there has always been culture), there has been a relationship between them. Historically, we observe a harmony of form and content. Local cultures often adopted traditional forms (folk music, oral histories, pagan rites and festivals) to preserve ancient customs *against* new theories, which were making important changes in the structure of legal subjectivity. Writing, for example, from the thirteenth century, began to profoundly change the reach and character of law; as did seventeenth-century notions of sovereignty, eighteenth-century notions of legal positivism and nineteenth-century notions of the market (Hobbes 1909, Horwitz 1979, Berkowitz 2005). All of these were far-reaching ideological changes in the purposes and language of law which implemented radical changes in the balance of social power. Throughout these periods cultural representations and performances of law were often backward-looking, a site of active resistance on behalf some earlier and still meaningful legality.

The work of E.P. Thompson is a crucial point of departure for this argument. In his classic work on 'the moral economy' (1971, 1993) Thompson posits that while the European merchant and ruling classes eagerly adopted the ideology, legal principles and techniques of the market economy, the consequence for many local communities was a period of extraordinary social dislocation. The highland clearances and the Irish Famine are two catastrophes that spring to mind. Accordingly, many local communities upheld a strong tradition of resistance to the developing ideology of modernity. In times of shortage, for example, they fell back on the pre-existing language of a 'moral economy', with its roots in St. Thomas Aquinas (1251–1273) according to which sellers were required to provide staples such as flour or corn at a just price rather than a market price. Thompson does a remarkable job of resuscitating the role this hidden principle played in popular disturbances right into the nineteenth century. He demonstrates that what had been previously described by historians and commentators as a 'riot' was in fact the conscious appeal to ancient practices representing ideas about economic justice which still circulated. The culture of the underclass emerges here as a powerful conservative force with its own concepts of law and justice, its own practices and its own memories. In conformity with modernity's central conceit about itself – new, rational and past-less (Fitzpatrick 1991) – these practices had until Thompson's work been stripped of their underlying memory and legality and portrayed as simply an outburst of irrational violence.

Thompson sought to recuperate these customs as the articulation of a coherent vision of law. *Customs in Common: Studies in Traditional Popular Culture* (1993) brings together a range of examples that retrieve the legal forms and practices of early modern communities. 'Rough music', for example, subjected those who had breached local standards (typically pertaining to sexual behavior) to humiliating and noisy demonstrations by masked participants who used kitchen, household and farm implements to create an intimidating cacophony. Rough music was a highly effective practice of ostracism. It found its counterparts in the French *charivari*, in US *shivarees*, and in many related techniques involving the enforcement of local and traditional legal norms: lynching, shunning, tarring and feathering, and riding out of town on a rail. The two con artists in *Huckleberry Finn* befell such a fate:

> [And] here comes a raging rush of people with torches, and an awful whooping and yelling, and banging tin pans and blowing horns; and we

> jumped to one side to let them go by; and as they went by I see they had the king and the duke astraddle of a rail—that is, I knowed it *was* the king and the duke, though they was all over tar and feathers, and didn't look like nothing in the world that was human—just looked like a couple of monstrous big soldier-plumes.
>
> Well, it made me sick to see it; and I was sorry for them poor pitiful rascals, it seemed like I couldn't ever feel any hardness against them any more in the world. It was a dreadful thing to see. Human beings *can* be awful cruel to one another.
>
> (Twain 1985, pp. 340–341).

Thompson shows us, in many contexts, that what is categorized as random 'noise' from the perspective of modernity was in fact replete with normative power. Cultural representation – and action – is the repository of prior norms which continue to circulate, albeit informally. The 'chaos', which modernity reads back into the past and against which it categorically defines itself, is in fact possessed of its own legal logic and legal history. Clearly, understood in this way, culture is not a *depiction* of or merely parasitic upon formal systems of law. It is a *source* of law, a record and memory of alternative practices, which have not lost their power to constitute actions and ideas.

This argument is an aspect of legal pluralism. The defining feature of legal pluralism is its insistence that the State does not have a monopoly on the development and application of legality. Law is *not* essentially territorial and monopolistic in character. Instead, multiple legal orders co-exist as complex relations of force and discourse (Cover 1984, Griffiths 1986, Melissaris 2009). Boaventura de Sousa Santos famously compares law to a 'map' (2002). Like all maps, legal orders distort reality so as to emphasize certain relationships, to encourage certain functions or behaviors, by turns to facilitate and to inhibit, to name and to silence. And just as many different maps co-exist over the same territory, focusing on different functions, relationships or behaviors, so too do many different legal orders co-exist, using different vocabularies and resources to accomplish different ends. This bottom-up social theory of the production, circulation and enforcement of law is central to Thompson's theory.

Against modernity's myth of the past and the primitive as static (Hart 1961, Fitzpatrick 1991) we see here a vision of a polyglot and 'living law' (Ehrlich 2001) constantly responsive to social practices and circumstances. Culture's law is not filled with the embalmers' fluid; it courses with life. Thompson sought to demonstrate that the legal resources of a culture do not merely *vanish* with the emergence of modern hegemonies and structures. The normative orders represented by the moral and market economies, for example, were synchronous not diachronous. That too is a central insight of legal pluralism, which first came to prominence when scholars noticed the enduring relevance of indigenous legal orders although they had allegedly been superseded by colonial powers – a transition ideologically total but in practice highly variable (Popsopil 1956, de Sousa Santos 1977, Sugarman 1983, Fitzpatrick 1989). More recently, legal pluralists have applied this sensitivity to the synchrony of overlapping legal orders within metropolitan societies no less than in colonial and post-colonial law. They have explored the endurance of local, religious, ethnic, domestic, institutional and associative normative structures as well as the emergence of international, globalized or multi-national legal orders (Falk Moore 1973, Engle Merry 1988, Belley 1996, de Sousa Santos 2002, Melissaris 2009).

What Thompson demonstrated about the plurality and plasticity of the law/culture relationship in the eighteenth and nineteenth centuries still holds true. The field of culture continues to recollect and circulate alternative and prior modes of understanding law. Culture is not the site of the depiction of formal law but resistance to and constitution of it — memory and echo of a half-forgotten past, a counterpoint, a trace.

The active constitution of law

Let me draw out two features of this continuity of cultural representations of law: its constitutive power, and the *longue durée* of its memory and tradition. Both can be seen, for example, in a TV show like '24'. The series ran from 6 November 2001 to 24 May 2010, overtaking *Mission: Impossible* and *The Avengers* as the longest-running espionage series in television history. At its peak it generated a mass following with close to 14 million viewers in the USA alone. The series spawned numerous soundtracks, novels, cartoon books, video and board games and action figures. To describe the show as the glorification of the abandonment of the rule of law is to put it mildly. In the name of preventing terrorist acts Jack Bauer, the show's hero, and officials in Counter Terrorism Unit, the secret government agency he runs, routinely engage in breaches of privacy, profiling, unauthorized computer surveillance, violence, murder and torture. Each season represents a day in the life of CTU, and in the first six 'days', Bauer killed 185 people.[1] Parents' Television Council identified 67 scenes of torture in the first five seasons of *24* alone. Almost without exception, it is the government and not the terrorists that engage in this violence. As Melissa Caldwell, the council's senior director of programs, said, '*24* is the worst offender on television: the most frequent, most graphic, and the leader in the trend of showing the protagonists using torture (Mayer 2007)'. Just as significantly, when CTU engages in it, torture *always* succeeds: information is prised, disaster averted and freedom saved. Time and again, those who express legal or moral qualms about the use of torture are depicted as weak, naïve or complicit (Mayer 2007).

The absence of any meaningful legal constraint on Bauer's actions did not amount to a simple abandonment of law. It amounted to a theory of law.

24 premiered not two months after the World Trade Centre attacks, in a climate of unprecedented anxiety about the vulnerability of the USA to terrorism (Faludi 2007), and about the need to resort to 'the dark side' (Dick Cheney, September 2001) to defeat it. The program channeled and articulated those anxieties with uncanny promptness and accuracy. The Bush Administration, academics and public officials who have defended the violation of the rule of law and the use of torture have done so by reference to three fundamental principles. Exceptionalism – the rule of law must be overridden in the face of new and unanticipated circumstances. Efficacy – torture is presented as extremely effective as an 'information-gathering technique to avert a grave risk'. Urgency – it is 'the immediacy of the situation', of which the so-called 'ticking bomb hypothetical' is the most frequently evoked example, which justifies extreme measures (Dershowitz 2004, Bagaric & Clarke 2005, Greenberg & Dratel 2005). Relying on these three assumptions the Bush Administration insisted on its sovereign right to act entirely as it saw fit in the 'war on terror', including by the use of torture and unconstrained by either domestic or international law (see US Department of Defence and Alberto Gonzales Memos, in Greenberg & Dratel 2005). Indeed, these practices encouraged significant legal changes in countries around the world in matters of security, interrogation and intelligence, changes, which have given unprecedented levels of freedom, and absence of oversight, to government actors.

(1) *24* framed the issues of the 'war on terror' exactly as did the US government.[2] In *24,* the three *assumptions* we noted above were transformed into narrative necessities. Like any frame or set of premises, then, they become exceptionally hard to notice, question or abandon (Derrida 1987). In the first place, exceptionalism is articulated over and over again by Bauer and the other main characters. The implications of this exceptionalism, for example, on broader questions of foreign policy or international reputation, are not broached for a moment.

(2) The efficacy of torture is not simply 'assumed', let alone doubted, but also displayed – 67 times. The success of this technique runs counter to most scholarship in the area, including from military officers and interrogation experts who have had experience with it (Mayer 2007). But *24 performs* the opposite – it provides convincing evidence, emotionally and psychologically if not empirically, for the successful deployment of torture. The torture of Jack Bauer himself in the sixth season of *24,* far from undermining this perspective, sustains it. Jack's goodness (and his masculinity) ensures his capacity to endure torture while the terrorists' evil guarantees that they never do. Just as in earlier eras, torture becomes a test of virtue and silence proof of innocence.[3] Indeed, the fact that the villains in *24* always confess only confirms their villainy. The *justification* of torture is therefore not just that it elicits useful information, but – and what a relief to all those who commit it – that it simultaneously proves their guilt.

(3) The urgency which justifies Jack Bauer's every disregard of the limits of the law is embedded within the series' most distinct elements, its form and style. The series unfolds in 'real time'. Each season depicted a 24-hour period in the life of Bauer, and each one-hour episode corresponded to a single hour in the fictional world. This temporal conceit, together with the show's multiple plots, while straining credulity, allow for an unusually fragmented narrative arc. While our affective sympathy is unswervingly allied to Bauer, actions are seen from the perspective of other CTU agents, government officials, politicians, family members and even the terrorists themselves. As opposed to orthodox police, detective or forensic dramas, which privilege, by and large, a single perspective, events are depicted from multiple standpoints. Within *24*'s 'real time' frame, this challenges narrative techniques. 'Meanwhile, back on the ranch...' is the classic reduction of temporal synchrony to narrative diachrony; the use of flashbacks is another; the use of third person narratives is another. But these devices would breach the show's real-time rule. The adoption of the perspective of a single character throughout would solve this problem but at the expense of the detail and complexity which multiple perspectives provide. Accordingly, the show makes considerable use of 'split frames' in order to depict conversations and events simultaneously.

As Bob Cochran, one of the show's creators, says, 'Most terrorism experts will tell you that the "ticking time bomb" situation never occurs in real life, or very rarely. But on our show it happens every week' (Mayer 2007). This urgency is expressed formally through the show's 'real time' conceit, which gives viewers, and the characters, no time to think. The show's countdown clock, portentously chiming the seconds and minutes as they slip by, intrudes on the action throughout each episode of *24*, constantly reminding us of the urgency and emergency of decision-making. Likewise, the use of split frames draws our attention to the priority of action over reflection in a circumstance in which multiple events keep spiraling out of our control. Time and the multiple demands upon it are *24*'s two key aesthetic choices. They are presented as the enemy of law and the servant of necessity.

Most importantly, the narrative design of the show grants us the luxury of complete confidence in Bauer's judgment. The multiple perspectives that are the show's hallmark gave viewers the compelling illusion of omniscience. The crude and stereotypical depictions of 'the terrorist' as a self-identifying and immediately recognizable phenomenon, about whose pain we feel no guilt and about whose guilt we have no doubt, generates this absolute confidence. Jack Bauer is always right – and we know that Jack is always right, and Jack knows that Jack is always right. Our certainty about what the villains know and our certainty about Jack's judgment about what to do assuages any concerns we might have about his use of torture. Torture is a response to uncertainty, but not in *24*. The narrative perspective of *24* removed the very problems that actually confront us in such a situation — the possibility of error and the uncertainty of knowledge. *24* framed Bauer (and by extension all those who acted like him) not as a fallible agent of the law but as the infallible angel of justice.

The power to construct a narrative is the power to silence choices. The influence of '24' on the way in which US action in the aftermath of 9/11 was framed and justified is I think well established:[4] a framing in which uncertainty was replaced by certainty, reflection was replaced by reaction, and 'exceptional circumstances' required exceptional measures. Law is always a response to fiction: the 'what if' and the 'as if' are precisely what drives the development of our norms and procedures (Cover 1984, Derrida 1992). Law is 'made up', as Elaine Scarry says, before ever it is 'made real' (Scarry 1992). But the *terms* of this invention are critical. In other words, the stories to which we attend, the perspective from which they are told and the shape they are given in the telling are of the utmost importance to law's response. Do we think about the problem from the point of view of an infallible torturer or from that of an innocent victim of torture? The former is ever-present in *24*, while the latter is almost invisible. If we feel that *24*'s hypothetical scenarios accurately express the urgency and exceptionality of the problem, and that the efficacy of torture is made plausible, then our attitude to the rule of law will correspondingly alter. *24* presented to the viewer a series of assumptions, perspectives and narratives. No matter how discredited these may have been in other disciplines, their currency and their affective power pushed critics to respond to them on their own terms. Entering the public imaginary, *24's* stories, structure and assumptions were active players in the legal *nomos* of the time. 'Judges are like the rest of us', wrote Robert Cover. 'They make and interpret law' (Cover 1984). Cover's radical decentering of the role of the judge is of special significance in the context of the power of legal discourse, where there is a fluid and ongoing exchange between formal law and culture, fact and fiction.

The longue durée of memory and tradition

The constitutive power of the field of cultural representation on and as law is pretty clear, the *longue durée* of its memory and tradition perhaps less so. Yet, the figure of a justice *outside* of law draws on a philosophical tradition whose tendrils extend deeply into nineteenth- and twentieth-century thought. In Friedrich Nietzsche's *Thus Spake Zarathustra*, most obviously, the *Übermensch* surpasses man's conventionalism, Christianity and its 'slave morality', and all those established structures that inhibit his potential (Nietzsche 1973, 1961). Jack Bauer did not shore up orthodox legality: he actively dismissed its futility and constituted himself *against* it. Such an approach has clear echoes in Nietzschean and Heideggerian thought. It would not be going too far to see in

Jack Bauer the embodiment of Nietzsche's 'will to power'.[5] Writers like Derrida and Levinas, while inspired by Nietzsche's efforts to break through the limits of a *system,* whether of rules or of morals, nonetheless, supplement it by a higher commitment to ethics or justice which is not based in rules but is constantly beset by doubt. In Derrida and in Levinas, the singularity of circumstances, the uniqueness of *every* situation, requires us to transcend or reinvent the rules (Levinas 1981, 1968, Balkin 1994). The distinction which first Levinas and then Derrida drew between accountability and responsibility is acutely relevant here (Derrida 1996, Manderson 2006). The former is a defensive maneuver which enables us to justify our actions by reference to established rules or chains of command. The latter thinks of our obligations to others as inherently uncodifiable. Accountability is an external structure of justification, predictable and limited. Responsibility is an internal structure of obligation, unpredictable and unlimited. Jack Bauer exemplifies this difference. Poor Jack was accountable to no one, and responsible for everyone.

At the same time, '24' showed clear connections with the Superhero genre that emerged in America in the late 1930s (*Action Comics #1* 1938) likewise against a background of geo-political crisis, and whose resonance with contemporary culture remains powerful (Haslem *et al.* 2007). Just like Nietzsche's *Übermensch*, Superman and all those who have followed in his footsteps do not promise justice by thinking in terms of rules or democracy. Instead, it is their *personal* character and their *special* powers that justify their actions at the very moment that law and society fails. They are heroes precisely *because* their actions transcend laws, physical or social. The promise of 'truth, justice, and the American way', of defeating 'evil and injustice' [the legal definition, I might add, of Superman (see Detective v. Bruns 1940, Coogan in Haslem *et al.* 2007)] is achieved not through law but outside of it and indeed utterly apart from it. Justice is friendless, alien and masked. Look, for example, at the social dysfunction that backgrounds recent movie versions of *Batman,* or in *V for Vendetta.* By eschewing any structural solutions to social problems but instead resorting to some *deus ex machina* to swoop down and rescue us from them, Superman's legacy is a gesture of desperation against the mainstream world rather than either acceptance or reform of it (Eco 1979).

The dream of isolated transcendence – of a savior from outside or beyond the law – itself recalls the vigilante tradition of the Wild West. The gunslinger, the lawman or the cowboy impose justice rather than law and they do so through the natural integrity of their character (Wright 2001, Lubet 2004). By force of will and speed of action he conquers a wildness in which the structures and systems of civilization are not yet born, and when those structures and systems intrude he rides off again into the sunset.[6] *24* echoed not just these familiar cultural narratives, but as Susan Faludi argued, paralleled their astonishing re-emergence at the heart of the American imaginary in the wake of 9/11 (Faludi 2007). Yet I need hardly add that this dream of a unique and unaccountable decision-maker responding only to the immediate problem before them runs directly counter to the rule of law which seeks to encode, in other words to remove from the realm of the singular, the qualities and outcomes of decision making, to expel the quality of vengeance from it, to regularize its judgments and to disperse its violence institutionally (Derrida 1992).

The alternative legality that these traditions of cultural representation keep alive is much more deeply rooted in the Western legal tradition than that. The rule of law, though in some respects going back to Aristotle (1932), has been very much a modernist project (Tamanaha 2004, 2006). Its notion of the virtues of rules and procedures, of checks and balances, set out to replace a vision of justice as deriving from God with a vision of justice as deriving from Man. By contrast, the world of medieval and early modern Europe was suffused by the image of Christ. Representations of justice in art and literature drew consistently on a Christ-centred model of justice (Jacob 1994). Christ is seen as both the giver of justice and the archetype for the judge. In his magisterial study of images of justice in the Middle Ages, Robert Jacob demonstrates how often the artwork that adorned the courts, tribunals, and cathedrals of Europe in the Middle Ages, depicted justice and the trial as an intimate drama centred on two figures. On the one hand Christ, to whom the judge must ultimately answer. And on the other, the judge himself who is responsible for what transpires before him and whose soul is on trial. The lineaments which bind Christ and judge together, the parallel juxtaposition of the human judge and the divine judge, are explicitly represented in many of these images.[7]

But the image and the teaching of Christ employs the language of love and of inspiration, not of commandments, rules or authority. That was what made Christ a rebel and the Old Testament different from the New. In the Middle Ages, then, legal judgment was intensely personal and dynamic. Just as Christ appears as the model of one whose character was the guarantee of justice, so too the principal criterion for the judge lay in *his* goodness and character, and therefore his capacity to access this divine insight. As Jacob notes, the medieval judge therefore occupied an exalted but vulnerable office since judgment was tied to his personal capacity and the achievement – or failure – of justice was his personal responsibility (1994, p. 70). We see this most sharply in a painting such as Gerard David's (1498) diptych, *The Judgment of Cambyses,* which (itself citing Herodotus) depicts the flaying alive of a corrupt judge, his skin the fabric on which his son in turn would sit as judge (Lippens 2009). The paintings were hung in the town hall of Bruges – presumably *pour encourager les autres.* It is exceptionally hard to imagine an image like this being considered appropriate to a courtroom now. One doubts whether the judges would find its message congenial. Modernity has humbled the judge as the price of limiting his responsibility. The empiricist and secular revolutions of Europe replaced divine with human authority; as Richard Mohr notes, the image of Christ which typically emblazoned the literal or figurative seat of judgment was replaced by the coat of arms (Mohr 2009). The crucial move to secular authority led to the modern obsession with the construction of hierarchical institutions and interpretative norms in which the role of the judge could be circumscribed and subservient. Thus the promise of justice was replaced by the guarantee of law — the spirit of justice by the letter of the law, the subjectivity of judgment by the technical objectivity of a machine (Berkowitz 2005).

Contemporary cultural representations of law and justice look back before this revolution and sustain a memory and continuity between past and present. Returning to EP Thompson, the cultural representation of law continues to recall a distinction between 'moral legality' and 'market legality' or perhaps, more accurately, between 'moral jurisprudence' and 'legal jurisprudence'. A show like *24* still reflects cultural traditions and a popular memory of law's alterity. We live in a world in which judges and lawmakers are participants in legal consciousness but do not determine its exclusive source or its definitive form: a world in which law is produced not only hierarchically but also discursively. In such a world, this role and these traditions remain vitally important.

Contradictions: cultural representations and the problems of modernity

The question of trust

In the modern world this continuity has been destabilized in two notable ways. In the first place, though it draws on a whole lineage of cultural archetypes, the vision of moral responsibility unanchored to law finds itself now shorn of the religious and cultural understandings that used to keep it in check. Jack Bauer never tries reason. He never listens to alternatives or engages in discussion. Within the framework of *24,* there is no time for that. 'Trust me' is the mantra of *24;* but this appeal to trust, like the superhero's mask, costume and secret identity, is an aspect of his perfect alienation from the world. The idea that true justice is not only transcendent but mysterious and secret seems characteristic of a great deal of contemporary cultural production. In soap operas and in dramas, characters — mainly lead characters, mainly male characters — consistently refuse to explain themselves or to reflect on their judgment. They simply *demand* to be trusted; and it is their failure to be trusted that creates the secrecy, conflict, drama and action on which television thrives.

Neither is this trope only to be found on television. Shortly after 9/11 US Vice President Dick Cheney remarked that 'one of the things that's changed so much since September 11 is the extent to which people do trust the government — big shift'. But as Bob Woodward wrote, with prophetic foresight, at the time:

The problem for Bush in the long run, or even the short run, may be managing and balancing trust and secrecy — and credibility... At any time the Presidency has a spellbinding power. In crisis and national emergency it can be blinding. The public, even the media, want to trust. Balancing trust and secrecy in the coming period is going to be a giant task.

(Woodward 2001)

Recent testimony before a US Congressional Committee demonstrated the extent to which Cheney tried to undermine Congressional oversight and to circumvent established procedures of holding executive decisions accountable.[8] Much like Jack Bauer, Cheney's approach to the 'war on terror' was to demand extraordinary relaxations on legal constraints accompanied by a single mantra — 'trust me'. Before the UK Chilcot Inquiry former British Prime Minister Tony Blair displayed the same lack of accountability — 'Righteous, responsible, but no regrets' (*Manchester Guardian*, 2010) — and generated the same public rage. Here too, the appeal to trust is not an argument or a reason but an end to arguments and reasons, a 'why-stopper'. It removes any idea of justice as emerging through dialogue or discussion, any sense of it as a social activity. The language of ineffable trust echoes the image of the lone vigilante for whom responsibility is a burden but accountability is a curse.

This dichotomy rings false. Justice and the giving of reasons are not opposites; they are in fact symbiotically related. Think about teaching. Teaching is not the mere manifestation of insight but its painful emergence (in the teacher no less than the student) under the pressure imposed by our students to give reasons, to explain our views, and to comprehend the stories of others. Tobias Wolff writes, 'Teaching made him accountable for his thoughts, and as he became accountable for them he had more of them, and they became sharper and deeper' (Wolff 2003). That is profoundly true of the teaching experience and it ought to be profoundly true of the legal experience too. In the giving of reasons and in subjecting decision-makers to standards of accountability and justification we *learn* something that we did not know before. Our concepts of justice, and the way in which the interpretation of rules both illuminates and transforms those concepts, thus develop. Insight and understanding are not secured in secret. They are chiseled out of us by the constant demands and interrogations of others, the painful *result* of reasons and not by sidestepping them (Gibbs 1991).

The appeal to blind trust is the gutted and corrupted shell of the Christological tradition and its cultural and philosophical variants. It is nothing but a rhetorical posture that undermines the only conditions on which, in *our* world, that trust could develop. Trust cannot be demanded: certainly not in the absence of that communal or theological or aristocratic consensus on which it might once have been based. It is no longer an entitlement. It must always be earned and re-earned, by just these processes of open communication, explanation — and listening (Govier 1997, 1998). We cannot be trusted if we are not prepared to trust. The arrogance of blind trust generates a vicious circle from which the authority figures of our world, in politics and in culture, cannot escape. Ultimately such a posture cannot establish what most it craves and, being increasingly mistrusted, resorts to a furious tyranny.

Furthermore, the pluralist vision of law I have defended in this essay, which gives to cultural representations a normative role which orthodox legal theories fail to credit, is thus rendered increasingly vulnerable. From a pluralist standpoint, popular culture's ability to echo and to express alternative visions of legality is not anachronistic: it continues to contribute to legal ideology and to legal change. But the inescapable irony that pluralist theories of culture and law confront is this: what law 'is' is not a brute fact about the world; it is necessarily a consequence of how we *represent* it.[9] By presenting an image of law in which communication is depicted as weakness, and trust is synonymous with secrecy, cultural representations themselves constitute justice as unresponsive, non-reciprocal and external to discourse. Such an approach undermines the relevance and power of a pluralist approach to law itself.

The paradox of technology

In the second place there is a contradiction between the two dimensions of the study of culture and law with which I began this essay: the modernity of its form, on the one hand, and the traditionalism of its content, on the other. While *24* gestures towards the remembrance of justice past, it does so through a visual vocabulary steeped in ultra-modernity. Again it is merely exemplary in this regard. The *CSI* franchise and its many comparators likewise attempt to rescue law's promise of objectivity and certainty by transferring what we might literally call 'the moment of truth' from the judge or lawyer or policeman to the scientist. The amnesia of modernity is performed in every frame of these series, in an ultra-modern aesthetics, gleaming steel and glowing clinical lighting, and in computerized and otherwise pseudo-scientific technologies of investigation and surveillance. Science – precise, certain and impersonal – represents here an almost magical antidote to the failure of law. Thus while the narrative arc of these shows typically gestures towards a transcendent subjectivity and the cult of personality, their form and aesthetics re-inscribe the ethos of positivism through which modern law attempted to do away with subjectivity and personality in judgment. Such depictions of law all point to the past with their voice but to the future with their eyes.

What does the figure *24* represent but modernity itself? One of the greatest achievements of the modern world has been the transformation it has wrought in our understanding of time. Clockwork is the very image of the modern world: its law, its society, its physics (Melzer *et al.* 1993). The clock, day in and day out, unstoppable, unchangeable, relentless and unceasing, was one of the great technological agents of modernization (De Grazia 1994). Again, as E.P. Thompson showed, this did not take place without considerable social resistance. But eventually, the rigours of clock-time disciplined seasonal workers to conform to the unbending demands of industrial life. The clock replaced the cathedral as the focal point of the town square. The cycle of the year and the seasons, with all its rhythms and rituals – its Michaelmas and Trinity, its market days and Sundays – was replaced by a purely human structure, abstract and objective, in which day and night were commensurable, winter and summer irrelevant, and time could be measured and spent and lost. The digital '24', even more than the analogue clock-face, is a positivized human construction which has not ceased to terrify us with its exact and pitiless ticking – an alphabet, a subdivision, an order: human beings molded and produced by scientific knowledge.[10] The digital clock conveys an uncompromising urgency in which the relentless onslaught of numbers permits no pause for memory or for reflection. For Jack Bauer, whether the day started at 1:00 am. or at 8:00 am. or at noon made no difference; every hour was like every other hour. Time is against us and we must submit to it: this is not just the conceit of *24*; it is one of the founding conceits of the modern world (Elias 1993). The number that best describes this world is not 9/11. It is 24/7.

The contradiction between form and content is a question not just of the representation of technology but of the technology of representation itself. Mass culture, in particular, now has a link to technological innovation, in stark contrast to the exclusivity of earlier technological developments. The book was once a rare commodity and literacy a feature of elites. The organ was an astonishing technical achievement but of exceptionally limited access. On the other hand, Troubadours and mummers wandered and played, folk songs and nursery rhymes circulated informally, broadsheets made their way from hand to hand. In pre- and early-modern Europe, the technical *simplicity* of cultural forms was a necessary component of its social accessibility. But in the twentieth- and twenty-first centuries, on the other hand, the technical complexity of mass media – its films, TV and music recording – is equally a necessary component of *its* accessibility.

Yet, these two accessibilities are not the same: the former makes production accessible; the latter makes consumption accessible. The forms, aesthetic languages, and institutional relationships distinctive of the relationship between technology and modernity clearly influence the messages they convey to their audiences, and indeed are constitutive of the audiences they define. As Walter Ong (1988) argues, oral practices, for example, are fluid and participant in ways that literate practices are not (see also Grant 1969/1986, Clanchy 1993, Illich 1996). Writing is a marvelous disseminator of information but it is also leads to ossified traditions and fundamentalist interpretations. Technology in modernity reflects its myths – it communicates a relentless newness; where it does not discard the past entirely, it transcribes it (as for example, in relation to folk music[11] or in documentaries about indigenous societies) but simultaneously freezes it in time and distorts it forever. We observe the products of high technology such as films, video games, television and the music industry. We admire the skill and we worship the spectacle — that is what is made instantly and multiply accessible to us. Modern technology has turned culture into a commodity, and exchanged media to which performers had easy access for media to which consumers have easy access.[12] Participation is thereby replaced by observation, and a dynamic tradition replaced by the fetish of authenticity. In short, the power of modern technology reproduces the power of modern positivism: to reify its objects and to pacify its subjects.

Conclusion

The contemporary cultural representation of law highlights the fault-line with which I began this essay, between form and substance. The ideology it expresses contradicts the modernity that expresses it. The memories it stirs are undermined by the technological and social amnesia it encourages. Thus *24* wants it both ways: to be simultaneously the nemesis of modernity and its apotheosis. Thinking about the relationship between culture and law requires us to explore not one but two dimensions, an analysis of what it says and an analysis of how it says it; a sensitivity to historical memory on the one hand, and a sensitivity to the amnesia of technological and social change on the other. In the contemporary world, these two trajectories are often at odds. What is condemned on the level of conscious meaning is glorified on the level of — what? — form? medium? sub-conscious? Slavoj Zizek once said in relation to *The Sound of Music,* 'maybe we could even call it "writing"'.[13] Yes, perhaps that is it. Whatever we call it, the hills are alive with it.

Notes

1 There are many online sites devoted to counting Bauer's killings and the subject has attracted a rather recondite scholasticism. See www.bauercount.com

2 It is not my intention in this article to argue about the way in which torture has been discussed and understood in this context. See Desmond Manderson, 'Another Modest Proposal' in Gani and Mathew (2008).

3 *24* here reproduces very old assumptions about torture: du Bois 1991. See also variations on the theme in popular culture, e.g. *Wanted* (2008).

4 For extended analysis of the relationship between '24' and law, see Desmond Manderson 2011; for a careful documentation of the ways in which '24' began to influence legal thinking, public policy, and military action, see Mayer 2007.

5   For further reading on the links between the superhero genre and Nietzsche and Heidegger, see Raymond Younis, 'Restlessly, Violently, Headlong,' in Haslem et al. 2007.
6   See in particular Home Box Office, *Deadwood* (2004–2006), which explores the relationship of law, justice, and power in just such a void.
7   See for example, German school, *Tribunal terrestre et tribunal celeste* (Wurzbourg, early 15th Century).
8   See the evidence of Leon Pancetta in Pam Benson (2009).
9   Emmanuel Melissaris (2004) pp. 57–79. John Griffiths (1986) famously declares that 'Legal pluralism is the fact. Legal centralism is the myth, an ideal, a claim, an illusion:' 'What is Legal Pluralism', pp 1–54. But this argument fails to come to terms with the point I am making here: because law is not a material reality but an intentional, ideational object, constructed by a culture's beliefs and social structures, the 'myth' of legal centrism, if believed by the whole community to be the correct definition of law, would also constitute its reality.
10 See Michel Foucault (1966).
11 Two examples: Bela Bartok's work in recording and then transcribing the folk music of Hungary; and the work in the USA to record blues and bluegrass music. See John A. Lomax (1938); Nolan Porterfield (2001); Daniel Albright (2003). Elliott Antokoletz et al. (2000).
12 I am aware that rather different arguments might be made about web technologies, self-publication and so forth, and while I think there is some truth to these ideas I think they can and are fancifully overstated.
13 See Slavoj Zizek on *The Sound of Music*.

References

Action Comics #1 (1938) New York, DC Comics.
Albright, D., (ed.) (2003) *Modernism and music*, Chicago, University of Chicago Press.
Antokoletz, E., Fischer, V., Suchoff, B. eds. (2000) *Bartók perspectives: man, composer, and ethnomusicologist*, Oxford, Oxford University Press.
Aristotle (1932) *Politics*, trans. H. Rackham, Boston, Loeb Classical Library.
Bagaric, M. & Clarke, J. (2005) 'Not Enough Official Torture in the World? The Circumstances in which Torture is Morally Justifiable', *University of San Francisco Law Review*, vol. 39, pp. 581–617.
Balkin, J. (1994) 'Transcendental Deconstruction, Transcendent Justice', *Michigan Law Review*, vol. 92, pp. 1131–1187.
Belley, J. G., (ed.) (1996) *Le Droit Soluble*, Paris, LGDJ.
Benson, P. (2009) 'Senator: Cheney and Alleged Secret CIA Program "A Problem"', *CNNPolitics.com*, [online] Available at: http://www.cnn.com/2009/POLITICS/07/11/cheney.surveillance/ (accessed 18 August 2009).
Berkowitz, R. (2005) *The Gift of Science*, Boston, Harvard University Press.
Clanchy, M. (1993) *From Memory to Written Record*, Oxford, Blackwell.
Cover, R. (1984) 'Nomos and narrative', *Harvard Law Review*, vol. 97, pp. 4–69.
David, G. (1498) *The Judgment of Cambyses*, Groeninge Museum, Bruges.
De Grazia, S. (1994) *Of Time, Work, and Leisure*, New York, Vintage.
Derrida, J. (1987) *The Truth in Pointing*, trans. Geoffrey Bennington & Ian McLeod, Chicago, University of Chicago Press.
Derrida, J. (1992) 'Before the Law', in *Acts of Ligerature*, ed. D. Attridge, New York, Routledge, pp. 188–220.
Derrida, J. (1996) *Gift of Death*, trans. D. Wills, Chicago, University of Chicago Press.
Dershowitz, A. (2004) 'The Torture Warrant: A response to Professor Strauss', *New York Law School Review*, vol. 48, pp. 275–295.
Detective Comics v. Bruns Publications, Inc. (1940) 111 F.2d 432.
du Bois, P. (1991) *Torture and Truth*, London, Routledge.
Eco, U. (1979) *The Role of the Reader*, Indianapolis, Indiana University Press.
Ehrlich, E. (2001) *Fundamental Principles of the Sociology of Law*, New Brunswick, Transaction Publishers.
Elias, N. (1993) *Time: An Essay*, Oxford, Blackwell.
Faludi, S. (2007) *The Terror Dream: Fear and Fantasy in Post-9/11 America*, New York, Metropolitan Books.
Fitzpatrick, P. (1991) *The Mythology of Modern Law*, London, Routledge.
Fitzpatrick, P. (1989) 'The Desperate Vacuum', *Droit et Societe*, vol. 13, p. 347.
Foucault, M. (1966) *Les Mots et les Choses: Une archéologie des sciences humaines*, Paris, Gallimard.
Gani, M. & Mathew, P., eds. (2008) *Fresh Perspectives on the 'War on Terror'*, Canberra, ANU Press.

Gibbs, B. (1991) 'The Other Comes to Teach Me', *Man and World*, vol. 24, pp. 219–233.
Govier, T. (1998) *Dilemmas of Trust*, Kingston, McGill-Queen's University Press.
Govier, T. (1997) *Trust and Human Communities*, Kingston, McGill-Queen's University Press.
Grant, G. (1969/1986) *Technology and Empire*, Toronto, Anansi.
Greenberg, K. & Dratel, J. eds. (2005) *The Torture Papers: The Road to Abu Ghraib*, New York, Cambridge University Press.
Griffiths, J. (1986) 'What is legal pluralism?' *Journal of Legal Pluralism and Unofficial Law*, vol. 24, pp. 1–57.
Haslem, W., Ndalianis, A. & Mackie, C., eds. (2007) *Super/Heroes: From Hercules to Superman*, Washington, New Academia Press.
Hart, H. L. A. (1961) *The Concept of Law*, Oxford, Clarendon Press.
Hobbes, T. (1909) *Leviathan*, New York, Collier.
Home Box Office, *Deadwood* (2004–2006).
Illich, I. (1996) *In the Vineyard of the Text*, Chicago, University of Chicago Press.
Jacob, R. (1994) *Images de la Justice*, Paris, Le Leopard d'Or.
Levinas, E. (1968) *Otherwise than Being, or Beyond Essence*, trans. Alphonso Lingis, Pittsburgh, Duquesne University Press.
Levinas, E. (1981) *Totality and Infinity*, trans. Alphonso Lingis, Pittsburgh, Duquesne University Press.
Lippens, R. (2009) 'Gerard David's *Cambyses* and Early Modern Governance', *Law and Humanities*, vol. 3, pp. 1–24.
Lomax, J. A. (1938) *Cowboy Songs and Other Frontier Ballads*, New York, Collier Books.
Lubet, S. (2004) *Murder in Tombstone: The Forgotten Trial of Wyatt Earp*, New Haven, Yale University Press.
MacNeil, W. (2007) *Lex Populi*, Stanford, Stanford University Press.
Manderson, D. (2006) *Proximity, Levinas, and the Soul of Law*, Montreal, McGill-Queen's University Press.
Manderson, D. (2011) 'Trust us Justice: 24, Popular Culture and the Law', in *Imagining Legality: Where Law Meets Popular Culture*, ed. A. Sarat, Tuscaloosa, University of Alabama Press, pp. 22–52.
Mayer, J. (2007) 'Whatever It Takes', *New Yorker*, 19 February, pp. 68–82.
Melissaris, E. (2004) 'The More the Merrier? A New Take on Legal Pluralism', *Social and Legal Studies*, vol. 13, pp. 57–79.
Melissaris, E. (2009) *Ubiquitous Law: Legal Theory and the Space for Legal Pluralism*, Surrey, Ashgate.
Melzer, A., Weinberger, J. & Zinman, R. eds. (1993) *Technology in the Western political Tradition*, Ithaca, Cornell University Press.
Merry, S. E. (1988) 'Legal Pluralism', *Law and Society Review*, vol. 22, pp. 869–897.
Mohr, R. (2009) 'The Christian Origins of Secularism and the Rule of Law,' seminar presentation (work in progress), *Institute for the Public Life of Arts and Ideas*, Montreal.
Moore, S. F. (1973) 'Law and Social Change', *Law and Society Review*, vol. 7, pp. 719–747.

Moran, L., et al., eds. (2004) *Law's Moving Image*, London, Cavendish.
Nietzsche, F. (1961) *Thus Spake Zarathustra*, trans. R. J. Hollingdale, London, Penguin.
Nietzsche, F. (1973) *Beyond Good and Evil*, trans. R. J. Hollingdale, London, Penguin.
Ong, W. (1988) *Orality and Literacy: The Technologizing of the World*, New York, Methuen.
Popsopil, L. (1956) *Law among the Kapauku*, New Haven, HRAF Press.
Porterfield, N. (2001) *Last Cavalier: The Life and Times of John A. Lomax, 1867–1948*, Chicago University of Illinois Press.
de Sousa Santos, B. (2002) *Toward a New Legal Common Sense*, 2nd edition, London, Butterworths.
de Sousa Santos, B. (1977) 'The Law of the Oppressed: The Construction and Reconstruction of Law in Pasargada', *Law & Society Review*, vol. 12, pp. 5–126.
Sarat, A., Douglas, L. & Umphrey, M. M. eds. (2005) *Law on the Screen*, Stanford, Stanford University Press.
Scarry, E. (1992) 'The Made Up and the Made Real', *Yale Journal of Criticism: Interpretation in the Humanities*, vol. 5, pp. 239–264.
Zizek, S. on *The Sound of Music*, [online] Available at: http://www.youtube.com/watch?v=wiTum8eQ51E (accessed 18 August 2009).
Sugarman, D. (ed.) (1983) *Legality, Ideology and the State*, London, Academic Press.
St. Thomas Aquinas (1251–1273) *Summa Theologica*.
Tamanaha, B. (2004) *On the Rule of Law*, Cambridge, Cambridge University Press.
Tamanaha, B. (2006) *Law as a Means to an End*, Cambridge, Cambridge University Press.
Thompson, E. P. (1971) 'The Moral Economy of the English Crowd in the 18th Century', *Past & Present*, vol. 50, pp. 76–136.
Thompson, E. P. (1993) *Customs in Common: Studies in Traditional Popular Culture*, New York, New Press.
Twain, M. (1985) *Huckleberry Finn*, New York, Penguin.
Wolff, T. (2003) *Old School*, New York, Vintage.
Wintour, T. & Norton-Taylor, R. (2010) 'Righteous, responsible but no regrets: Tony Blair's day in the dock', *Guardian* (U.K.) 29 January 2010, [online] Available at: http://www.guardian.co.uk/uk/2010/jan/29/responsible-no-regrets-blair-iraq (accessed 13 August 2011).
Woodward, B. (2001) 'Credibility Fails if Trust, Secrecy, Out of Balance,' *The Ledger*, 28 October 2001 (reproduced from *The Washington Post*).
Wright, W. (2001) *The Wild West: The Mythical Cowboy and Social Theory*, London, Sage.

Austin Sarat and Martha Merrill Umphrey

TEMPORAL HORIZONS

On the possibilities of Law and Fatherhood in *To Kill a Mockingbird*

> To Kill a Mockingbird *is a classic of American cultural—legal studies, and it offers in Atticus Finch an iconic hero who, as Stephen Lubet suggests, is popular culture's most important embodiment of lawyerly virtue. As other scholars have noted, however,* To Kill a Mockingbird *is not just, or primarily, a law story. Rather, Scout Finch's portrait of Atticus as a father is regarded by many as the key to the text's cultural resonance. Told as a daughter's memory of her father, her brother, and the town in which she grew up, the text frames the era's conflicts over race, gender, and justice through the lens of Scout's admiration for Atticus. From our perspective, however, it is the conjunction of lawyer and father that fuels* To Kill a Mockingbird's *appeal and importance, and in this paper we argue that such a conjunction, particularly in its filmic incarnation, provides an opportunity to explore the role that fathers and fatherhood play in cultural imaginings of law and in exemplifying the various faces of law's power. We argue that Atticus Finch is a father/lawyer committed to a particular vision of fatherhood and law, one in which both can transcend, if not transform, the context in which they exist, one in which orienting oneself to the future takes precedence over controlling the present, one in which the temporal horizon of law and fatherhood is kept firmly in view. In the figure of Atticus,* To Kill a Mockingbird *suggests that law and fatherhood are powerful and yet limited in their power, and that both exist in the present but are oriented towards an as yet unrealized future.*

To Kill a Mockingbird is a classic of American cultural—legal studies[1] and it offers in Atticus Finch an iconic hero who is one of popular culture's most important embodiments of lawyerly virtue. Indeed in 2003, the American Film Institute named Atticus Finch the greatest movie hero of the twentieth century. As Stephen Lubet (1999, p. 1340) puts it:

> No real-life lawyer has done more for the self-image or public perception of the legal profession than the hero of... *To Kill a Mockingbird*. For nearly four decades, the name of Atticus Finch has been invoked to defend and inspire lawyers, to rebut lawyer jokes, and to justify (and fine-tune) the adversary system.
>
> (see also Schlag 1990, p. 189)

Although some have criticized Atticus for being too accommodating to the segregated world in which he lived and practiced law (Freedman 1994, Osborn 1996, Holcomb 2002, Phelps 2002) many, nonetheless, acknowledge that Atticus is an antidote to much common criticism of law and the legal profession (Lubet 1999).

Other scholars have noted, however, that *To Kill a Mockingbird* is not just, or primarily, a law story (Asimow 1996, p. 1136). Rather, Scout Finch's portrait of Atticus as a *father* is regarded by many as the key to the text's cultural resonance. As Bruzzi (2005, pp. 85–86) puts it: from a psychoanalytic perspective 'Atticus Finch... is the perfect fairytale father...' Told as a daughter's memory of her father, her brother and the town in which she grew up, the text frames the era's conflicts over race, gender and justice through the lens of Scout's admiration for Atticus.

From our perspective, however, it is the *conjunction* of lawyer and father that fuels the appeal and importance of *To Kill a Mockingbird*, and in this essay we argue that such a conjunction, particularly in its filmic incarnation, provides an opportunity to explore the role that fathers and fatherhood play in cultural imaginings of law and in exemplifying the various faces of law's power (Sarat 2000). Atticus Finch is a father/lawyer committed to a particular vision of fatherhood and law, one in which both roles can transcend, if not transform, the context in which they exist; in which orienting oneself to the future takes precedence over controlling the present; and in which the temporal horizon of law and fatherhood is kept firmly in view. In the figure of Atticus, *To Kill a Mockingbird* suggests that law and fatherhood are powerful and yet limited in their power and that both exist in the present but are oriented towards an as yet unrealized future.[2]

Scout's reflections on her father render the two roles – father and lawyer – inseparable, fusing what she represents as Atticus' almost magical parenting with his deep integrity and sense of justice. Moreover, her dual position as child protagonist and post-hoc narrator alerts us to the significance of the film's complex temporality, both in its narrative vision and in the social landscape of its reception (on the temporality of film spectatorship see Garber 1998). That the film, set during the Great Depression, was released in 1962 locates its earliest viewers in the midst of the civil rights struggles of the early 1960s, after *Brown v. Board of Education* but before the 1964 Civil Rights Act. They were and, in a different way, we are situated in the future that the film imagines. In 1962, the conflicts of the 1930s that were represented in the film remained palpable, as did its portrait of the South's hotly contested visions of justice and injustice. Viewed today, close to 50 years after its release, viewers know that Atticus' cause will be substantially, if not completely, vindicated. Yet at the time of its release, the film's horizon of hope remained largely prospective.

Scout's reflective voiceovers invite viewers to accept her idealized perspective ('There just didn't seem to be anyone or anything that Atticus couldn't explain', she observes) and to take a child's point-of-view on the events portrayed in the film. Her invitation to imagine law as a father — and a very particular kind of father — in *To Kill a Mockingbird* resonates with, and yet departs from, a Judeo-Christian cultural tradition that, historically, has aroused desire and anxiety. The Abraham and Isaac story is, of course, a paradigmatic exemplification of law's claims and its powers, of the presentation of law as the Father but also the father as law (Hartman 1996, p. 35). In a different vein legal scholars, following Freud (1950), regularly have called attention to the complex psychological associations of paternity and legality, portraying law as the focal point for a deep-seated longing for paternal authority (Althusser 1971, p. 212). Jerome Frank in *Law and the Modern Mind* (1949, pp. 196–197) suggests that law, like religion, is a projection of a widely shared human need for certainty and security in a world of danger and invites us to think of law as the father or, more precisely, as the father-substitute. 'Despite advancing years', Frank (1949, p. 19) argues, 'most men are at times, the victims of the childish desire for complete serenity and the childish fear of irreducible chance. They then will to believe that they live in a world in which chance is only appearance, not reality....' Frank (1949) further suggests:

> to the child the father is the Infallible Judge, the Maker of definite rules of conduct. He knows precisely what is right and what is wrong and ... sits in judgment and punishes misdeeds. The Law ... inevitably becomes a partial substitute for the Father-as-Infallible-Judge....'
>
> (p. 18)

Exploring similar themes, Peter Goodrich (1997) recently noted that:

> Freud and those who follow him depict a law that is modeled upon the power of the father. They elaborate a symbolic order that is patriarchal in its norms and methods. To some extent that account of the legal order reflects an institution embedded in a history of homosocial power and continuing male privilege.
>
> (p. 1047)

To Kill a Mockingbird offers a view of law and fatherhood quite different from the model of father/law as command or father/law as infallible judge (for a contrasting view see Meyer 2013). In it, fatherhood and law conjure a normative world of *becoming* more than *being*, one concerned with legitimate authority rather than raw power. Like Moses leading the Jews out of Egypt, Atticus believes in a 'promised land' that he himself may never enter or attain and he acts, in his role as father/lawyer, as a bridge between the past and the future (for this view of Moses see Walzer 1986). The entailments[3] of the past are legacies against which Atticus sets himself. He resists the norms and customs of racism and race privilege and of violence that were deeply intertwined in the mid-twentieth century American South.

In attempting to undo those legacies, Atticus offers his children an example, a different way of being in the world, a model of adult values and sensibilities that foreshadow and also constitute the ideals of liberal legality. Many are the moments when Atticus tries to teach Scout how to live a principled life in ways underwritten by those ideals. In one instance, as he tries to convince Scout that she cannot stop going to school he says, 'Scout, do you know what a compromise is?' to which Scout responds, 'Bending the law?' Atticus corrects her, as if delivering a lesson from a first year contracts course:

> No, Scout, it is an agreement reached by mutual consent. Now, here's the way it works. You concede the necessity of going to school and we'll keep right on reading every night just as we always have. Is that a bargain?

This fusion of father and lawyer is perhaps most explicitly made after Scout has been caught fighting with children who accused her father of being a 'nigger lover'. Atticus (Bruzzi 2005, p. 88):

> sits her down on the front steps and teaches her white liberal ideology: how she should substitute "Negro" for "nigger" and how he "couldn't hold my head up in this town. *I couldn't even tell you and Jem not to do something again*" if he did not defend Robinson.
>
> (emphasis added, see also Papke 2001 and Holcomb 2002, p. 36)

To Kill a Mockingbird dramatizes the aspirations of mid-twentieth century manhood – its benign paternalism and willed repression of violence – as well as what Kaja Silverman (1992, p. 38) calls 'the vulnerability of conventional masculinity' in Atticus' incapacity to impose his will on the world around him. Yet the film suggests that sacrificing the present for a better future is one key constituent element of a father's duty to his children and of law's commitment to justice. The film's temporal flux – the nostalgia of its narrative voice intertwined with its imagined trajectory towards a new world of racial equality – exposes a complex structure of desire and anxiety that attaches law to fatherhood. In *To Kill a Mockingbird*, Scout and Jem embody the hope that, through the relation between a lawyer/father and his children, law will reach forward towards justice rather than be mired in a restrictive and unjust past. At the same time, we see vulnerability in those figures of hope as well as the incapacity of their father fully to protect them from the dangers of the present.

'What kind of man are you?'

To Kill a Mockingbird is in fact a film concerning conflict primarily between two fathers and their versions of fatherhood: Atticus Finch and Robert E. Lee (Bob) Ewell. Both are single parents.[4] Ewell's daughter Mayella is the victim of the alleged rape whose perpetrator, Tom Robinson, Atticus defends. If Atticus is a fairytale father, Ewell is a fatherly nightmare, crude and abusive with a demonic look (Bruzzi 2005, p. 86). In ways both bold and subtle, the film marks and highlights contrasts between them: while Atticus is soft spoken, polite and generally unflappable, Ewell is loud, profane and threatening; while Atticus is always dressed impeccably in a suit and hat, Ewell wears overalls and is generally dishevelled; while Atticus eschews violent confrontation, Ewell seems to crave it (Osborn 1996, p. 1140). In cultural terms, Ewell represents the governing moral order of Old South – honour, violence, racism – and Atticus the emerging liberal order of the New South – respect, restraint and racial equality.

Indeed, the film highlights the contrast between them in a number of scenes in which they appear together. After a preliminary hearing in Tom Robinson's case, for example, Ewell and Atticus meet outside the courtroom. Atticus, holding his hat in his hand, talks to another man as Ewell, hat cocked defiantly, challenges him. In a voice part sneering, part insinuating, Ewell reveals an ever-present inclination towards violence. 'Captain, I'm real sorry they picked you to defend that nigger who raped my Mayella', Ewell says. 'I don't know why I didn't kill him myself instead of going to the sheriff. It would have saved you and the sheriff and the taxpayers a lot of trouble'.

While he spits these words out with venom, 'I don't know why I did not kill him myself . . .' is a question not just for Ewell, but also for the film's viewers. From one perspective, it suggests that Ewell sees himself as the legitimate embodiment of a racist legal system that allows white men to take the law into their own hands against African-Americans. Yet from another, the question suggests that in spite of his constant aggressiveness and threatening demeanour, Ewell is capable of actual violence only against children and the weak. While he is the kind of man who, during their conversation, pokes an index finger into Atticus' chest with his thumb pointing upward, as if to mimic a gun, he may not be one who could pull an actual trigger (Figure 1). Atticus, on the other hand, seldom shows anger and never aggressiveness; but when, later in the film, he is called on by the sheriff to shoot a rabid dog, we (and his children) discover that he is the best shot in the county.

Ewell's menacing but flaccid display of violence is a metaphor for the structure of violence underpinning the era's white supremacist values. Those values depend on a kind of racial solidarity that evacuates the promises of liberalism, on racial loyalty over factual truth, on caste status over individual merit, and on violence over reason. In their courthouse exchange, even as he notes Atticus's superior status ('Hey Captain') Ewell calls Atticus to account in response to an accusation of racial betrayal, casting his question as an issue of alliance:

FIGURE 1 Atticus Finch and Bob Ewell.

> Hey Captain, someone told me just now that they thought you believed Tom Robinson's story again our'n. You know what I said. I said you are wrong man, you are dead wrong. Mr. Finch ain't takin his story against our'n. Well they was wrong wasn't they?

Atticus avoids answering the question about whether he believes Tom, taking on the mantle of liberal legality. 'I've been appointed to defend Tom Robinson', he says, 'Now that he has been charged that's what I intend to do'.

As Atticus departs, walking down the stairs out of the frame, the camera closes in on Ewell, his teeth clenched, calling after Atticus: 'What kind of man are you? You've got children of your own'. Ewell's question might be read as asking 'What kind of (white) man are you?' – meaning, are you one who will protect his white daughter from the dangers of racial intermixing? one who will enforce the race line at all cost? Read this way, Ewell's accusation of betrayal raises questions about law's proper role in relation to racial hierarchy and privilege. His is a call to serve the present, to acknowledge and protect white supremacy. Atticus's flat, matter-of-fact response points to a future in which African-American men accused of raping white women routinely will be afforded the full protections of the law.[5]

Of course, that future remains over the horizon; in spite of overwhelming evidence to the contrary, Tom Robinson is found guilty by an all-white, all-male jury. Sometime later, Tom is shot trying to escape as he is transported to jail in a neighbouring town. The law of the present, it seems, is allied with the entailments of the past. Yet, Atticus's cross-examination of Bob and Mayella Ewell during the trial leaves a cloud of suspicion that Ewell had beaten his daughter for her willing dalliance with an African-American man and fabricated the rape allegation to cover up Mayella's transgression. The cloud of that dishonourable imputation provokes Ewell to menace Atticus and his children, and that menace lays bare the promise as well as the limitations of Atticus's redefinition of fatherhood and law. In emphasizing the fact that Atticus is also a father, Ewell suggests that lawyerly niceties ought to matter less than remembering what it means to have children. For Ewell, having children is an occasion for and a call to violence, and it is precisely this call that Atticus refuses to hear and heed, for better or worse.

Ewell's spiteful critique of Atticus's manhood marks one way in which Atticus is vulnerable to violence in the present: through his children, whether it be their verbal harassment in the schoolyard or Ewell's final attack on them in the woods. While Bruzzi (2005, p. 88) observes that Atticus is there 'to protect Jem and Scout from the brutalizing adult world Mayella's father embodies', early in the film Atticus articulates a more tragic understanding of fatherhood. 'There's a lot of ugly things in this world, son', he tells Jem. 'I wish I could keep 'em all away from you. That's never possible'.[6] Knowing that, Atticus embraces a model of fatherhood and law that aims to build a new and different future rather than remaining tethered to entailments of the past and present. 'You're gonna hear some ugly talk about this [Atticus's representation of Tom Robinson] in school', he tells Scout after her fight with young Walter Cunningham. 'But I want you to promise me one thing: that you won't get into fights over it, no matter what they say to you'.

This move away from reflexive violence is paradigm-shifting in the Depression-era South for both men (insult demands response in honour-based cultures) and for law (contrast, for example, the lynch law demanded by townsmen with Tom Robinson's actual trial). Once again Atticus embodies that shift. Late in the film, after hearing of Tom's death, Atticus and Jem go to Tom's home to convey the tragic news to his wife and family. As Jem sits in the car, Ewell appears out of the shadows and orders one of Tom's relatives to fetch Atticus from the house ('Boy, go inside and tell Atticus Finch I said to come out here. Go on boy', he says to a grown man). While they wait for Atticus to appear, the camera brings Ewell and Jem into the same frame. They glance at each other, visually connecting, registering yet again Ewell's awareness of Atticus's vulnerability as a father. In this moment, viewers take on Jem's perspective as the conflict between Atticus and Ewell plays out (Figure 2).

As Atticus exits the Robinson's house and slowly walks towards him, Ewell suddenly spits in Atticus's face. Startled by the violent act, seemingly about to lose control at its deep insult, Atticus takes one step forward, anger finally registering for the first and only time in the film. Shifting quickly, the camera captures Jem's frightened reaction to the impending violent confrontation. We watch Ewell and over his shoulder Jem, anxiously waiting to see what Atticus will do in response to this gross provocation. Yet instead of resorting to violence, Atticus stops, wipes the spit off his face with disgust, and

FIGURE 2 Jem and Ewell.

steps around Ewell. As he drives away, the car's lights illuminate Ewell's scowling face.

Yet again Ewell has been frustrated, unable to draw Atticus into his world – now not in the racialized alliance contemplated in their earlier interaction, but instead in a confrontation between white men over insults to their honour. Atticus models for his son (and for the film's viewers) the answer to Ewell's question 'What kind of man are you?' His version of manliness shows restraint in the face of a crude attack and evokes in that restraint a choice between the world that Ewell inhabits and the one that Atticus seeks to create, a world in which manliness resides in self-control and moral rectitude, not violence or physical confrontation.

Disobedient children/non-compliant jurors

While the film portrays Atticus as an idealized figure, it remains the case that whether during Tom Robinson's trial or in daily dealings with his children, Atticus Finch is often unable to work his will in the present. A single father still mourning for his lost wife, he gives Jem and Scout considerable freedom (e.g., in the highly formalized world in which they live they call him 'Atticus') and relies on others to enforce the few rules that govern the children's everyday lives. Calpurnia, Atticus's African-American maid and the household's mother substitute, certainly exerts some amount of authority over them, but her racial otherness prevents her from carrying the moral and affective weight of the children's actual mother. If she helps on the margins to maintain propriety in the domestic sphere, she does not (particularly in the film) become a parental figure like Atticus, who infuses his injunctions with deep love and displays what we might call a commitment to equity rather than rule-based governance at home.

Yet his general absence from the children's daily world lessens his immediate authority. Indeed, drawing a parallel between the non-compliant jury in Tom's case and Atticus' disobedient children, the film suggests that, if the present is the touchstone of his efficacy as a father and a lawyer, Atticus is oddly impotent. The viewer's embrace of him and his vision of fatherhood and law depends, then, upon the affection and ratification the narrator's post-hoc voice-over provides. Seeing Atticus as his children see him and knowing that the disobedience of the present is part and parcel of the future Atticus seeks to build, we are able to take the long view of his immediate failings as both a lawyer and father even as we understand their costs.

Atticus frequently is unable to make his children obey him at all. Indeed, six minutes into the film, we first meet Jem in a moment of stubborn defiance, sitting in a tree-house refusing to come down until Atticus agrees to play football. Atticus calmly walks over to the tree, looks up, as if offering a prayer, and asks, 'Son, why don't you come down out of there now and have your breakfast?' 'No sir', Jem responds, 'not until you agree to play football for the Methodists.... I ain't coming down'. Atticus response highlights what Jem sees as a kind of weakness: 'Oh, son, I can't do that. I'm too old to get out there'. Yet as in his confrontations with Bob Ewell, when Jem continues his protest Atticus turns, walks away and offers a calm rejoinder: 'Suit yourself'. Jem stays in the tree.

Moreover, despite his best efforts, Atticus has difficulty stopping Scout from fighting with other children at school. 'Scout I don't want you fighting....', he explains, 'I don't care what the reasons are, I forbid you to fight'. In a voice-over, Scout acknowledges Atticus' point:

> Atticus had promised me he would wear me out if he ever heard of me fighting anymore... I was far too old and too big for such childish things and the sooner I learned to hold it in, the better off everybody would be.

But, as she puts it, 'I soon forgot'.

If Scout and Jem's childishness proves frustratingly resistant to Atticus's incessantly reasonable injunctions, it offers an opening onto a world in which social norms have not completely colonized the children's every thought and action. In their relative innocence, Scout and Jem relate to those around them in ways, though mildly defiant, that unravel the tight fabric of racism bit by bit. In so doing, they provide a vision of a more just social order that is, in the world of the film, incipient and ready for cultivation.

The film conjures that alternative most powerfully in a scene midway through the narrative in which Atticus and his children avert a lynch mob on the jailhouse steps. Atticus is called to the jail by the sheriff the evening before Robinson's trial is to begin, and he posts himself on the front step with a chair, a lamp, and a law book — ready to confront impending violence with reason and enlightenment. After Atticus leaves his house, the children and Dill sneak out and follow him to see what is going on. Hiding in bushes across from the jail, Jem tells Scout, 'I just wanted to see where he was and what he was up to. He's alright', he says as if he were responsible for protecting Atticus. 'Let's go back home'.

Just as they are about to leave, a group of armed men arrive at the jail and demand that Atticus turn over Tom. At this point, the children run through the crowd of men to Atticus. 'Jem, go home and take Scout and Dill home with you', Atticus demands when they appear. Jem, slowly surveying the crowd of men, refuses to leave. 'Son I said, go home', Atticus insists, to which Jem replies 'No sir'. Someone in the crowd tells Atticus that he had better get the children out of there. 'Jem, I want you to please leave', Atticus says. 'No sir' Jem repeats. 'Jem', Atticus intones, anxiously raising his voice. 'I tell you I ain't going', Jem insistently replies.

Jem's defiance paradoxically is rooted in a deep identification with Atticus. It is almost as if Jem projects himself into the future and acts as he imagines Atticus himself would act — indeed, is acting: on principle. It is Scout, however, who pierces the tension of the moment. She spots Walter Cunningham Sr., a leader of the mob, and, too young to understand his purpose, calls to him in a friendly way. 'Hey, Mr. Cunningham...How's your entailment going?' She has met him once before, in the film's first scene when he drops by her house to pay Atticus in hickory nuts for legal work 'as part of his entailment', and she knows his son Walter, Jr. 'Tell him "hey" for me, won't you?' she says to Walter Sr. She then forays innocently into a topic with much deeper resonance across the film. 'You know something, Mr. Cunningham?' she says, 'Entailments are bad...' (Figure 3).

FIGURE 3 Scout and the lynch mob.

Cunningham, who has so far been avoiding her gaze shamefaced, begins to look at her quizzically. 'It takes a long time, sometimes', Scout continues (to play entailments out? get rid of them? Or, perhaps, to lift the burden of the entailments that structure a social inheritance of inequality and injustice?). Then, thinking she might have offended him with her forwardness, she quietly retreats. 'What's the matter? I sure meant no harm, Mr. Cunningham', she says worriedly. Finally he looks at her and replies, 'No harm taken, young lady. I'll tell Walter you said "hey".' Turning to the mob he says, 'Let's clear out of here; let's go, boys'.

Scout, more credulous than defiant, breaks the frame of meaning that has structured the conflict between Atticus and the mob. She reaches across lines of class and racial antagonism and, as her father has always enjoined her to do, tries to stand in the shoes of someone else to understand the weight of the entailments Mr. Cunningham feels as a poor man – but also, in the wider world of the film, perhaps as he also stands ready to help lynch a black man. In this scene, Jem and Scout disobey Atticus in service of some value or principle that Atticus himself might have espoused. By teaching his children about the proper way to live and act, Atticus has given them grounds for disobeying his more immediate paternal commands. The children bring his values to bear, however prematurely, in ways that suggest they have already learned lessons about the kinds of adults Atticus wants them to become. Jem and Scout exist both in the here and now and in an incomplete vision of what they can and should be.

For obviously different reasons, Atticus is equally unable to get the jury to do justice in the present. His reasoned, careful parsing of evidence, so persuasive to contemporary viewers, is of no avail before the film's white, male jury. He cannot convince them to embrace and ratify his civics book belief in equal justice for all. As Asimow (1996, p. 1136) puts it, '... (T)he reality was that Atticus' defense was doomed from the start...' 'Now gentlemen', he tells the jury as if anticipating *Brown v. Board of Education* and the Warren Court, 'in this country the courts are the great levelers. In our courts all men are created equal'. Atticus is uncharacteristically animated in his plea to the jury to review the evidence dispassionately and restore Tom Robinson to his family. 'In the name of God', he says his voice raised, 'do your duty'. 'In the name of God', Atticus implores, 'believe Tom Robinson'.[7]

As he utters these lines the camera closes in on Jem, who is intently surveying the scene from the coloured balcony. With the scene's focus on Jem, who has begun to identify powerfully with his father, the film transforms the legal argument before the jury into an instruction from father to son and into an inter-generational, family legacy (Holcomb 2002, p. 40).[8] What Atticus cannot bring to fruition in Tom Robinson's case is left to his children's generation to complete. As he explains to Tom after the guilty verdict, 'I'll go to see Helen first thing tomorrow morning. I told her not to be disappointed, that we'd probably lose this one'. Losing 'this one' refers to the trial, but also to the legal present. Atticus knows the obstacles he confronts in the Alabama courts, and losing 'this one' is Atticus's acknowledgment that law of the here and now cannot overcome the racism of its cultural surround.

Later, after learning of Tom's death, Atticus despairingly tells his children, their friend Dill, and a neighbour, 'The last thing I told him was, not to lose heart, that we'd ask for an appeal. We had such a good chance. We had more than a good chance'. To whom would Atticus have made his appeal? What gave him such confidence in its success? Atticus would appeal to the courts but also to an indeterminate future in which the promise of justice could, and would, be redeemed, a future where courts might indeed be great levellers.

The coloured balcony

This dual orientation to the future is captured visually in the positioning of Atticus's children as spectators in Tom Robinson's trial.[9] The courtroom, like the town in which it is located, is rigidly segregated, with whites seated on the first floor and African-Americans in the balcony. That Dill, Jem and Scout cannot find a seat on the first floor among Maycomb's whites, but can comfortably join the balcony crowd, seems to foretell something about the world into which they will grow up. They find their place as spectators hovering over a classic southern race trial, looked after by an African-American minister, Reverend Sykes.

The camera places viewers alongside them, merging our gaze with theirs as we watch the trial proceed. But we also often look up from below to see three white children surrounded, indeed enveloped, by the African-American community in a vision of racial integration imaginable within the confines of the law long before it is imaginable in the world outside the courtroom.[10] It is to that imagining that Atticus as lawyer/father orients himself, offering a vision of formal legal equality, embraced in spite of social difference, to the law and his children. When Bob Ewell later tries to kill Jem and Scout, he avenges his own humiliation at Atticus's hands during the trial but also tries to short circuit the future that Atticus's children embody (Shaffer 1981, p. 191).

The spectators in the coloured balcony act as an audience for the jury's verdict in Tom Robinson's case and another kind of jury for Atticus' arguments, for his vision of equal justice under law. Viewers focus on their reaction to the verdict as it occurs: the camera shifts to the African-Americans in the balcony and then returns to the jury below. When Tom Robinson is found guilty, we are returned to the balcony where Jem sits, head down and crying, and Scout stares out glumly, as if imprisoned between the slots of the balcony's railing.

After the rest of the courtroom empties, spectators in the balcony remain to watch Atticus pack his briefcase. The camera moves behind him to show the

FIGURE 4 The black balcony.

African-Americans in the balcony standing in silent tribute as he leaves (Figure 4). They rise, Bruzzi (2005, p. 87) argues, 'to honor Atticus as 'the great protector who stands up for the weak and the good'. Jem immediately joins them in standing, but the still-untutored Scout remains seated until Reverend Sykes tells her, 'Miss Jean Louise, stand up'. Scout complies without protest as the Reverend puts his hand around her and adds, 'Your father is passing'.

The word 'passing' in this deeply affecting scene suggests not just physical movement out of the courtroom but the passing on of a legacy. The lawyer's appeal and the work of the father in passing on his values are joined. The African-Americans in the balcony rise for Atticus the way the spectators at a trial stand when the judge enters and exits the courtroom. For Maycomb's African-American community, and for his children who stand with them, Atticus is the true embodiment of law, of a law whose gaze is oriented beyond this courtroom to a time when equality is achieved, segregation ended, and African-Americans and whites sit side-by-side.

Conclusion

In its temporal orientation, *To Kill a Mockingbird* captures a constituent element of both law and fatherhood. With respect to law, as Drucilla Cornell (1990, p. 1697) reminds us, 'Legal interpretation demands that we remember the future'. In that phrase, Cornell suggests that law fixes it gaze temporally, not just on the possibilities (or impossibilities) of the present, but on a future promise of justice. Justice, Cornell (1990, p. 1697) argues, 'is precisely what eludes our full knowledge'. We cannot 'grasp the Good but only follow it. The Good... is a star which beckons us to follow'. While justice, what

Cornell (1988. p. 1587) calls the Good, is, on her account, always present *to* law, it is never completely realized *in* law. Cornell reminds us that there are, in fact, two audiences for every legal act, the audience of the present and the audience of the future (which stands as a figure of law's redeeming promise of justice). Both audiences seem to be very much part of the legal and paternal world of Atticus Finch.

Perhaps no one had a deeper and more penetrating understanding of the centrality of the temporal duality that Cornell highlights than Robert Cover (1983). 'Law', Cover (1983, p. 9) argued:

> may be viewed as a system of tension or a bridge linking a concept of reality to an imagined alternative... Thus, one constitutive element of a *nomos* is the phenomenon George Steiner has labeled 'alterity': the 'other than the case', the counterfactual propositions, images, shapes of will and evasions with which we charge our mental being and by means of which we build the changing, largely fictive milieu for our somatic and our social existence.' But the concept of a *nomos* is not exhausted by its 'alterity'; it is neither utopia nor pure vision. A *nomos*, as a world of law, entails the application of human will to an extant state of affairs as well as toward our visions of alternative futures.

The *nomos* that law helps to create, Cover believed, always contains within it visions of possibility not yet realized, a better world not yet built. Yet law is not simply, or even primarily, a gentle, hermeneutic apparatus; as Cover (1986, p. 1601) reminds us, it always exists in a state of tension between a world of meaning in which justice is pursued, and a world of violence in which 'legal interpretation takes places on a field of pain and death'.

Taking Cornell's and Cover's perspective, one might say that Atticus Finch's effort to save an African-American man accused of raping a white woman in *To Kill a Mockingbird*, while it had little chance of immediate success, provides such a bridge and participates in the logic of what Cover (1983, p. 34) called 'redemptive constitutionalism'. Atticus refused to recognize the injustice of the time and place in which he lived as the defining totality of law and, as such, acted as the carrier of a vision of a future in which justice might prevail. For people like Atticus, as Cover (1983, p. 34) argues, 'Redemption takes place within an eschatalogical schema that postulates: (1) the unredeemed character of reality as we know it, (2) the fundamentally different reality that should take its place, and (3) the replacement of one with the other'.

Cover (1983, p. 39) uses the example of anti-slavery activism in the mid-nineteenth century to suggest that the work of 'redemptive constitutionalism' reveals 'a creative pulse that proliferates principle and precept, commentary and justification, even in the face of a state legal order less likely to hold slavery unconstitutional than to declare the imminent kingship of Jesus Christ on Earth'. In this view, lawyers like Atticus Finch speak in a prophetic voice even as they supply the argumentative and interpretive resources to bridge the gap between the present and the beckoning possibility of justice.

To Kill a Mockingbird suggests that fathers also are called on to remember the future and to imagine for their children a time different from, and perhaps better than, the present (Dollahite and Hawkins 1988). As a father and figure of law, Atticus cultivates a way of being with his children and his community that recognizes who they are while never forgetting who he hopes they will become (see Shaffer 1981, p. 221). Looking back from the perspective of the film's future we can say that however partial Atticus Finch's vision of justice may have been, and however compromised a parent he was, seen through his daughter's eyes he, nevertheless, deserves to be viewed as a 'hero' who held firmly to hope for the law he served and the children he raised.

Acknowledgements

We are grateful for the skilled research assistance of Matthew Brewster, and to Sara Knox and Cristyn Davies for their insightful comments on an earlier draft of this paper. All images courtesy of Universal Studies Licensing LLC.

Notes

1. *To Kill a Mockingbird* first appeared as a novel in 1960, winning a Pulitzer Prize, and was made into an Academy-Award winning film two years later. See Harper Lee, *To Kill a Mockingbird* (Philadelphia: J.P. Lippincott and Co., 1960); *To Kill a Mockingbird*, dir. Robert Mulligan (Universal Pictures 1962). The novel cast a long shadow on the film's reception, and remains arguably the more important and influential of the two versions. Even so, in 2008 the American Bar Association polled a panel of experts to identify and rank the 25 greatest law films ever made. While it was not a scientific survey, ranked first was *To Kill a Mockingbird*. See Brust (2008). Moreover, the American Film Institute ranked it as #34 in its list of the top 100 films of the last 100 years. http://www.afi.com/tvevents/100years/movies.aspx. See also Holcomb (2002).
2. In this essay we focus particularly on the filmic version of the story. Its visual presentation and certain alterations in the novel's narrative intensify the thematic focus on fatherhood. The film's opening credits insert viewers into a nostalgic re-examination of childhood as the camera slowly pans across a landscape of old toys and knickknacks as a child's hand wanders over them. Small visual cues emphasize a child's perspective throughout; we often watch visually self-reflexive moments as Scout and Jem stare intently at their father and the world around them. The film shows two other fathers from

this childlike vantage, the frightening and prohibitive Mr. Radley, who along with Bob Ewell is another paternal gauge against which we measure Atticus Finch's liberality as a father.

Additionally, the film draws upon and extends a specific set of mid-century Hollywood ruminations on law, racism and democratic values. They are thematized either explicitly or implicitly in a cluster of films that have a distinct understanding and iconography of justice and injustice: *12 Angry Men* (1959), *Inherit the Wind* (1960), *Judgment at Nuremberg* (1961) and *The Man Who Shot Liberty Valance* (1962), to name but a few. While as a film *To Kill a Mockingbird* hews relatively closely to Lee's original text, it also has a cultural life of its own within this genealogy.

3   An entailment, one of the running motifs in the text of which more below, is at common law:

> an interference with and curtailment of the ordinary rules pertaining to devolution by inheritance; a limitation and direction by which property is to descend different from the course which it would take if the creator of the entailment, grantor, or testator, had been content that the estate should devolve in regular and general succession to heirs at law in the statutory order of preference and sequence.
>
> Black's Law Dictionary (1968, p. 652)

4   Indeed, a third, single father plays a subsidiary role: Boo Radley's father, whom Jem describes as 'the meanest man who ever drew breath'. Where in the novel Boo's father has died, in the film he effectively imprisons Boo and acts as a barrier between Boo and Atticus's children. His meanness stands in stark contrast with Atticus's gentility and generosity. Thanks to Sara Knox and Cristyn Davies for this insight.

5   However unsuccessfully, Atticus enacts that future as an answer to Ewell's question. After the trial is complete and the verdict rendered, when Atticus exits the courtroom moving down the same centre aisle that Ewell had used earlier, the camera shows people looking down on Atticus from the segregated, 'coloureds-only' balcony where the African-American community has risen to pay homage to Atticus. If Ewell's question called forth the logic of racial solidarity under Jim Crow, the homage of the African-American community is their tribute to a vision of the future in which law can live up to its promise of equal treatment.

6   In fact, Jem and Scout are saved from Ewell's attack by their neighbour, the reclusive Boo Radley, rather than their father Atticus. Boo is able to take on the mantle of protector perhaps because he has lived fully apart from the norms of the community and so remains outside the controversies of the Robinson case. He is at least reputedly capable of violence, where Atticus is reluctant, and he has observed, and in his own way, befriended Jem and Scout as they have grown, though without actually meeting them. He sees

7   them and understands their world and its dangers in ways Atticus, otherwise occupied with the future, does not. Indeed, it is precisely as an outsider that Boo brings Ewell to justice, doing what neither Atticus nor law itself could do. As one critic puts it:

> Finch wants his all white, all male jurors to do the right thing. But as a good Jim Crow liberal he dare not challenge the foundation of their privilege. Instead, Finch does what lawyers for black men did in those days. He encourages them to swap one of their prejudices [about race] for another [about class and respectability] (parentheticals added).
>
> See Gladwell (2009)

8   Holcomb (2002) calls attention to what he labels 'Jem's nascent activism . . .'.

9   That they attend the trial at all marks another instance of their defiance of Atticus. As they sit on the side of the road watching a parade of neighbours heading down to the courthouse, Jem suddenly gets up and begins to join that parade. He says, 'I can't stand it any longer. I'm going down to the courthouse and watch'. Scout replies, 'You better not. You know what Atticus said'. 'I don't care if he did', Jem answers, 'I'm not going to miss the most exciting thing that ever happened in this town'.

10 Holcomb, in contrast, suggests that the film actually has little to say about race, that it displays 'an implicit desire for race and class to simply not matter'. See Holcomb (2002, p. 39).

References

12 Angry Men (1959) Dir. Sidney Lumet, United Artists.

Althusser, L. (1971) 'Freud and Lacan', in *Lenin and Philosophy and Other Essays*, trans. Ben Brewster, London, Monthly Review Press, pp.189–219.

American Film Institute (2003) '100 Years: Heroes and Villains', [online] http://connect.afi.com/site/DocServer/handv100.pdf?docID=246 (accessed 19 June 2012).

Asimow, M. (1996) 'When lawyers were heroes', *University of San Francisco Law Review*, vol. 30, pp. 1131–1138.

Black's Law Dictionary (1968) *Black's Law Gladwell*, 4th edn, revised, St. Paul, MN, West Publishing Co.

Brust, R. (2008) 'The 25 greatest legal movies', [online] http://www.abajournal.com/magazine/article/the_25_greatest_legal_movies/ (accessed 19 June 2012).

Bruzzi, S. (2005) *Bringing Up Daddy: Fatherhood and Masculinity in Postwar Hollywood*, London, BFI Publishing.

Cornell, D. (1988) 'Post-structuralism, the ethical relation, and the law', *Cardozo Law Review*, vol. 9, pp. 1587–1628.

Cornell, D. (1990) 'From the lighthouse: the promise of redemption and the possibility of legal interpretation', *Cardozo Law Review*, vol. 11, pp. 1687–1714.

Cover, R. (1983) 'The supreme court, 1982 term-foreword: nomos and narrative', *Harvard Law Review*, vol. 97, pp. 4–68.

Cover, R. (1986) 'Violence and the word', *Yale law Journal*, vol. 95, pp. 1601–1630.

Dollahite, D. & Hawkins, A. (1988) 'A conceptual ethic of generative fathering', *The Journal of Men's Studies*, vol. 7, pp. 109–132.

Frank, J. (1949) *Courts on Trial: Myth and Reality in American Justice*, Princeton, Princeton University Press.

Freedman, M. H. (1994) 'Atticus finch-right and wrong', *Alabama Law Review*, vol. 45, pp. 473–482.

Freud, S. (1950) *Totem and Taboo*, trans. James Strachey, New York, Norton.

Garber, M. (1998) 'Cinema scopes: evolution, media, and the law', in *Law in the Domains of Culture*. eds. A. Sarat & T. R. Kearns, Ann Arbor, University of Michigan Press, pp. 121–160.

Gladwell, M. (2009) 'The courthouse ring: Atticus Finch and the limits of southern liberalism', *The New Yorker* (August 10, 2009) [online]. www.newyorker.com/reporting/2009/08/10/090810fa_fact_gladwell (accessed 19 June 2012).

Goodrich, P. (1997) 'Maladies of the legal soul: psychoanalysis and interpretation in law', *Washington & Lee Law Review*, vol. 54, pp.1035–1074.

Hartman, G. (1996) 'The blind side of the Akedah', *Raritan*, vol. 16, pp. 28–39.

Holcomb, M. (2002) 'To Kill a Mockingbird', *Film Quarterly*, vol. 55, pp. 34–40.
Inherit the Wind (1960) Dir. Stanley Kramer, United Artists.
Judgment at Nuremberg (1961) Dir. Stanley Kramer, United Artists.
Lee, H. (1960) *To Kill a Mockingbird*, Philadelphia, J.P. Lippincott and Co.
Lubet, S. (1999) 'Reconstructing Atticus Finch', *Michigan Law Review*, vol. 97, pp. 1339–1384.
Meyer, L. (forthcoming 2013) 'I would kill for you: Love, Law and Sacrifice in To Kill a Mockingbird', in *Re-imagining To Kill a Mockingbird: Family, Community and the Possibility of Equal Justice Under Law*, eds. Austin Sarat and Martha Merrill Umphrey, Boston, University of Massachusetts Press.
Osborn, J. J. (1996) 'Atticus Finch-The End of Honor: a discussion of *To Kill a Mockingbird*', *University of San Francisco Law Review*, vol. 30, pp. 1139–1342.
Papke, D. R. (2001) 'Law, cinema, and ideology: hollywood legal films of the 1950s', *UCLA Law Review*, vol. 48, pp. 1473–1494.
Phelps, T. G. (2002) 'Atticus, Thomas, and the meaning of justice', *Notre Dame Law Review*, vol. 77, pp. 925–936.
Sarat, A. (2000) 'Imagining the law of the father: loss, dread, and mourning in *The Sweet Hereafter*', *Law & Society Review*, vol. 34, pp. 3–46.
Shaffer, T. (1981) 'The moral theology of Atticus Finch', *University of Pittsburgh Law Review*, vol. 42, pp. 181–224.
Schlag, P. (1990) 'Normative and Nowhere to Go', *Stanford Law Review*, vol. 43, pp. 167–192.
Silverman, K. (1992) *Male subjectivity at the margins*, New York, Routledge.
The Man Who Shot Liberty Valance (1962) Dir. John Ford, Paramount Pictures.
To Kill a Mockingbird (1962) Dir. Robert Mulligan, Universal Pictures.
Walzer, M. (1986) *Exodus and Revolution*, New York, Basic Books.

Peter J. Hutchings

ENTERTAINING TORTURE, EMBODYING LAW

> Torture appears as an image: once, of sovereign power, more recently, of acts performed on people not even defined as prisoners. It served to instruct, now it serves to entertain, as image and spectacle. Law's entertaining of torture both enables the spectacles seen (and not seen) since Abu Ghraib, and intersects with wider cultural practices, especially in cinema and television. Torture has been a form of entertainment as much as it has been a subject of revulsion. Recent justifications of torture have sought cinematic backing. The US Justice Department torture memos, and the scandals of Abu Ghraib and beyond, link attitudes towards torture with a culture of entertainment and spectacle, up to the point at which the law comes to entertain torture. At stake in both spectacle and actual practices is a form of corporeal sovereignty: the wholeness of the sovereign against the brokenness of any body that would threaten such wholeness. This paper explores these intersections, along with the logic of a sovereign disregard for the body, through readings of the torture memos, First Blood, and the investigations into prisoner abuse in Afghanistan and Iraq.

> Secretary Rumsfeld: I think that — I'm not a lawyer. My impression is that what has been charged thus far is abuse, which I believe technically is different from torture. ... I don't know if the — it is correct to say what you just said, that torture has taken place, or that there's been a conviction for torture. And therefore I'm not going to address the torture word.
> (US Department of Defense 2004)

In the post 9/11 world of the Global War on Terror, torture appeared as an image. Until the release of the Abu Ghraib photos, torture was barely a word to be mentioned by those in power. With the appearance of those photos,

---

This essay develops a paper delivered at *Trans(l)egalité*, the Law and Literature Association of Australia and Law and Society Association of Australia and New Zealand Joint conference (Griffith University, 2–5 December 2009).

torture was still something that could be seen more than spoken, subsumed in the more vague term 'abuses'.

Torture is the perquisite of the sovereign: as a punishment for treason, it was the thing itself, with no necessity defences invoked (Foucault 1979, Scarry 1985, Santner 2011). The reduction of a treacherous subject to a brute and broken body was a display aimed at asserting the potent wholeness of the sovereign's body. As sovereign spectacle, it entertained, instructed and enacted.

As an immediate spectacle, torture became invisible with the transformation of the operations of sovereign force, as Foucault has argued. The application of sovereign force upon bodies became more indirect but also more widespread, constituting what has been termed a 'bio-politics' (Foucault 1997, Agamben 1998). Recently, torture has returned to public sight as a mediated spectacle, the stuff of film and television, of photographic and video souvenir and evidence. This mediation of torture effects a disembodiment of torture, one which enables casual violence to occur within a realm in which any distinctions between torture and entertainment seem to have been blurred. That is, to the extent that torture becomes a general spectacle, or is 'spectacularized' (Hutchings 2001), it is both easier to entertain as an idea, and to be experienced as a form of entertainment.

The cinematic roots of torture run from cinema's outset, from the early Edison short *Electrocuting an Elephant* (1903), to the actuality footage of Chinese executions *Execution of the Hung-Hu* (1904, Pathé Frères, Paris), through to Godard's *Le petit soldat* (1960–1963), which was banned from release in France until 1963 due to its depictions of torture in the Algerian war, on to Pontecorvo's *La battaglia di Algeri* (1966), to any James Bond film. Throughout cinema's history, torture has been a form of entertainment as much as it has been a subject of revulsion. In the era of the Global War on Terror, justifications of torture have sought cinematic backing in the archetypally cinematic ticking time bomb scenario, while the Pentagon was reported to screen *The Battle of Algiers*, perhaps looking to brush up on intelligence-gathering techniques (Kaufman 2003). The US Justice Department torture memos, and the scandals of Abu Ghraib and beyond, link attitudes towards torture with a culture of entertainment and spectacle, up to the point at which the law comes to entertain torture.

Torture joins bodies and images in complex interactions. I want to trace those interactions through a number of key texts and events:

1. The Bybee torture memo;
2. *First Blood*;
3. The transformation of SERE techniques into torture practices; and
4. The Abu Ghraib images and the related revelations of the practices of torture first entertained by a clique of US government lawyers.

The Bybee torture memo

In August 2002, the US Justice Department's Office of Legal Counsel (OLC) produced the first of a series of memoranda concerning 'the standards of conduct under the Convention Against Torture . . . as implemented by . . . the United States Code'. The first of these is known as the Bybee Memo (Bybee 2002). The purpose of all of these legal opinions was to enable torture to come out from 'under the color of law' (Bybee 2002, p. 3). In legal terms, 'the color of law' refers to an illegal act performed while acting under use of governmental authority, and the Bybee memorandum sets out a series of arguments that would enable torture to be performed under the colour of law and not constitute a criminal act.

The arguments begin by addressing the question of what happens outside the US (as this is what is dealt with by the law but also by the practices of overseas incarceration and interrogation designed to avoid the bulk of US law), and will become a question related to what happens to non-US citizens, to aliens. The relevant law is Title 18 of the US Code, which deals with Crimes and Criminal Procedure, and defines torture as a crime, defining it as 'an act committed by a person acting under the color of law specifically intended to inflict severe physical or mental pain or suffering (other than pain or suffering incidental to lawful sanctions) upon another person within his custody or physical control'; and offers definitions of 'severe mental or physical pain' (18 USC §2340). Title 18 further defines torture committed outside the USA as an offence that may, in the case of death, amount to a capital offence.

The Bybee torture memo commences with an inability to imagine the severity of pain that would amount to torture. Turning to dictionaries and laws related to health benefits, the memo operates in a strange world of unspecified 'extreme acts' and various acts of faith. To perform acts which the Convention Against Torture (CAT 1984) directly defines as torture – but which Bybee recasts as something less than torture but still likely to elicit urgently needed intelligence – would be legal, Bybee argues, if those acts were performed in the belief that they were both necessary and legal, a belief in turn founded upon a particular belief in the constitutional omnipotence of the President as Commander in Chief.

As Elaine Scarry has suggested, this inability to imagine the pain of torture is inherent in the relationship between the body and language:

> The act of misdescribing torture or war, although in some instances intentional and in others unintentional, is in either case partially made possible by the inherent difficulty of accurately describing any event whose central content is bodily pain or injury.
>
> (Scarry 1985, p. 13)

Torture works through establishing a relationship between the body and language in which the body is brought to speak out of, but not about, its pain. The verbal dimension of torture, the justification of the interrogation, is its alibi, and Bybee's memo searches for a legal language capable of justifying the physical pain it is designed to licence.

In pursuit of this licence, there are a number of distinct moments in the staging of the OLC arguments.

The first is to remove acts of torture from any definition of torture: it is an ascendant argument because it puts the definition at so great an extremity that very little can satisfy it. The memorandum then comes up with the following definition of 'severe pain or suffering', drawn from the law relating to health benefits:

> Although these statutes address a substantially different subject ... they are nonetheless helpful for understanding what constitutes severe physical pain. They treat severe pain as an indicator of ailments that are likely to result in permanent and serious physical damage in the absence of immediate medical treatment. Such damage must rise to the level of death, organ failure, or the permanent impairment of a significant body function. These statutes suggest that 'severe pain', ... must rise to a similarly high level — the level that would ordinarily be associated with a sufficiently serious physical condition or injury such as death, organ failure, or serious impairment of body functions — in order to constitute torture.
>
> (Bybee 2002, p. 6)

The 'substantially different subject' turns out to be not entirely different: the prime legal reference here is USC Title 8, which deals with Aliens and Nationality, and the section drawn upon for a definition of 'severe pain or suffering' concerns 'Treatment of expenses subject to emergency medical services exception'. The law refers to a category of persons who aren't US citizens: 'an individual who is an alien not lawfully present in the United States' (8 USC §1369 (a)). It offers a definition of the level of 'severe pain or suffering', which necessitates medical intervention, the cost of which will be covered if the alien or anyone else can not be made to pay (8 USC §1369 (d)). The definition is about what would occur in the 'absence of immediate medical attention', and so sets a standard at which medical intervention must occur. It is an unlikely threshold for the setting of the kinds of pain that can be deliberately inflicted on the same alien body.

As the argument develops, it becomes clear that Bybee's aim is to put a whole range of practices outside of the definition of torture, which is positioned as above these practices in its severity:

> Each component of the definition emphasizes that torture is not the mere infliction of pain or suffering on another, but is instead a step well removed.... In short, reading the definition of torture as a whole, it is plain that the term encompasses only extreme acts.
>
> (Bybee 2002, p. 6)

If this disposes of torture by defining it out of the realm of the actual infliction of severe pain and suffering, then there is also the matter of the necessity of what might otherwise be termed torture. That is, even if these interrogation techniques did amount to torture, their necessity would give them legitimate colour of law:

> a detainee may possess information that could enable the United States to prevent attacks that potentially could equal or surpass the September 11 attacks in their magnitude. Clearly, any harm that might occur during an interrogation would pale to insignificance compared to the harm avoided by preventing such an attack, which could take hundreds or thousands of lives.
>
> Under this calculus, two factors will help indicate when the necessity defence could appropriately be invoked. First, the more certain that government officials are that a particular individual has information needed to prevent an attack, the more necessary interrogation will be. Second, the more likely it appears to be that a terrorist attack is likely to occur, and the greater the amount of damage expected from such an attack, the more that an interrogation to get information would become necessary.
>
> (Bybee 2002, p. 41)

Here, the necessity of interrogation inheres in those words, to be spoken under extreme duress, which will save some bodies at the expense of another.

Finally, there is a further exemption provided courtesy of the President's sovereign power to conduct military campaigns:

> Even if an interrogation method arguably were to violate Section 2340A, the statute would be unconstitutional if it impermissibly encroached on the President's constitutional power to conduct a military campaign. As Commander-in-Chief, the President has the constitutional authority to order interrogations of enemy combatants to gain intelligence information concerning the military plans of the enemy.... Any effort to apply Section 2340A in a manner that interferes with the President's direction of such core war matters as the detention and interrogation of enemy combatants thus would be unconstitutional.
>
> (Bybee 2002, p. 31)

In short, the Executive Orders can overrule any laws: they become law.[1]

This argument for the necessity of torture rests on at least two presuppositions:

1. The certainty that a detainee has information relevant to a pending attack (the cinematic 'ticking time bomb' scenario); and
2. The likelihood of an imminent attack.

Both suppositions are fictions: the recently declassified CIA Inspector General Report found that torture was frequently applied without anything to support these suppositions:

> Agency officers report that reliance on analytical assessments that were unsupported by credible intelligence may have resulted in the application of EITs [Extreme Interrogation Techniques] without justification. Some participants in the Program, particularly field interrogators, judge that CTC [Counterterrorist Center] assessments to the effect that detainees are withholding information are not always supported by an objective evaluation of available information and the evaluation of the interrogators but are too heavily based, instead, on presumptions of what the individual might or should know.
> (Office of Inspector General, CIA 2004, pp. 104–105)

While that analysis does not question the premise that withheld information might be justifiably obtained through torture, that is the justifying premise that requires closer examination, particularly as it is based on a cinematic and televisual exemplar: the ticking time bomb (see Manderson, forthcoming).

At the time of the writing of the torture memo, the television programme entirely structured around the ticking time bomb premise was *24* (2001–10). The programme's scenario involves 24 episodes, each unfolding over a televisual hour, in which counter-terrorism operative Jack Bauer (Kiefer Sutherland) races against the clock to avert a terrorist incident. As its co-creator, Robert Cochran admitted, 'Most terrorism experts will tell you that the "ticking time bomb" situation never occurs in real life, or very rarely. But on our show it happens every week' (Mayer 2007). That fictional scenario is the programme's license for torture, always with the justification that 'There isn't time!' We are in the world of the permanent emergency, the permanent exception, the absence or exceptional suspense of law.

Jane Mayer, who has written extensively on US practices of torture, reported the following claim on the part of the programme's co-creator Joel Surnow:

> The series, Surnow told me, is 'ripped out of the Zeitgeist of what people's fears are—their paranoia that we're going to be attacked,' and it 'makes people look at what we're dealing with' in terms of threats to

national security. 'There are not a lot of measures short of extreme measures that will get it done,' he said, adding, 'America wants the war on terror fought by Jack Bauer. He's a patriot'.

(Mayer 2007)

Jack Bauer the patriot always decides the exception: his *modus operandi* seems to consist almost entirely of ignoring the law and any service protocols because of the urgency of his mission. In that world of the exception, torture appears to be normal practice, as Adam Green remarked in a discussion of season four of the programme:

> torture has gone from being an infrequent shock bid to being a main thread of the plot. At least a half-dozen characters have undergone interrogation under conditions that meet conventional definitions of torture. The methods portrayed have varied, and include chemical injection, electric shock and old-fashioned bone-breaking. Those subjected to these treatments have constituted a broad range, too, from an uncooperative associate of the plotters to a Middle Eastern wife and son linked to an operative to the teenaged son of the current season's secretary of defense.

(Green 2005)

Surnow's definition of patriotism involves the acceptance of torture as what an older television programme might have termed 'the American way'. By contrast, as Mayer has reported, US Army Brigadier General Patrick Finnegan, the Dean of the United States Military Academy at West Point and three experienced military and FBI interrogators consider that *24* sets a dangerous example, one that endangers the US national interest and the security of military forces (Mayer 2007). This expression of military and civil opposition to torture is consistent with a broader disquiet among the military and domestic law enforcement agencies with the Bush administration's embrace of torture.

In *24*, torture is normalized in a manner that is complicit with the logic of the Bybee memo, in contrast to the way that, as we will see, torture is a traumatic flashpoint in *First Blood*.

First Blood

> SHERIFF TEASLE: People start fucking around with the law and all hell breaks loose.

We now shift from contemporary legitimations of torture to a less contemporary film character who has come to be seen as an American warrior icon, John Rambo, who made his appearance in the film *First Blood* in 1982. In its initial context, *First Blood* is a fable of the post-war traumatic nomadism of Vietnam veterans, a secondary trauma overlaid upon their experience of war and, in Rambo's case, torture at the hands of the North Vietnamese. In its popular reception, and through its sequels, the Rambo character became a Reaganesque figure of consolation for the loss of the Vietnam War, opening out a processing of that trauma through the presentation of an exuberant return to an active, potent, successfully interventionist America. Now, *First Blood* can also be seen as containing all of the elements of the post-9/11 Global War On Terror debacle: casually brutal ignorance of human rights leading to a violent, bloody insurgency in which hapless, poorly trained regular forces are totally out-flanked and out-fought. As we will see, the figure of Rambo, the ex-Green Beret, also relates to contemporary practices of torture, which variously take inspiration from his training and heroic status.

The film opens with Rambo journeying to a farm in the Pacific north-west in search of an old army buddy — Delmar, an African-American — whom he finds has died from Agent Orange-related cancer a year before. He then continues on foot, reaching the town of Hope. He has long hair, is unshaven and wears a green combat jacket with an American flag on it. As he approaches the town he is stopped by Sheriff Will Teasle. Teasle questions him but quite misreads his identity, taking him for a draft-dodging hippy, wearing a combat jacket with irony. This introduces one of the poetic tensions of the film's scenario between the military and the civilian population, around the Vietnam War and the nature of American identity, and around forms of masculinity and embodiment. The Sheriff offers Rambo some advice: 'Wearing that flag on that jacket, looking the way you do — you're asking for trouble around here, friend'. He also explains to Rambo that he is the law: that the sheriff is the local sovereign. After Rambo refuses to leave the town, he is arrested and taken to the town jail.

At the jail he is processed: he resists being fingerprinted, but one of the policemen notices that he is wearing military dog tags, and removes them to check on his identity. The Sheriff then orders that he be prepared for his court appearance the following day, which involves having him cleaned up: showered and shaved. The sergeant in charge, Galt, takes an instant dislike to Rambo: the information that he has served in the army only antagonizes him. Galt displays a total disinterest in identifying Rambo, and is angered by the latter's refusal to allow himself to be fingerprinted.

As Rambo undresses to prepare for his shower, we see his muscular torso, covered with long scars. Seeing the scars Mitch, the policeman who noticed his dog tags, wonders what 'the hell he's been into', while Galt orders Rambo's hands above his head, and then steps behind him and strikes his lower back with his baton, knocking Rambo to the floor. Galt then kicks the prisoner before ordering that he be showered. This is done with a high-pressure hose.

After the shower, Rambo is returned, clothed, to the shower area to be shaved with a straight razor. It is at this point that the traumatic flashbacks of his Vietnam experiences which began when he was first taken down to the cells become stronger: the sight of the razor recalls a bayonet-waving North Vietnamese torturer, the choke hold that is applied with a baton recalls his crucifixion strapped to a bamboo pole, and the move to beginning to shave him with the razor recalls the cutting he received from a bayonet. The presentation of the flashbacks becomes increasingly detailed, and the climactic cutting recollection is the trigger for Rambo to lash out and fight his present-time tormentors. He disables all three men who are in the shower area, before escaping from the police station with his survival knife.

The 'enhanced techniques' featured in this scene include a choke hold, baton beating from behind, and compulsory grooming: that is, shower with high pressure hose, and a threatened dry shave with a straight razor. None of these techniques would have been out of place in Afghanistan, Iraq or Guantànamo (see Amnesty International 2005, Office of Inspector General, Central Intelligence Agency 2004, Schlesinger 2004, Human Rights Watch 2005, Office of the Inspector General of the Department of Defense, Deputy Inspector General for Intelligence 2006). After these actions reignite Rambo's traumatic experience of torture, leading him to react as if he were in hostile territory, the police discover that he is a former Green Beret, a highly decorated Vietnam war hero.

At first mistaken for a hippy, which arouses the Sheriff's animosity, Rambo's identification as a soldier arouses an equivalent animosity. The conflict that ensues also pits police and civilians against Rambo's military training, their local woodsmen's knowledge against his survival skills, their comfortably hetero-normative small town bodies against his army trained veteran's body which has its own non-small town significations through his long hair and mistaken association with the counter-cultural anti-war movement with its connections to sexual liberation. All of which results in positioning the returned soldier as alien in the apparent small town heartland of the country for which he has fought (albeit in the wrong kind of war). John Rambo is not just alien because he is from somewhere else, he is an alien as the incarnation of the structural alienation produced by his military service for a country that does not want to remember the war that it had lost, nor the men that it had sent (predominantly the white urban and rural poor, or African-Americans). Within a sphere of popular sovereignty, this scenario features the people against themselves.

David Morrell's novel, upon which the screenplay is based, is founded on the exploration of this tension, and the film works well to play out the subtexts through its costume (the military jacket is not in the book) and through Stallone's embodiment of Rambo. Writing about the genesis of his story, Morrell begins by describing the juxtaposition of two stories on the *CBS Evening News* in the summer of 1968: one showing a firefight in Vietnam, the other showing National Guardsmen during the Baltimore riots following the assassination of Martin Luther King. The thread is troops using M-16s: 'if I hadn't heard each story's reporter explain what I was watching, I might have thought that both film clips were two aspects of one horror' (Morrell 1988, p. viii). Morrell is inspired by the violent tensions played out through America's transformation in the late sixties, at a time when the form of the state and the forms of embodiment of its citizens were being drastically renegotiated.

I want to pick out a few elements from this scenario.

The first is Rambo's subjectivity as being 'ineradicably tortured.' As the Nazi torture victim Jean Améry has put it:

> Whoever was tortured, stays tortured. Torture is ineradicably burnt into him, even when *no clinically objective traces* can be detected.
>
> (Améry 1980, p. 34)

Unlike the OLC lawyers, Améry is a witness to the reality of torture, not a legal observer and apologist for the forms of 'severe pain and suffering', which fall below a definition of torture. For Améry, torture involves a very specific form of embodiment:

> only in torture does the transformation of the person into flesh become complete. Frail in the face of violence, yelling out in pain, awaiting no help, capable of no resistance, the tortured person is only a body, and nothing else beside that.
>
> (Améry 1980, p. 33)

Stallone's performance of the tortured Rambo involves some complexities which might have been erased by the subsequent series of Rambo films. Rambo's body is the paradoxically hardened carapace of a tortured subject – in both the merely physical and psychological senses of 'tortured' – and the attempt to reduce that body is the very effort made in the prisons of Afghanistan, Iraq and Guantánamo Bay. What the police do in this film is now recognisable as the reflexive cruelty of US troops in Afghanistan and Iraq. One alibi for torture, comes from the SERE training which was designed to prepare troops to resist the very experience we see in Rambo's flashback to this torture (a point addressed in more detail in the next section).

The aggressively homoerotic elements of Rambo's abuse further connect it to the forms of physicality at stake in prisoner abuse. Rambo's smoothly muscular, rounded body is both an ideal and a threat: a form of masculinity that arouses hostile masculine desire (particularly in its associations with the then gay associated sub-culture of body building). Galt, the abusive police sergeant, approaches Rambo from behind, striking him to force him into submission, kicking him while prone, then taking him in a violent embrace from behind, choking him and cooing to him when he turns more submissive. As Morrell notes in his reflections on the source of his novel, the aggression directed towards counter-cultural otherness also focused on long hair as a confusing marker of gender. He recalls 'the harassment that my own recently grown mustache and long hair had caused me. "Why don't you get a haircut? What the hell are you, a man or a woman?"' (Morrell 1988, pp. ix–x).

We have seen that the Sheriff sees himself as the local sovereign: his deputies attempt to enact their own sovereignty in the subjection of Rambo, in the manner recognized by Améry as he reflected upon the motivations of his torturers, arguing that the sadism of torture was part of the torturer's desire to 'realize his own total sovereignty'. Sovereignty, here, is biopolitical, relating as much to the control of bodies and their borders as to the polity. Thinking of the pervasiveness of the eroticized abuse in Iraq and Afghanistan, we might think of a gendered sovereignty.

The second point is that Rambo's incarnation of self-sufficient, sovereign masculinity – in both this film and in the later series, as well as through the *Rocky* films – is the very trope enacted by torturers, even as they assault the very possibility of such a self-sovereignty in their prisoners. Lynndie England, the woman featured in the Abu Ghraib photographs, cited Rambo as an inspiration for her military career:

> I always wanted to be in the military. My whole life. I just didn't know what branch — Navy, Army, Coast Guard, Marines, Air Force. I just wanted to serve my country and be a patriot, I guess. As a child I mainly grew up on military gung-ho movies so that's where I got the idea. Old Chuck Norris movies, 'Delta Force', 'Rambo', 'Missing in Action', 'Platoon'.
>
> (England 2008)

Imagining, desiring themselves to be that physically potent incarnation of US exceptionalism – that is, imagining themselves as Rambo the Green Beret – England and her fellow soldiers played the policemen's parts. Rambo is, thus, both the icon of the tortured and of the torturer.

From tortured to torturer

Further complicating Rambo's relation to the torturer, as a Green Beret he has been schooled in the SERE techniques – Survival, Evasion, Resistance, Escape – which were to become both further alibis, and the very programme, for torture after 9/11. As Jane Mayer explains, the SERE programme 'was founded during the Cold War in an effort to re-create, and therefore understand, the mistreatment that had led thirty-six captured U.S. airmen to give stunningly false confessions during the Korean War' (Mayer 2008, p. 158):

> It taught these potential captives how to resist torture and other extreme forms of abuse should they have the misfortune to fall into the hands of a dishonorable enemy. ... The theory behind it was that by subjecting U.S. soldiers to the worst treatment the world could meet out, but doing so in a limited and carefully controlled setting, the soldiers could inoculate themselves emotionally, increasing their chances of resisting should they ever be subjected to torture in real life.
>
> (Mayer 2008, p. 157).

The techniques which troops were prepared to resist drew their origins from both North Korean and Soviet Russian KGB interrogation practices. As Mayer puts it, 'SERE was a repository of the world's knowledge about torture.... But in the CIA's hands after September 11, critics close to the program said, it was "reverse-engineered" into a blueprint for abuse'. In 2002, the CIA decided to introduce the techniques developed to resist torture as a means for interrogating prisoners in the war on terror. The person they chose to lead this was James Mitchell:

> The apparent leader of the CIA team was a former military psychologist named James Mitchell, whom the intelligence agency had hired on a contract. Oddly, given the Agency's own dearth of experience in the area of interrogating Islamic extremists, he had no background in the Middle East or in Islamic terrorism. He spoke no Arabic and he knew next to nothing about the Muslim religion. He was himself a devout Mormon. But others present said he seemed to think he had all the answers about how to deal with Zubayda. Mitchell announced that the suspect had to be treated 'like a dog in a cage,' informed sources said. 'He said it was like an experiment, when you apply electric shocks to a caged dog, after a while, he's so diminished, he can't resist'.
>
> (Mayer 2008, p. 156)

Mitchell's religious fervour, dogmatic application of a misplaced scientific principle, and absence of any experience in interrogation, are characteristics which connect him to a wider pattern in the entertainment of torture. The drive to use these techniques within the CIA came from people with little field experience and little knowledge of interrogation.

By contrast, the opposition to these techniques came from the FBI interrogators, who were skilled in traditional non-violent forms of interrogation, from the military, particularly those with extensive experience in the SERE programme, and subsequently from someone who had actually experienced torture at the hands of the North Vietnamese, Senator John

McCain (2011). As with Améry's understanding of torture, theirs was not a disembodied, theoretical understanding of torture: this issue of embodied understanding will come up again in the discussion of Abu Ghraib and Bagram Air Base. The entertainment of torture entails both a biopolitics that involves the desire to break down and subjugate an alien body and subject, and a capacity for disregarding the other predicated upon a lack of embodied experience. Furthermore, we need to question the aim of these practices, as they seemed to have very little do with eliciting intelligence. As one critic of the use of SERE, Steve Kleinman, a reserve Air Force colonel and experienced interrogator, put it:

> 'Learned Helplessness was [Mitchell's] whole paradigm.' . . . 'It starts with isolation. Then they eliminate the prisoner's ability to forecast the future — when their next meal is — when they can go to the bathroom. It creates dread and dependency. It was the KGB model. But the KGB used it to turn people who had turned against the state to confess falsely. The KGB wasn't after intelligence'.
>
> (quoted in Mayer 2008, p. 164)

Despite Dick Cheney's claims for the important intelligence elicited by torture, there is little evidence that it produced any useful intelligence, and it has had a particularly negative impact on the capacity of the USA to prosecute any of the detainees. Recent cases have rejected evidence tainted by torture (see Farhi Saeed Bin Mohammed, v. Barack H. Obama, United States District Court for the District of Columbia 2009).

Returning to the earlier discussion of the torture memoranda, the SERE programme was used as a legal rationale for torture in the memorandum produced by Steven Bradbury, Principal Deputy Assistant Attorney General in May 2005. Bradbury's memorandum starts at a slightly different place from Bybee's attempt to define 'severe pain and suffering': Bradbury writes three years after Bybee's exculpation of torture, at a point where official policy now appears to say that the US does not conduct torture. Bradbury seeks to normalize a culture of torture by reference to what might 'shock the conscience'. This is a very specific legal argument, involving the Fifth and Fourteenth amendments, and a body of case law dealing with restrictions on actions that would produce self-incriminating and other forms of coerced testimony, as Bradbury notes in his opening: 'As detailed below in Part III, the relevant constraint here, assuming Article 16 did apply, would be the Fifth Amendment's prohibition of executive conduct that "shocks the conscience"' (Bradbury 2005, p. 2).

The nub of Bradbury's case is that anything which has been done to US troops is acceptable to do to enemy prisoners:

> the CIA interrogation techniques have all been adapted from military Survival, Evasion, Resistance, Escape ('SERE') training. Although there

> are obvious differences between training exercises and actual interrogations, the fact that the United States uses similar techniques on its own troops for training purposes strongly suggests that these techniques are not categorically beyond the pale.
>
> (Bradbury 2005, p. 3)

That is, that what the US military had imagined that its enemies would do to its troops became the model for how it broke the laws of war in treating its enemies. As with the 'reverse-engineering' of SERE training, Bradbury ignores the fact that the standard found in SERE training is not normative for the US: it is an alien standard, drawn from non-US treatment of prisoners. The practices, which are supposed to be 'not categorically beyond the pale', are exotic practices that have been domesticated as an inoculation against torture. SERE training was to be a form of protection against, but not to be a model for enacting, interrogation. The point he misses is that, in adapting prevention to the purposes of warfare, the CIA had become the KGB whose practices it now implemented.

Throughout the memorandum, Bradbury relies on the 'we do it to our own, so we can do it to others' argument (see, for example, Bradbury 2005, p. 12), leading to the conclusion that:

> in light of 'an understanding of traditional executive behavior, of contemporary practice, and of the standards of blame generally applied to them,' the use of the enhanced interrogation techniques in the CIA interrogation program as we understand it does not constitute government behavior that 'is so egregious, *so* outrageous, that it may fairly be said to shock the contemporary conscience'.
>
> (*Lewis,* 523 U.S. at 847 n8, cited in Bradbury 2005, p. 38)

In short, Rambo the tortured provides the rationale for Rambo the torturer.

Abu Ghraib and the image of torture

> Am I being considered human being or animal, or is USA my God?
>
> (Saifullah Paracha, Amnesty International 2005, p. 123)

> To Améry, the world devised and realized by German Fascism was the world of torture in which 'man exists only by ruining the other person who stands before him'.
>
> (Sebald 2004, pp. 156–7)

How did torture come to be so widely entertained, and not just in the US? And through what twisted logic can there be a link between one of the most abject reductions of a human being – torture, from the latin *torquere*, to twist – and entertainment?

> On their day off people would show up all the time. Everyone in camp knew if you wanted to work out your frustration you show up at the PUC [Persons Under Control] tent. In a way it was sport.
> (Account of Sergeant A, 82nd Airborne Division, quoted by Human Rights Watch 2005)

At Bagram Air Base it went further than sport: it was considered funny to beat one prisoner, in a line of humour that led to his death.

One rather simple answer to the question is: lack of training, aggravated by troop shortages and significant confusion concerning the rules concerning prisoners, aggravated by media depictions of torture as being acceptable. England might have been inspired to join the military by Rambo, but her actions, and those of the other troops at Abu Ghraib, owe more to examples such as *24*.[2] Another answer involves the adoption of behaviour related to the SERE training which, as we have seen, was applied by people untrained in interrogation, and was designed as a means of resisting interrogation rather than performing it. The more complex answer goes to the reason for the confusion: the high level disavowal of both the Geneva Conventions and the CAT, leading to the 'migration of techniques... the introduction of interrogation techniques from one theater of operation to another' (Office of the Inspector General of the DOD, 2006, p. 24), involving interrogation techniques developed at Guantànamo being used as general techniques for dealing with any prisoners.

As an example of the lack of training, let us not start in Abu Ghraib but in Afghanistan. Bagram Air Base became home to the 377th Military Police Company, who had had only the most basic training in handling prisoners before their deployment. One lesson that they learnt too well was a pressure point technique referred to as a 'peroneal strike': a blow applied to the side of the leg above the knee (Golden 2005). Their training did not seem to include instruction in the Army Field Manual or the laws of war.

Bagram was where beating prisoners became a recreational activity: at least two deaths were recorded as a consequence. One death involved a man known as Dilawar, who had been arrested by mistake:

> When one of the First Platoon M.P.'s, Specialist Corey E. Jones, was sent to Mr. Dilawar's cell to give him some water, he said the prisoner spit in his face and started kicking him. Specialist Jones responded, he said, with a couple of knee strikes to the leg of the shackled man.
>
> 'He screamed out, 'Allah! Allah! Allah!' and my first reaction was that he was crying out to his god,' Specialist Jones said to investigators.

'Everybody heard him cry out and thought it was funny'.
Other Third Platoon M.P.'s later came by the detention center and stopped at the isolation cells to see for themselves, Specialist Jones said. It became a kind of running joke, and people kept showing up to give this detainee a common peroneal strike just to hear him scream out 'Allah', he said. 'It went on over a 24-hour period, and I would think that it was over 100 strikes'.

(Golden 2005)

The New York Times story points out that the man whose spit was so threatening weighed approximately 54 kg. He died of his injuries. The military coroner later remarked that she had 'seen similar injuries in an individual run over by a bus' (Golden 2005).

This culture of torture as entertainment might have remained hidden: it certainly did not when the photos from Abu Ghraib were published, even if they showed less about the systematic torture in pursuit of information apparently licensed by the OLC memos. As the Schlesinger report noted:

The events of October through December 2003 on the night shift of Tier 1 at Abu Ghraib prison were acts of brutality and purposeless sadism. We now know these abuses occurred at the hands of both military police and military intelligence personnel. *The pictured abuses, unacceptable even in wartime, were not part of authorized interrogations nor were they even directed at intelligence targets.* They represent deviant behavior and a failure of military leadership and discipline. However, we do know that some of the egregious abuses at Abu Ghraib which were not photographed did occur during interrogation sessions and that abuses during interrogation sessions occurred elsewhere.

(Schlesinger 2004, p. 5; emphasis added)

Between 'torture' and 'abuse' there is a distinction that involves a particular understanding of torture. Torture is motivated, abuse unmotivated. Torture's sovereign motivation is called up in its justification. Abuse is a casual exercise of power, apparently not part of sovereignty: it does not have the authority of the sovereign, as it is not in the service of sovereignty: it is a private initiative, not an outcome of public policy. This distinction breaks down if we consider that torture takes its alibi from the needs of sovereign power — the acts may be identical to those acts labelled abuse — whereas abuse is a mimicry of the techniques of the sovereign's servants.

What the Abu Ghraib photos revealed was an image of torture that could not be justified by any necessity argument. The most telling images involved female soldiers, and the sexual humiliation of prisoners, reiterating a theme begun in *First Blood*. It is also been argued that these images concealed more than they revealed, displacing the issue of infringements of the Geneva Convention and the CAT:

> In an odd way,' Kenneth Roth, the executive director of Human Rights Watch, said, 'the sexual abuses at Abu Ghraib have become a diversion for the prisoner abuse and the violation of the Geneva Conventions that is authorized.' Since September 11th, Roth added, the military has systematically used third-degree techniques around the world on detainees. 'Some JAGs hate this and are horrified that the tolerance of mistreatment will come back and haunt us in the next war', Roth told me. 'We're giving the world a ready-made excuse to ignore the Geneva Conventions. Rumsfeld has lowered the bar'.
>
> (Hersh 2004)

Distressing as it is to consider the details of torture, there is an inadvertent dark humour in the behaviour of troops who were somewhat trained to kill, but not at all trained to interrogate or torture, whereupon they made it up for themselves with hints derived from what had been licensed by the torture memos, taught to be expected in SERE training, taken from film and TV, and practiced by the CIA.

Fantasy runs through all of this: Dick Cheney, the enthusiastic player of doomsday scenarios to prepare for the kind of conflict which never eventuated (see Mann 2004, Kurtz 2004), making up reality. The SERE programme – the imagination of what an unscrupulous enemy would do to US troops – turned on its head as the basis for the torture of prisoners under US control, and the very justification for extreme torture techniques in the Bradbury memo.

The scandals concerning the torture and abuse of US-held detainees in the Global War on Terror bring together a number of complex issues concerning the relationship between images and sovereign power.

At one level, what is remarkable about the Abu Ghraib scandal is that the photographic and video documentation was provided by the perpetrators of the torture as a form of digital souvenir. It was this leaked archive of materials (not all of which have been released publicly), which allegedly brought the seriousness of what had hitherto been written reports to the attention of Defence Secretary Donald Rumsfeld. With such vivid images, not even one of Bush's Cabinet could ignore what was going on, arguably at his direction. Similarly, the brutal 'disciplinary' methods at Guantánamo Bay have been carefully documented, this time as an official record of Emergency Response Force (ERF) interventions (ERF-ing, as the inmates and victims term it). Those images have yet to be released, yet indicate the extent to which breaches of international law have been so routinized as to form part of a bureaucratic record. Without needing to stretch the analogy with earlier incarnations of such camps, this is a further instance of what Hannah Arendt termed the 'banality of evil' (Arendt 1965).

For all the detail of the reports of abuse, and all of the detail of what was legitimated through the torture memos, it was the images of torture that made real the act to one of its architects. As Seymour Hersch noted, Donald Rumsfeld did not seem to have understood what was happening until he saw the photos in the media, citing Rumsfeld as saying:

> You read it, as I say, it's one thing. You see these photographs and it's just unbelievable. . . . It wasn't three-dimensional. It wasn't video. It wasn't color. It was quite a different thing.
>
> (Hersh 2004)

Rumsfeld's remarks demonstrate a point made in Scarry's distinction between the spectacle of the physical act of torture and its verbal dimension:

> Almost anyone looking at the *physical* act of torture would be immediately appalled and repulsed by the torturers. It is difficult to think of a human situation in which the lines of moral responsibility are more starkly or simply drawn, in which there is a more compelling reason to ally one's sympathies with the one person and to repel the claims of the other. Yet as soon as the focus of attention shifts to the *verbal* aspects of torture, those lines have begun to waver and change their shape in the direction of accommodating and crediting the torturers.
>
> (Scarry 1985, p. 35)

Rumsfeld's relation to torture started in the realm of language: torture as justified for the purposes of interrogation. These mute images paradoxically reintroduce the physicality of torture, in a twisted logical knot (the other side of which disregards torture's bodies: an aspect explored by Joseph Pugliese (forthcoming), through his linking of the corporeal status of tortured bodies, reduced to being a 'carcass', CIA black sites, and the practices of textual redaction which remove even these carcasses from the purview of law). While, as we have seen, the disassociation between torture and its effects occurs in a specular economy in which violence appears to be removed from bodies, and the relation to the other is severely attenuated, the scandal of these images lay in showing what torture was without any verbal justification. These images show torture as a form of entertainment, and circulate as entertaining souvenirs, as Susan Sontag immediately recognized in her response to the Abu Ghraib images:

> [t]he horror of what is shown in the photographs cannot be separated from the horror that the photographs were taken — with the perpetrators posing, gloating, over their helpless captives.
>
> (Sontag 2004)

Sontag, however, saw more in these images, seeing just what the media circus around them tended to obscure: the denial of torture in the admission of 'abuse', amounting to a 'disregard' for the torture of others:

> The Bush administration and its defenders have chiefly sought to limit a public-relations disaster — the dissemination of the photographs — rather than deal with the complex crimes of leadership and of policy revealed by the pictures. There was, first of all, the displacement of the reality onto the photographs themselves. The administration's initial response was to say that the president was shocked and disgusted by the photographs — as if the fault or horror lay in the images, not in what they depict. There was also the avoidance of the word "torture". The prisoners had possibly been the objects of "abuse", eventually of "humiliation" — that was the most to be admitted. "My impression is that what has been charged thus far is abuse, which I believe technically is different from torture", Secretary of Defense Donald Rumsfeld said at a press conference. "And therefore I'm not going to address the 'torture' word".
>
> (Sontag 2004)

In this disregard, through which the other ceases 'to be visible to us' (Scarry 1985, p. 22), in this sovereign failure to see the other, we find the basis of an entertainment of torture.

Notes

1. This is an interpretation built upon a particular understanding of the Commander in Chief powers: yet Article 2, section 2 'Civilian Power over Military, Cabinet, Pardon Power, Appointments' of the US Constitution describes no such specific power attending the President's Commander in Chief role. It is certainly an understanding that has been rejected by the US Supreme Court, as Justice Sandra Day O'Connor put it quite succinctly: 'We have long since made clear that a state of war is not a blank check for the President when it comes to the rights of the Nation's citizens' (Hamdi v. Rumsfeld 542 US 507 2004 at 29).
2. As Mayer reports, Tony Lagouranis, a former Army interrogator in Iraq:

   > told the show's staff that DVDs of shows such as '24' circulate widely among soldiers stationed in Iraq. Lagouranis said to me, "People watch the shows, and then walk into the interrogation booths and do the same things they've just seen." He recalled that some men he had worked with in Iraq watched a television program in which a suspect was forced to hear

tortured screams from a neighboring cell; the men later tried to persuade their Iraqi translator to act the part of a torture 'victim', in a similar intimidation ploy.

(Mayer 2007)

References

Agamben, G. (1998) *Homo Sacer: Sovereign Power and Bare Life*, trans. Daniel Heller-Roazen, Stanford, Stanford University Press.

Améry, J. (1980) *At the Mind's Limits: Contemplations by a Survivor on Auschwitz and its Realities*, trans. Sidney Rosenfeld and Stella P. Rosenfeld, Bloomington & Indianapolis, Indiana University Press.

Amnesty International. (2005) *United States of America — Guantánamo and beyond: The continuing pursuit of unchecked executive power*, [online] Available at: http://www.amnesty.org/en/library/info/AMR51/063/2005 (accessed 22 September 2011).

Arendt, H. (1965) *Eichmann In Jerusalem: A Report on the Banality of Evil*, Penguin Books, Harmondsworth.

Bradbury, S. (2005) *Memorandum For John A. Rizzo, Senior Deputy General Counsel, Central Intelligence Agency, Re: Application of United States Obligations Under Article 16 of the Convention Against Torture to Certain Techniques that May Be Used in the Interrogation of High Value al Qaeda Detainees*, [online] Available at: http://www.gwu.edu/~nsarchiv/news/20120403/docs/Bradburymemo.pdf

Bybee, J. (2002) *Memorandum for Alberto R. Gonzales, Counsel to the President, Re: Standards of Conduct for Interrogation under 18 U.S.C. §§ 2340–2340A*, [online] Available at: http://news.findlaw.com/hdocs/docs/doj/bybee80102ltr.html (accessed 22 September 2011).

Convention against Torture and Other Cruel, Inhuman or Degrading Treatment or Punishment (United Nations General Assembly resolution 39/46 of 10 December 1984).

Electrocuting an Elephant. (1903) Dir. Thomas Edison. Edison Manufacturing Company, USA.

England, L. (2008) 'Rumsfeld knew', Interview in *Stern*, 17 March, [online] Available at: http://www.stern.de/politik/ausland/lynndie-england-rumsfeld-knew-614356.html (accessed 22 September 2011).

Execution of the Hung-Hu (1904). Pathé Frères, China.

Farhi Saeed Bin Mohammed, v. Barack H. Obama, United States District Court for the District of Columbia 2009, [online] Available at: http://s3.amazonaws.com/propublica/assets/detention/gitmo/farhi_mohammed_unclassified_opinion.pdf (accessed 22 September 2011).

First Blood (1982) Dir. Ted Kotcheff. Anabasis N.V. and Elcajo Productions, USA.

Foucault, M. (1979) *Discipline and Punish: The Birth of the Prison*, trans. Alan Sheridan, New York, Vintage Books.

Foucault, M. (1997) 'The birth of biopolitics', in *Ethics: Subjectivity and Truth*, ed. Paul Rabinow, New York, The New Press, pp. 73–79.

Golden, T. (2005) 'In U.S. Report, Brutal Details of 2 Afghan Inmates' Deaths', *New York Times*, 20 May, [online] Available at: http://www.nytimes.com/2005/05/20/international/asia/20abuse.html?pagewanted=1&_r=1 (accessed 22 September 2011).

Green, A. (2005) 'Normalizing Torture on '24'', *New York Times*, 22 May, [online] Available at: http://www.nytimes.com/2005/05/22/arts/television/22gree.html (accessed 22 September 2011).

Hamdi v. Rumsfeld 542 US 507, 2004, [online] Available at: http://caselaw.lp.findlaw.com/scripts/getcase.pl?court=US&vol=000&invol=03-6696&friend (accessed 22 September 2011).

Hersh, S. M. (2004) 'The Gray Zone: How a secret Pentagon program came to Abu Ghraib', *The New Yorker*, 24 May, [online] Available at: http://www.newyorker.com/archive/2004/05/24/040524fa_fact (accessed 22 September 2011).

Human Rights Watch. (2005) *Leadership Failure: Firsthand Accounts of Torture of Iraqi Detainees by the U.S. Army's 82nd Airborne Division*, [online] Available at: http://www.hrw.org/en/reports/2005/09/22/leadership-failure-0 (accessed 22 September 2011).

Hutchings, P. J. (2001) *The Criminal Spectre in Law, Literature and Aesthetics: Incriminating Subjects*, London and New York, Routledge.

Kaufman, M. T. (2003) 'The World: Film Studies; What Does the Pentagon See in 'Battle of Algiers'?' *New York Times*, 7 September, [online] Available at: http://www.nytimes.com/2003/09/07/weekinreview/the-world-film-studies-what-does-the-pentagon-see-in-battle-of-algiers.html (accessed 22 September 2011).

Kurtz, H. (2004) "'Armageddon' Plan Was Put Into Action on 9/11, Clarke Says', *The Washington Post*, Wednesday 7 April, p. A29, [online] Available at: http://www.washingtonpost.com/ac2/wp-dyn/A55877-2004Apr6 (accessed viewed 22 September 2011).

La battaglia di Algeri (1966) Dir. by Gillo Pontecorvo. Igor Film, Casbah Film, Algeria.

Le petit soldat (1963) Dir. by Jean-Luc Godard. Les Productions Georges de Beauregard, Société Nouvelle de Cinématographie, Switzerland.

Manderson, D. (forthcoming) 'Memory and echo: pop cult, hi tech and the irony of tradition', doi: 10.1080/09502386.2012.722292

Mann, J. (2004) 'The Armageddon Plan', *The Atlantic Monthly*, March, [online] Available at: http://www.theatlantic.com/past/docs/issues/2004/03/mann.htm (accessed 22 September 2011).

Mayer, J. (2007) 'Whatever It Takes: The politics of the man behind '24'', *The New Yorker*, 19 February, [online] Available at: http://www.newyorker.com/reporting/2007/02/19/070219fa_fact_mayer (accessed 22 September 2011).

Mayer, J. (2008) *The Dark Side: The Inside Story of How the War on Terror Turned into a War on American Ideals*, New York, Doubleday.

McCain, J. (2011) 'Bin Laden's death and the debate over torture,' *The Washington Post*, 12 May, [online] Available at: http://www.washingtonpost.com/opinions/bin-ladens-death-and-the-debate-over-torture/2011/05/11/AFd1mdsG_story.html (accessed 22 September 2011).

Morrell, D. (1988) 'Rambo and Me', in *First Blood*, New York, Warner Books.

Office of Inspector General, Central Intelligence Agency (2004) *Special Review: Counterterrorism Detention and Interrogation Activities (September 2001–October 2003)*, [online] Available at: http://graphics8.nytimes.com/packages/images/nytint/docs/c-i-a-reports-on-interrogation-methods/original.pdf (accessed 22 September 2011).

Office of the Inspector General of the Department of Defense, Deputy Inspector General for Intelligence (2006) *Review of DoD-Directed Investigations of Detainee Abuse*, Report No. 06-INTEL-10, August 25, 2006, Evaluation Report, Arlington, Office of the Deputy Inspector General for Intelligence.

Pugliese, J. (forthcoming) 'Instrumental and gratuitous violence: the torture and death of Gul Rahman in the cia salt pit', doi: 10.1080/09502386.2012.722299

Santner, E. L. (2011) *The Royal Remains: The People's Two Bodies and the Endgame of Sovereignty*, Chicago and London, The University of Chicago Press.

Scarry, E. (1985) *The Body in Pain: The Making and Unmaking of the World*, New York and Oxford, Oxford University Press.

Schlesinger, J. (2004) *Final Report of the Independent Panel to Review Department of Defense Detention Operations*, Arlington, Department of Defense.

Sebald, W. G. (2004) 'Against the Irreversible: On Jean Améry', in *On the Natural History of Destruction*, trans. Anthea Bell, London, Penguin Books.

Sontag, S. (2004) 'Regarding the Torture of Others', *New York Times*, 23 May, [online] Available at: http://www.nytimes.com/2004/05/23/magazine/23PRISONS.html (accessed 22 September 2011).

US Department of Defense. (2004) Defense Department Operational Update Briefing May 4, [online] Available at: http://www.defense.gov/transcripts/transcript.aspx?transcriptid=2973 (accessed 22 September 2011).

24 (2001–2010) Created by Robert Cochran and Joel Surnow. Imagine Entertainment, 20th Century Fox Television, Real Time Productions, Teakwood Lane Productions, USA.

8 United States Code (USC) — Aliens and Nationality.

Joseph Pugliese

INSTRUMENTAL AND GRATUITOUS VIOLENCE

The torture and death of Gul Rahman in the CIA Salt Pit

This essay examines the torture and death of Gul Rahman in the CIA secret prison/black site known as the Salt Pit, located in northern Kabul, Afghanistan. Virtually excised from the public record, his name and death are mentioned in footnote 28 of the Classified Response to the US Department of Justice Office of Professional Responsibility Classified Report. This report, prepared by Counsel for Jay S. Bybee, is a detailed and lengthy repost to the accusation made by the Office of Professional Responsibility (OPR) that Judge Bybee's memo (1 August 2002) to Alberto R. Gonzales, Counsel to the President, authorized some forms of torture that contravened the US Torture Statute − 18 U.S.C. § 2340, which defines torture and declares it to be a federal crime. In its Report, the OPR concludes that Judge Bybee 'committed professional misconduct'. In what follows, I proceed to discuss the details of Gul Rahman's torture and death in the CIA Salt Pit in the context of the Bybee memo and his Counsel's response to the OPR's condemnatory report in order to flesh out the relations of legal and governmental power that were instrumental in establishing US regimes of torture and death in the CIA secret prisons. In delineating the forces that were operative in the torture and death of Rahman, I proceed to identify two intersecting modalities of violence − instrumental and gratuitous. In the concluding section of this essay, my analysis of the torture and death of Rahman is framed by the literal and tropological dimensions of redaction, as that legal process that edits and censors a document of any secret or sensitive information. I argue that the process of redaction must be seen as producing, analogically, its own discursive black sites of silence, loss and death.

Gul Rahman is an Afghan torture victim who died on 20 November 2002 in the CIA secret prison/black site known as the Salt Pit, located in northern

Kabul, Afghanistan.[1] His body has never been recovered. Virtually excised from the official public record, his name and death are mentioned in footnote 28 of the Classified Response to the US Department of Justice Office of Professional Responsibility Classified Report (2009). This report, prepared by Counsel for Jay S. Bybee, is a detailed and lengthy repost to the accusation made by the Office of Professional Responsibility (OPR) that Judge Bybee's memo (1 August 2002) to Alberto R. Gonzales, Counsel to the President, authorized some forms of torture that contravened the US Torture Statute — 18 U.S.C. § 2340, which defines torture and declares it to be a federal crime. In its report, the OPR (2008, p. 180) concludes that Judge Bybee 'committed professional misconduct'. In what follows, I proceed to discuss the details of Gul Rahman's torture and death in the CIA Salt Pit in the context of the Bybee memo and his Counsel's response to the OPR's condemnatory report in order to flesh out the relations of legal and governmental power that were instrumental in establishing US regimes of torture and death in the CIA secret prisons. In attempting to delineate the forces that were operative in the torture and death of Gul Rahman, I proceed to identify two modalities of violence — instrumental and gratuitous. Instrumental violence, I argue, is the direct application of violence on the body of the torture victim through the deployment of an arsenal of torture technologies such as shackles, electrical wires, waterboarding and so on. Gratuitous violence, however, refers to the indirect exercise of violence on the body of the victim through the use of 'no-touch' torture, in which an ecology of torture is established that produces a type of self-inflicted violence.

Whilst the specific focus of the essay is on the fate of one torture victim, Gul Rahman, I want to stress at the outset that the violent techniques deployed in his torture and death must be seen as situated within what I term a 'torture continuum' that encompasses multiple sites (including Abu Ghraib, Bagram, Guantánamo Bay and a number of other black sites). This torture continuum was enabled by the so-called 'torture memos' produced by US Government policy and the 'torture lawyers'. 'The torture lawyers', writes Luban (2006, pp. 71, 51), 'aimed to construct a judicially-endorsed practice of permissible torture'; they 'were constructing a torture culture'. Moreover, as I have argued in detail elsewhere (Pugliese 2007a, 2007b), this US torture continuum must be seen as having its roots within a complex genealogy that precedes the events of 9/11 and that is inscribed with histories of colonial and racist violence.

In the concluding section of this essay, my analysis of the torture and death of Gul Rahman is framed by the literal and tropological dimensions of redaction, as that legal process that edits and censors a document of any secret or sensitive information through the application of a black marker over designated text. In the context of the CIA Salt Pit — and its ensemble of torturers, legal advocates and its victims — the process of redaction must be seen as producing, analogically, its own discursive black sites of silence, loss and death.

Torture law

In the wake of the 9/11 attacks against the USA, President Bush called on the US Department of Justice, Office of Legal Counsel, to establish guidelines for the interrogation of captured 'enemy combatants', as subjects who, under that designated rubric, failed to qualify as prisoners of war and who were thus disqualified from claiming the limited rights and protections outlined in the Geneva Convention on Prisoners of War (see Greenberg & Dratel 2005, pp. 134–135). Alberto R. Gonzales, White House Counsel, set the tone for the Office of Legal Counsel's response by suspending the Geneva Convention and declaring it 'quaint' and 'obsolete' in the context of the 'new paradigm' of the war on terror (Greenberg & Dratel 2005, p. 119). Judge Jay S. Bybee, as Legal Counsel to the President, produced the Memorandum for Alberto R. Gonzales, Counsel to the President, articulating the 'Standards of Conduct for Interrogation under 18 U.S.C. §§ 2340-2340A' in the context of interrogations conducted outside of the USA. The Bybee memo is concerned with defining torture in order to establish certain interrogation practices that could be used by US interrogators without risking prosecution for violating the US torture statute. Significantly, the rhetoric of the memo is concerned with 'examining *possible defenses* that would negate any claim that certain interrogation methods violate the statute' (Bybee 2005, p. 172, my emphasis). As I demonstrate below, in my discussion of Gul Rahman's torture and death, it was precisely the Bybee memo's establishing of 'possible defenses' against claims that actual torture had taken place that enabled the CIA interrogators responsible for Rahman's death to evade prosecution.

Bybee (2005, p. 172) opens his memo by outlining his legal definition of acts of torture: 'Physical pain amounting to torture must be equivalent in intensity to the pain accompanying serious physical injury, such as organ failure, impairment of bodily function, or even death'. This definition was later reproduced across many of the so-called 'torture memos'. It effectively delimits torture to the infliction of pain such that it causes death or, alternatively, places the victim within the fatal parameters of 'organ failure, or impairment of bodily function'. This definition, as I have discussed elsewhere, serves to enable a range of violent practices that can be performed on the victim as long as they do not result in death (Pugliese 2007b). In the context of this potentially fatal circumscription, torture is officially sanctioned along a continuum of carefully managed intensities, punctuated by levels of pain that, the torturer *knows*, must not the push the victim over a fatal threshold. I underscore the term *knows* as it is pivotal to the escape clause that Bybee proceeds to establish for his prospective interrogators under the rubric of 'intent'. 'To violate Section 2340A', Bybee (2005, p. 174) argues, 'the statute requires that severe pain and suffering must be inflicted with specific intent. See 18 U.S.C. § 2340(1). In order for a defendant to have acted with specific intent, he must expressly intend to achieve the forbidden act'. Bybee (2005, p. 175) further elaborates:

> even if the defendant knows that severe pain will result from his actions, if causing such harm is not his objective, he lacks the requisite specific intent even though the defendant did not act in good faith. Instead, a defendant is guilty of torture only if he acts with the express purpose of inflicting severe pain or suffering on a person within his custody or physical control.

At this critical juncture in the Bybee memo, a strategically ambiguous area is opened up that effectively signals, by default, the sanctioning of a range of torture practices that can claim impunity from prosecution as long as the defendants can demonstrate that they deployed these practices without the specific intent to cause severe pain or to kill. I turn now to Gul Rahman's torture and death at the hands of his CIA interrogators in order to evidence the effective application of this escape clause of 'specific intent'.

Beyond US jurisdiction: the Salt Pit

Gul Rahman was captured by US agents on 29 October 2002. Habib Rahman, Gul's brother, has described his capture:

> [Gul] had come to Islamabad a day before the Oct. 29, 2002 raid for a medical checkup for his allergies and was planning to return the next day to the Shamshatoo refugee camp near Peshawar, where he lived with his wife and four children and sold wood...the agents surrounded the marble-fronted house at 1:30 a.m., arresting Rahman and four others.
> (CBS News 2010)

Rahman was imprisoned in the CIA secret prison in northern Kabul known as the Salt Pit. The Salt Pit was one of a number of so-called 'black sites': secret prisons established by the CIA across a number of 'host' countries, such as Afghanistan, Poland, Thailand, Egypt and Morocco. Situating these secret prisons within such 'host' countries effectively placed CIA agents operating in these prisons beyond US jurisdiction as these sites were outside US territory:

> The CIA wanted the Salt Pit to be a "host-nation facility," an Afghan prison with Afghan guards. Its designation as an Afghan facility was intended to give U.S. personnel some insulation from actions taken by Afghan guards inside, a tactic used by CIA prisons in other countries, former and current CIA officials said. The CIA, however, paid the entire cost of maintaining the facility, including the electricity, food and salaries for the guards, who were all vetted by agency personnel. The CIA also decided who would be kept

inside, including some "high-value targets," senior al Qaeda leaders in transit to other, more secure secret CIA prisons.

(Emptywheel 2010)

The CIA's black sites are sites of 'non-existence', as they render both the material prisons and their inmates 'non-existent' to either the public gaze or processes of accountability. The Salt Pit, an abandoned brick factory, was known by its inmates as the 'dark prison' because its cells were windowless. Goldman and Gannon (2010), the reporters who first brought Rahman's death to public attention, draw on information given by several former CIA officials in order to describe the prison: 'The Salt Pit contained a patchwork of small, windowless cells where detainees were subjected to harsh treatment and at least one mock execution'.[2] Goldman and Gannon (2010) cite the testimony of one of the Salt Pit prisoners, Dr Ghairat Baheer, in order to document what transpired in this secret prison:

'I was left naked, sleeping on the barren concrete', said Baheer. His toilet was a bucket. Loudspeakers blared. Guards concealed their identity with masks and carried torches. Baheer said his American interrogators would tie him to a chair and sit on his stomach. They hung him naked, he said, for hours on end.

Baheer's testimony of torture evidences the double logic of torture within these black sites: it is at once a secret torture, occluded from the public gaze and judicial accountability, *and* a spectacle of cruelty predicated on the theatricalization of pain and (mock) death, as the interrogators and guards don masks and train their torches on their victims. The testimonies of the tortured that have emerged from these secret prisons describe a phantasmagoria of physical torture that is further amplified by the use of disorienting strobe lighting and unbearably loud music that is played in repetitive loops. The theatricalization of pain and torture underscores the performative dimensions of these violent practices; in other words, they must be seen as material practices that achieve their cultural intelligibility through processes of iterative, performative codification. The spectacle of torture that is produced by this violent performative is circumscribed by a type of private scopic consumption that only becomes public through unintended leaks, such as occurred with the Abu Ghraib pictures (see Pugliese 2007a).

Captive flesh

The events that led to Gul Rahman's death are briefly described by Goldman and Gannon (2010):

At one point, the detainee threw a latrine bucket at his guards. He also threatened to kill them. His stubborn responses provoked harsher treatment. His hands were shackled over his head, he was roughened up and doused with water, according to several former CIA officials. The exact circumstances of Rahman's death are not clear, but the Afghan was left in the cold cell on the morning of Nov. 20, when the temperature dipped just below 36 degrees. He was naked from the waist down, said two former U.S. officials familiar with the case. Within hours, he was dead.

In an essay written over two decades ago, an essay that compels repeated returns because of its power and undiminished saliency, Hortense Spillers maps the contours of the violent colonial space within which Native Americans and African-Americans were confined during the construction of the white nation. She names this space 'the vestibule (or "pre-view") of a colonized North America' (Spillers 1987, p. 67). The vestibule of colonial white America is that other space in which those deemed as not embodying the subject position of human-personhood were quarantined, enslaved, tortured and executed: 'That order, with its human sequence written in blood, represents for its African and indigenous peoples a scene of actual mutilation, dismemberment, and exile' (Spillers 1987, p. 67). As Spillers argues, this order of violence cannot be relegated to the past. Her essay documents its reproduction and maintenance in the present.

I want to transpose Spillers' colonial vestibule and its inmates of 'captive flesh' to the Salt Pit, Afghanistan, in order to begin to trace the dimensions of transnational relations of US colonial power. This is not a transposition that I undertake lightly as this genealogy of US colonial power is marked by the specificities of the lived histories of Native Americans and African-Americans, and the trajectories of subjugation driven by a two-pronged exercise of power that is differently genocidal: both exterminatory-colonial and impelled by a genocidal economics of property-made-flesh through enslavement. In the wake of these fundamental differences, there remains a feature that is constitutive of this colonial violence: a seriality of violent power that survives precisely by being flexible and adaptive to different geopolitical sites, bodies and forms of violence.

The Salt Pit, in Spillers' (1987, p. 67) terms, must be seen as another instantiation of colonial 'vestibularity' that is absolutely disjunctive, on every level, from 'the *culture*' of the white order of the human-rights-bearing subject. This vestibularity is divided from the order of the hegemonic culture by that biopolitical caesura that determines in fundamental ways who will live and who will die (Agamben 2004, p. 16). Whether operative within the body of the nation or in that secret, transnational elsewhere of CIA black sites, the carceral vestibule produces one constant: 'the captive body reduces to a thing, becoming *being for* the captor' (Spillers 1987, p. 67). In the Salt Pit, Gul

Rahman becomes, through a series of violent instrumentalizations of his body, 'a thing' for his captors. I want to delineate the ensemble of dimensions – physical, ontological and juridical – that enable the transmutation of Gul Rahman's embodied being into 'thing'.

'[T]he captive body', writes Spillers (1987, p. 67), '...embodies sheer physical powerlessness'. Shackled with his hands above his head and hung from the ceiling hooks, Rahman is made to embody sheer powerlessness. Suspended from the ceiling with shackles, his agency is incapacitated at both physical and ontological levels. Physically, there is a suspension of basic motor control over his body. Ontologically, in the context of his blackened cell, Rahman's being is suspended over an abyss, as he loses touch with the ground, the base from which the subject phenomenologically makes sense of the world. What transpires is 'the elimination of world ground' (Scarry 1987, p. 37). The incapacitating of Rahman's sensorium is further exacerbated by the disorientation of darkness, by the blasting of loud speakers and by numbness resulting from the draining of his blood to his feet. The ensemble of torture techniques that are inflicted on his body collectively work to transmute Gul Rahman into a carcass of 'captive flesh', raised up and suspended, like a slain beast, from the metal hooks hanging from the ceiling.

These CIA black sites are not the prison-house of the human. They are the death chamber of the object-thing whose 'being for the captor' is a being towards death. As a being towards death, the object-thing becomes *carcass*. That is why these secret prisons must remain *black sites*, as within these gulags every convention on the human is breached through an array of somatechnologies of torture that render the human mere carcass. The moment of capture enunciates the crossing of the threshold into the horror of Spillers' 'vestibule', a crossing that will strip the subject of every ontological and legal claim to the category of the 'human'. Entry into the vestibularity of black site prisons marks the death of the 'subject-function' (Foucault 2006, p. 56) and the birth of the object-thing: carcass, 'a kind of absolute biopolitical substance' that embodies Agamben's (1998, p. 183, 2002, p. 156) 'bare life'. The flesh held captive within these prisons becomes, in Fanon's (1970, p. 77) haunting words, an 'object in the midst of other objects' – the cell, the shackles, the instruments of torture.

I deploy the unsettling term 'carcass' in order to disrupt the hold of residual humanisms that would demand of the victim, who has been stripped of every possible vestige of (human) personhood, the exercise of some redemptive (human) agency in the face of the most horrific of situations. This demand, as I have argued elsewhere, operates as a type of alibi that reassures the privileged western subject confronted by a site of utter subjection that something 'human' remains in the face of the horror that lies entirely on the hither side of their own ontological ground, even as they are, structurally, complicit in the production of the violence that they abhor (Pugliese 2007c). To proceed to demand, and extract, (human) agency from the victims of *fatal* torture regimes, and I underscore the qualifier 'fatal', would be tantamount to inflicting upon them yet another level of (symbolic) violence, by imposing upon them a redemptive narrative that is undone at every turn by their torture, death and unmarked graves. It would do nothing more than assuage my desire to maintain my own life, agency and will to power in the face of the victim's catastrophic loss – of power, agency and life. Situated in this context, 'carcass' signifies the non-(human)subject status of torture's object-thing. Carcass is that object-thing that will not be liberated or redeemed and for whom (as I discuss below in Gul Rahman's case) no justice will be served.

Laboratories of torture

In these secret prisons, Spillers' 'being for the captor' is thanatologically circumscribed and temporally delimited. The captive victim can only be for the captor for the duration that his or her body can hold out against the assaults and trauma of torture. The Bybee (2005, p. 176) memo establishes the possibility for these black sites to become laboratories of torture shadowed by the tenuous limits between life and death: severe pain, the memo declares, can be pushed to 'the level that would ordinarily be associated with a sufficiently serious physical condition or injury such as death, organ failure or serious impairment of bodily functions – in order to constitute torture'. I term these black sites *laboratories* of torture as the torturers test a number of techniques by which to torture their victim, often to the point of unconsciousness from the intensity of the pain, only to then deploy a series of counter-strategies that will revive the victim in order to keep the subject alive for more torture sessions. One of the victims held prisoner in one of these CIA black sites describes his sessions of torture as structured by repeated lapses into unconsciousness because of the pain and his consequent revival so that he could endure yet another session of torture [International Committee of the Red Cross (ICRC) Report 2007, pp. 29–30]. The laboratory-like conditions of these torture sites are evidenced by the CIA's use of medical and psychiatric personnel, employed to monitor the victim's life-signs during the torture sessions. The use of medical personnel to evaluate and monitor the health status of the torture victim is officially endorsed in the Memorandum for John A. Rizzo, Senior Deputy General Counsel, Central Intelligence Agency, 'Re: Application of 18 U.S.C. §§ 2340-2340A to Certain Techniques That May Be Used in the Interrogation of a High Value al Qaeda Detainee', 10 May 2005 (Rizzo Memo 2005). The Rizzo Memo (2005, p. 6) outlines that 'subsequent medical rechecks during the interrogation period should be performed on a regular basis', whilst also recommending that, as 'an additional precaution, and to ensure the objectivity of their medical and psychological assessments, OMS [Office of Medical Services] personnel do not participate in administering interrogation techniques; their function is to monitor interrogations and the health of the detainee'. As I argue below, however, the line between objective monitoring and complicity in torture becomes significantly blurred in light of the testimonies of the tortured detainees.

Drawing on a range of medical technologies, the medical personnel complicit in the torture sessions were not employed to safe-guard the health and safety of the victim; rather, in direct violation of the avowed ethics of the medical profession, they were employed to make sure that the victim never crossed the fatal threshold of organ failure or fatal injury that would render him or her dead and useless. The Report on the findings of the International Committee of the Red Cross (2007, pp. 21−22) on the torture of detainees by the CIA documents the following:

> Mr Khaled Shaik Mohammed alleged that, in his third place of detention, one of his interrogators stated that the greenlight had been received from Washington to give him a "hard time" and that, although they would not let him die, he would be brought to the 'verge of death and back again'.
> (ICRC 2007, p. 17)

The tortured body is here shown to be set on a halting trajectory towards not-quite-death: it is tortured to the point that it almost, but not quite, veers over the edge of the abyss, only to be hauled back, revivified and compelled to endure yet another session of torture. The ICRC testimonies of the CIA's torture victims repeatedly document this halting trajectory punctuated by torture sessions and reprieves.

In order to enable this risky shuttle between life and not-quite-death, medical personnel constituted a key element in the ensemble of torture agents:

> Throughout the course of initial phase of the detention, the ICRC received allegations that health personnel were directly involved in monitoring the health effects of ill-treatment. In some cases it was alleged that, based on their assessments, health personnel gave instructions to interrogators to continue, to adjust, or to stop particular methods ... For certain methods, notably during suffocation by water, the health personnel were allegedly directly participating in the infliction of the ill-treatment. In one case, it was alleged that health personnel actively monitored a detainee's oxygen saturation using what, from the description of the detainee of a device placed over the finger, appeared to be a *pulse oxymeter*.
> (ICRC 2007, pp. 21−22)

In the CIA laboratories of torture, the medical personnel clinically monitor all the relevant life-signs in order to keep the subject alive so that he may continue to be tortured:

> Mr Bin Attash (the detainee has had a right-sided below the knee amputation) alleged that while being held in a form of stress standing position with his arms shackled above his head, and his feet touching the floor, had his lower leg measured on a daily basis with a tape measure by a person assumed to be a doctor for signs of swelling.
>
> (ICRC 2007, p. 22)

The use of the tape measure to gauge the swelling of the victim's foot establishes a finely nuanced regime of torture calibrations: at what point does the swelling leg cross the irreversible line into necrosis? At what critical juncture will the blood oxygen level become so depleted as to risk organ failure? The attendant medical personnel will know. Operative here is the medicalized instrumentalization of torture, with its array of auxiliary weapons, including pulse oxymeter and tape measure, and the consequent enmeshment of the victim's body within regimes of biopower. Biopower, Foucault (1990, p. 143) writes, is designed to bring 'life and its mechanisms into the realm of explicit calculations'. It deploys a battery of somatechnologies of 'infinitesimal surveillances' in order to 'qualify, measure, [and] appraise' the subject in question (Foucault 1990, pp. 144, 146). The medical measuring of the swelling of the victim's leg with a tape measure will result in an appraisal that will determine whether or not the torture session can be productively continued, and not out of concern for the victim's health or life:

> Mr Hambali alleged that, after a period of the same form of prolonged stress standing, a health person intervened to prevent further use of the method, but told him that 'I look after your body only because we need you for information'.
>
> (ICRC 2007, p. 22)

Medical power is seen here to fold into a biopolitcs of torture and extortion: the body of the torture victim is kept alive only in order to render it viable for the extortion of information.

Instrumental and gratuitous violence

The production of the tortured carcass in these black sites is constituted by inflicting upon the captive flesh at least two intersecting modalities of violence: instrumental and gratuitous. Instrumental violence is enabled by a battery of somatechnical instrumentalities – loud speakers, shackles, strobe lighting, electrical wires, cables and so on – that are mobilized by the interrogator in the lived theatre of torture. These instruments of torture evidence the direct application of violence on the flesh of the victim. Working in tandem with this instrumental violence is gratuitous violence. Gratuitous violence operates indirectly on the flesh of the captive. It is enabled by the thanatological ecology of these cellular black sites: total darkness, damp concrete floors and freezing cold brick walls. Stripped naked of protective clothing, doused with a bucket of water and hung by his wrists, the lethal ecology of Gul Rahman's black site prison proceeded to enact its own regime of violence on the prisoner, inexorably exacting its pound of captive flesh, drawing the victim's life slowly, by hypothermic degrees, congealing his blood and freezing his life-force, gratuitously, without the assistance of a human actor. Neither the guard nor the interrogator was needed in order for this gratuitous violence to transform captive flesh into a carcass. In other words, there is operative here no 'specific intent', as meticulously argued in the Bybee memo.

The dousing of Rahman with a bucket of water must be understood as constituting 'torture lite' or 'no-touch' torture, two officially sanctioned ways of torturing one's victims without leaving any marks (see Phillips 2010, p. 138). Such forms of torture constitute what Rejali (2007, p. 4) terms '*clean* techniques in contrast to *scarring* techniques of torture'. 'Clean' techniques of torture, as Rejali (2007, p. 8) explains, are precisely those favoured by democratic states as they enable a type of torture by stealth, in which violence can be inflicted on the body of the victim without leaving the sort of evidentiary marks crucial to the forensic documentation of torture. Moreover, within these corporeal economies of torture, 'clean' techniques are often characterized by the use of stress positions that cause the victim to experience self-inflicted pain. In his documentation of the CIA's development of such techniques, Alfred McCoy (2006, p. 9) has underscored the fact that 'Although seemingly less brutal than physical methods, no-touch torture leaves deep psychological scars on both victims and interrogators'. Citing the work of a British journalist who had observed this form of torture, he writes that no-touch torture 'provokes more anxiety among the interrogatees than more traditional tortures, leaves no visible scars and, therefore, is harder to prove, and produces longer lasting effects' (McCoy 2006, p. 9).

Rahman's gesture of insurrection, his flaunting of the authority of his foreign captors to imprison him extra-judicially within his own land by besmirching them with the projectile waste of his flung latrine bucket, will only speed up his declination towards the status of carcass. As carcass, captive flesh can be humiliated, violated and mutilated before being dispatched to an unmarked burial pit, as Rahman's body was. What transpires for Gul Rahman in the time of being doused with a bucket of water, being left to freeze naked, and his solitary moment of dying? A void opens that will completely engulf him: as he is overcome by the lethal effects of gratuitous violence, and his death throes are borne with no auditor or witness, he becomes one and the same with the black site of his prison cell: he is become void, hollowed out of life and transmuted into dark matter, bodily disappeared, empirically unverifiable except analogously, in the black crypt of a redacted footnote – a redacted footnote in which Gul Rahman is opportunistically revivified only in order to vouch for the 'correct explanation' of law that will evidence the professional conduct and moral rectitude of the good judge who drafted the memo that legitimized the CIA's regime of torture.

Advance pardons

After his deposition, Gul Rahman's body was dispatched to a secret, unmarked grave. Only to reappear, marginalized and further subjugated to the violence of law, in footnote 28 of Judge Bybee's response to the OPR. I reproduce the footnote in full:

> 28 Notably, the declination memorandum prepared by the CIA's Counterterrorism Section regarding the death of Gul Rahman provides the correct explanation of the specific intent element and did not rely on any motivation to acquire information. Report at 92. If [redacted] as manager of the Saltpit [sic] site, did not intend for Rahman to suffer severe pain from low temperature in his cell, he would lack specific intent under the anti-torture statute. And it is also telling that the declination did not even discuss the possibility that the prosecution was barred by the Commander-in-Chief section of the Bybee memo.
> (Mahoney and Johnson 2009, p. 29)[3]

The redacted text in this footnote censors the name of the CIA officer in charge of the Salt Pit at the time of Gul Rahman's torture and death. I will presently analyse the systemic redactions in this text, but for now I want to discuss Gul Rahman's death in the context of the 'declination memorandum' and the 'lack [of] specific intent' mentioned in this footnote. In law, a *declination* refers to an agreement not prosecute. Sifton (2010) sardonically elaborates its definition in law: 'The word *declination* is similar to the word *indulgence* in Catholicism; it's about avoiding eternal damnation by obtaining forgiveness for your sins'. Sifton (2010), however, soon illuminates its 'more sinister' dimensions:

> The declination memo "regarding Gul Rahman's death" was essentially an after-the-fact blessing for Rahman's killer, in the form of a memo stating that DoJ [Department of Justice] would not prosecute the officers responsible. It is clear [that]...the criminal division of DoJ provided declination in cases of detainee abuse, thus giving individual officers de facto immunity from criminal prosecution.

Sifton (2010) argues that the 'facts of Rahman's death suggest at least a negligent homicide', yet 'To this day, not a single CIA officer has been prosecuted for detainee abuse'. On the contrary, several CIA officials have confirmed 'Kabul station CIA chief's career advancement inside the agency after Rahman died. Now a senior officer, the man was promoted at least three times since leaving Afghanistan in 2003' (Goldman and Gannon 2010).

The legal category of the declination (as, in Sifton's (2010) sardonic words, the 'get out of jail free card for torture') is intimately connected to the production of the Bybee memo. In its unpacking of the events that led to the writing of the Bybee memo, the OPR Report (2008, p. 26) draws attention to the manner in which the Department of Justice was approached by the CIA asking for 'pre-activity declination letters'. In other words, the:

> CIA had requested some sort of advance assurance that they would not be prosecuted for using EITs [Enhanced Interrogation Techniques]. According to Yoo [Deputy Assistant Attorney General, U.S. Department of Justice], Ashcroft [Attorney General U.S. Department of Justice] was sympathetic to the request, and asked Yoo if it would be possible to issue 'advance pardons'. Yoo...remembered that the concept of 'advance pardons' was discussed as the Bybee Memo was being finalised.
> (OPRR 2008, pp. 26–27)

The CIA request for the advance pardons offered by declinations was not directly drafted into the Bybee memo. However, a form of declination was inscribed in the final text of the memo as a result of the sheer latitude in the categorical description of what would constitute torture ['As noted by a number of critics, the Bybee memo's definition of severe pain could be interpreted as advising interrogators that they may legally inflict pain up to the point of organ failure, death, or serious physical injury' (OPRR 2008, p. 133)]. This immediately became evident to some in the US Department of Justice when they first read the Bybee memo: 'Yoo recalled that [Michael] Chertoff [Criminal Division Assistant Attorney General] was concerned that the memorandum could be interpreted as providing a "blanket immunity"' (OPRR 2008, p. 34). In the production of the Bybee memo, as the Office of Professional Responsibility (2008, p. 125) argues, Bybee, and his Office of Legal Counsel attorneys, crossed the line from acting as advisors to 'advocates' of the CIA request for immunity for conduct that would effectively 'violate federal [anti-torture] law'. The OPR Report (2008, p. 149) concludes that the Bybee memo 'in effect constituted an advance declination of prosecution for future violations of the torture statute, notwithstanding Criminal Division AAG Chertoff's refusal to provide a formal declination'. Another legal commentator is much more blunt in his assessment, arguing that the Bybee memo effectively worked 'to pre-authorize some torture and retroactively approve murder' through 'that giant loophole of intent' (Leisureguy 2010).

Counsel for Jay Bybee remarks that the 'declination memorandum prepared by the CIA's Counterterrorism Section regarding the death of Gul Rahman provides the correct explanation of the specific intent element' (Mahoney and Johnson 2009, p. 29). In other words, the CIA declination was successful precisely because it argued that torture and homicide had not transpired in the death of Gul Rahman as no specific intent had been exercised in the cause of his death. As discussed in my aforementioned analysis of the Bybee memo, the 'defendant is guilty of torture only if he acts with express purpose of inflicting severe pain or suffering on a person within his custody or physical control' (2005, p. 175). The OPR Report (2008, p. 137) views this as one of the 'key conclusions' of the Bybee memo:

> The infliction of severe physical pain or severe mental pain or suffering must be "the defendant's precise objective." Even if a defendant knows that severe pain will result from his actions, he may lack specific intent if 'causing such harm is not his objective, even though he does not act in good faith'.[4]

The CIA's declination regarding the death of Gul Rahman was 'correct', and therefore successful, precisely because it fulfilled Bybee's guidelines.[5] Technically, in leaving Rahman shackled, hanging and dripping wet, in a freezing cold cell, no specific intent to murder was exercised by the CIA officer, even though he acted in 'bad faith'.

What is instantiated here, I would argue, is a form of techno-legal rationality that disavows its own production of violence by the most disingenuous of legal circumscriptions. Violence, torture and homicide need to be located beyond the confines of 'specific intent' in order to flesh out the larger matrix of state violence that enabled the torture and homicide of Rahman. A series of macro- and micro-coordinates delineate this violent matrix. In the death of Rahman, an enabling continuum of torture was operative that effectively encompassed the discursive practices of the interrogators and guards – including shackling, hanging by the wrists, and dousing with water – and the extradiscursive dimensions of the prison – its damp walls, total darkness and freezing climate. Situated within this torture continuum, the legal question of 'specific intent' must be seen as constituted by relays of violence that are instrumental *and* gratuitous, where the instrumentalized torture-effects produced by interrogators are amplified by the gratuitous violence generated by the lethal ecology of the Salt Pit. This torture continuum must be expanded in order to encompass a diffuse network of diverse social agents (including judges, attorneys, legal counsels, politicians and medical personnel) and a range of somatechnologies of biopower (including legal texts, prisons, medical instruments and carceral apparatuses) that all work in tandem within the CIA's secret prisons.

Redactions

Reading through the official reports documenting the various incarnations of torture, I was struck by the innumerable redactions that scored these texts. The redactions encompassed everything from a single word to the blackening out of the entire page. Singularly absent from these texts are the names of the guards, interrogators and agents who were instrumental in the deployment of torture regimes on their victims. These redactions, I argue, are constitutive of a type of national forgetting through systematic occlusion and, through the ruse of declinations, exoneration.

These acts of redaction must also be seen as enabling a type of juridicide that exempts those responsible for the torture perpetrated in the CIA's secret prisons from open and transparent processes of juridical accountability. Redaction, in these official texts, is crucial to the production of state-regulated meaning. It establishes the very impossibility for justice to be served as it stages the state-sponsored disappearance of the principal actors in the theatre of torture that was the Salt Pit. The force of law animating these redactions produces, at one and the same time, a cloak of impunity for the agents of torture and the dispatch of the victim of torture, Gul Rahman, to an unknown burial pit. As such, the body of the victim of torture must be seen as not being placed 'under erasure'; rather, the body of the victim is, through these censorial acts of blackening, physically and symbolically annihilated.

These black slabs of redaction are meant, in legal terms, to liquidate the possibility of accessing confidential text. The redactional blackness generates a-signification, the impossibility of meaning, occlusions without referents. Yet, within these zones of blackened text, something persists, a perverse semiosis continues defiantly to (a-)signify. I want to attempt to read these redacted black slabs against the grain, to read for meaning where meaning has seemingly been completely obliterated. I situate this attempt in the context of a condition known, philologically, as 'redaction fatigue', where redacted texts often unintentionally display conflicting remainders of texts that signify earlier, unedited versions of the text. In mobilizing a form of redaction fatigue, I want to attempt to elicit possible palimpsests of signification that, because of the ineradicable metaphoricity of all texts, survive despite the redactions. A graphic example of redaction fatigue within these legal texts concerns another CIA torture-homicide victim named Hassan Ghul who was captured in January 2004. Sifton (2009), a former senior researcher on terrorism and counter-terrorism at Human Rights Watch, writes that: 'Ghul's interrogation was discussed in one of the 10 May 2005, Office of Legal Counsel memos signed by the OLC head Steven Bradbury. Ghul's name is mostly redacted but appears by mistake in one part of the memo'. In other words, the happenstance of redaction fatigue enables the accidental materialization of the name of one of the disappeared. Sifton (2009) suspects the worst in the case of Hassan Ghul:

I am starting to suspect that Ghul might be dead. After all, his name was redacted from the OLC memo, unlike that of other CIA detainees now at Guantánamo. Why would the CIA be afraid of mentioning Ghul? CIA doctors appear to have determined that Ghul was in poor health when he was captured, in fact, too unhealthy to be waterboarded. Unlike other former CIA detainees, human-rights groups have not confirmed that he was rendered to Pakistan or to a third country. Did the CIA perhaps torture Ghul to death? We do not know. He has now completely disappeared.

The black slabs of redaction in these official texts metaphorize, for me, the bodies of the disappeared. Every redaction gestures towards what must remain absent: the body of the victim that has been disappeared by the state. Every blackened slab of redaction functions to encrypt the body that cannot be located. As such, every redaction becomes the tomb-like proxy that holds the secret of the absent dead. They are the proxy gravestones that cannot be erected by the victim's families because they do not have the bodies of their disappeared. 'We want his body back', pleads Gul Rahman's brother, Habib Rahman, 'We want them to let us give him a religious burial' (CBS News 2010). Scarring these official texts, these redactions bespeak *unsayable* eulogies for their victims: unsayable because they are articulated without words, unsayable because they have been rendered unspeakable by the redactional hand of the state and its apparatuses of legalized violence. These black zones of occlusion emerge as their own forms of convoluted testimony, evidencing what has been secreted and obliterated. They are marked, violently, by a double logic: a censoring of the names of the perpetrators that, simultaneously, recalls the disappeared bodies of their victims.

In metaphorically defying their own non-meaning and a-referentiality, these redacted black slabs refer back to the very black sites of the secret prisons: they establish a discursive system of relation between texts, bodies and material sites. Reading through these redacted official texts is an experience similar to reading maps, as the textual redactions articulate cartographies that are homologous to the geopolitical black sites. They are equivalent to the 'blank spots' on the maps of the Pentagon's 'dark geographies' (Paglen 2009, p. 11), where names and places have been literally excised from official maps. This homology of secretive blackness, that holds between the redacted texts and the CIA black sites, pivots on the power of law to transmute knowledge into unknowledge. The material prisons and their redacted textual equivalents are animated at every turn by anti-epistemologies that thwart the possibility of a transparent judicial process, precisely as they interdict the realization of justice. The black redactions that mark the topography of these texts are voids generated by the force of law. They are the graphic spatializations of law's power to establish both the conditions of intelligibility and unintelligibility. As anti-epistemologies, these material and symbolic black sites unmake what it is to be a human rights-bearing subject, reducing the victim to the disposable biological material of captive flesh: carcass. As so many black holes that void meaning, they transfix their victims within event horizons that are beyond the remedial powers of law. 'The history of secret geographies', notes Paglen (2009, p. 140), 'shows that when they do come into contact with the legal system, the legal system tends to accommodate them. When the secret state wins, as it usually does, blank spots on maps create blank spots in the legal system'. The very fact that these heavily redacted texts have achieved a level of visibility, by being placed into circulation through Freedom of Information Acts, bears testimony to the assiduous labour of human rights activists and organizations to try to make the state accountable for its secret regimes of death and violence.

Reading these redacted legal texts, I reiterate, is tantamount to the reading of maps. As maps, these redacted legal texts must be seen as articulating topographies of ruin. Lodged between the *logos* of text are those redacted passages that stage the ruination of sense and signification. Nothing is recoverable in the face of their obdurate blankness – not the bodies of the victims tortured to death, nor the names of their executioners. Only by mobilizing the ruse of metaphor have I been able to recover 'something' from this ruination: unsayable testimonies of the tortured, the unmarked graves of the disappeared. In the face of the blank spaces that they both enact and preserve, these redacted legal texts evidence the incommensurability of law to justice.

Notes

1 Gul Rahman was not an al Qaeda operative, as initially claimed by the CIA:

> but rather an Afghan insurgent in Hizb-i-Islami, a mujahedeen group headed by the warlord Gulbuddin Hekmatyar. (Ironic twist: Hekmatyar's group received hundreds of millions of dollars in CIA assistance in the 1980s; it was one of the CIA's most favoured mujahedeen groups. It's also in the news for offering Karzai a peace plan)
>
> (Sifton 2010).

2 As Elaine Scarry (1987, p. 31) notes, 'the infliction of physical pain is always a mock execution'.
3 The Commander-in-Chief section of the Bybee memo effectively advised the client [the CIA] that the Department of Justice would not prosecute CIA interrogators for violating the torture statute during questioning of al Qaeda suspects, because such a prosecution would be an unconstitutional interference with the President's Commander-in-Chief power.

(OPRR 2008, p. 151)

The OPRR (2008, p. 151) critiques this position arguing that the memo 'should have addressed ways to comply with the law, not circumvent it: Accordingly, OLC [Office of Legal Counsel] must construe the torture statute as not applying to interrogations undertaken pursuant to the [President's] Commander-in-Chief authority'.

4 The OPR Report (2008, p. 136) draws attention to the Levin memo, published after the Bybee memo, which 'noted the complexity and ambiguity of this area of law'; it 'concluded that it would not be appropriate to rely on parsing the specific intent element of the statute to approve as lawful conduct that might otherwise amount to torture'.

5 In a closed-door interview with members of the House Judiciary Committee, 26 May 2010, Bybee refused to own any culpability in the torture regimes that his memo licensed: '"We might have been clearer in some places", Bybee said. "But, in terms of the analysis, I am going to stand by the memo"' (cited in Leopold 2010).

References

Agamben, G. (1998) *Homo Sacer*, Stanford, Stanford University Press.

Agamben, G. (2002) *Remnants of Auschwitz*, New York, Zone Books.

Agamben, G. (2004) *The Open*, Stanford, Stanford University Press.

Bybee, J. S. (2005 [2002]) 'Memorandum for Alberto R. Gonzales Counsel to the President, August 1, 2002', in *The Torture Papers*, eds K. J. Greenberg & J. L. Dratel, Cambridge, Cambridge University Press, pp. 172–217.

CBS News (2010) *Did CIA torture victim once rescue Hamid Karzai?*, Available at: http://www.cbsnews.com/stories/2010/04/06/world/main63610.shtml (accessed 17 May 2010).

Emptywheel (2010) *Salt pit victim, Gul Rahman, once rescued Hamid Karzai, April 6, 2010*, Available at: http://emptywheel.firedoglake.com/2010/04/06/

salt-pit-victim-guh-rahman-once-rescued-hamid-karzai/ (accessed 21 April 2010).

Fanon, F. (1970) *Black Skins White Masks*, London, Paladin.

Foucault, M. (2006) *Psychiatric Power: Lectures at the Collège de France 1974–1975*, Basingstoke and New York, Palgrave Macmillan.

Foucault, M. (1990) *The History of Sexuality*, vol. 1, London, Penguin.

Goldman, A. & Gannon, K. (2010) Salt pit death: Gul Rahman, CIA Prisoner, died of hypothermia in secret Afghanistan Prison, *Huffington Post*, 31 March 2010, Available at: http://www.huffingtonpost.com/2010/03/28/salt-pit-death-gul-rahman_n_516559.html (accessed 4 April 2010).

Greenberg, K. J. & Dratel, J. L. (eds.) (2005) *The Torture Papers*, Cambridge, Cambridge University Press.

International Committee of the Red Cross (2007) ICRC Report on the treatment of fourteen "High Value Detainees" in CIA Custody, Washington, DC, Available at: www.nybooks.com/media/doc/2010/04/22/icrc-report.pdf (accessed 29 April 2010).

Leisureguy (2010) *The salt pit and the Bybee memos*, Available at: http://leisureguy.wordpress.com/2010/03/28/the-salt-pit-and-the-bybee-memos/ (accessed 11 April 2010).

Leopold, J. (2010) Author of torture memos admits some techniques were not approved by DOJ, *truthout*, 15 July 2010, Available at: http://www.truth-out.org/author-torture-memos-admits-some-techniques-were-not-approved-by-doj63192 (accessed 20 July 2010).

Luban, D. (2006) 'Liberalism, torture, and the ticking bomb', in *The Torture Debate in America*, ed. K. J. Greenberg, Cambridge and New York, Cambridge University Press.

Mahoney, M. E. & Johnson, E. C. (2009) Classified response to the U.S. Department of Justice Office of Professional Responsibility Classified Report Dated July 29, 2009, Submitted on Behalf of Judge Jay. S. Bybee, Available at: http://judiciary.house.gov/hearings/pdf/BybeeResponse090729.pdf (accessed 21 January 2010).

McCoy, A. W. (2006) *A Question of Torture: CIA Interrogation from the Cold War to the War on Terror*, New York, Metropolitan Books.

Memorandum for John A. Rizzo, Senior Deputy General Counsel, Central Intelligence Agency (2005) 'Re: Application of 18 U.S.C. §§ 2340-2340A to certain techniques that may be used in the interrogation of a high value al Qaeda Detainee', 10 May 2005, by Steven G. Bradbury, Principal Deputy Assistant Attorney General, Available at: http://globalsecurity.org/intell/library/policy/national/olc_050510_bradbury46pg.htm (accessed 12 January 2011).

Office of Professional Responsibility Report (2008) Investigation into the Office of Legal Counsel's Memoranda Concerning Issues Relating to the Central Intelligence Agency's Use of "Enhanced Interrogation Techniques" on Suspected Terrorists, Available at: http://judiciary.house.gov/hearings/pdf/OPRReport090729.pdf (accessed 3 March 2010).

Office of Professional Responsibility Report (2009) Investigation into the Office of Legal Counsel's Memoranda Concerning Issues Relating to the Central Intelligence Agency's Use of "Enhanced Interrogation Techniques" on Suspected Terrorists, Available at: http://www.expose-the-war-profiteers.org/archive/government/2009-1/20090729.pdf (accessed 22 March 2010).

Paglen, T. (2009) *Blank Spots on the Map: The Dark Geography of the Pentagon's Secret World*, New York, Dutton.

Phillips, J. E. S. (2010) *None of us Were Like This Before: American Soldiers and Torture*, London and New York, Verso.

Pugliese, J. (2007a) 'Abu Ghraib's shadow archives', *Law and Literature*, vol. 9, no. 2, pp. 247–276.

Pugliese, J. (2007b) 'Geocorpographies of torture', *Australian Critical Race and Whiteness Studies Association ejournal*, vol. 3, no. 1, Available at: http://www.acrawsa.org.au/ (accessed 11 January 2011).

Pugliese, J. (2007c) 'The event-trauma of the carceral post-human', *Social Semiotics*, vol. 17, no. 1, pp. 63–86.

Pugliese, J. (2009), 'Apostrophe of empire: Guantánamo Bay, Disneyland', *Borderlands ejournal*, vol. 8, no. 3, Available at: http://www.borderlands.net.au/vol8no3_2009/pugliese_apostrophe.htm (accessed 11 January 2011).

Rejali, D. (2007) *Torture and Democracy*, Princeton and London, Princeton University Press.

Scarry, E. (1987) *The Body in Pain*, Oxford, Oxford University Press.

Sifton, J. (2009) The Bush administration homicides, *The Daily Beast*, Available at: http://www.thedailybeast.com/blogs-and-stories/2009-05-05/how-many-were-tortured-to-death/p/ (accessed 13 June 2009).

Sifton, J. (2010) The get out of jail free card for torture, *Slate*, March 29, 2010, Available at: http://www.slate.com/articles/news_and_politics/jurisprudence/2010/03/the_get_out_of_jail_free_card_for_torture.html (accessed 10 June 2010).

Spillers, H. J. (1987) 'Mama's baby, papa's maybe: An American grammar book', *Diacritics*, vol. 17, no. 2, pp. 64–81.

Cristyn Davies

CONSTRUCTING 'DECENCY'

Government subsidized cultural production during the culture wars

> *This article examines the production of normative subjectivity and the construction of 'appropriate' and exportable knowledge through cultural policy during the culture wars of the 1980s–1990s in the USA. During this time, the performing and visual arts, and mass media were increasingly seen as the cause, rather than the reflection, of social instability, and quickly became subject to governmental regulation. Focusing on a 1998 US Supreme Court case, National Endowment for the Arts v. Finley, I examine the construction and application of decency offered in the oral transcripts, and attend more broadly to the relationship between cultural policy and law. Cultural policy is a technique of governmentality, and a means through which citizenship and national identity is constituted and regulated, and self-governance inculcated. Similarly, law is a key technology through which governance, and subjectivity is produced, constituted and regulated. Policies such as the 'decency' clause depend on a series of coercive technologies and practices, which ensure that only particular kinds of individuals are understood as embodying norms that are constitutive of citizen-subjects that the State desires. The introduction of the 'decency' clause may be understood, in part, as a response to a perceived failure in the arts community of individuals to effectively self-regulate and embody standard sociocultural norms.*

Rhetorics of decency are deeply imbedded in American political and legal cultures, and continue to play out in a variety of contexts, from presidential campaigns to educational curricula. Analyses of cultural flashpoints where the concept of decency has converged with discourses around citizenship still require attention, and accordingly I turn here to look at those bitter years – culturally and politically speaking – of the so-called 'culture wars' of the 1980s and 1990s. Throughout that troubled era, the performing and visual arts and mass media were increasingly seen as the cause, rather than the reflection, of social instability, and quickly became subject to governmental regulation (Foerstel 1997, Davies 2008). The ongoing struggle over American cultural values and the representation, production and consumption of those values has made for a tenuous relationship between cultural production, regulation and the law. In this article, I examine the construction and application of a cultural and legal concept of decency in the transcripts of the 1998 US Supreme Court case, *National Endowment for the Arts v. Karen Finley*,[1] in which the court upheld the 'decency' clause.[2]

In the work to follow, I begin by outlining the role of law and policy in the production of (sexual) subjects through the framework of governmentality, examining law as a key technology through which governance, and subjectivity is produced, constituted and regulated. I then turn to briefly map the history of the concept of decency in the USA, and its formation in relation to obscenity. Third, I outline the socio-political and the legal context to *NEA v. Finley*. Examining the discursive production of 'decency' in *NEA v. Finley*, I argue that the concept of decency is grounded in values that reflect Christian morality, constituted through white, heteronormative, middle-class values, and therefore primarily concerned with regulating the production and consumption of sexuality.

The decency clause was introduced, in part, to facilitate the production of normative subjectivity and to inform the construction of 'appropriate' and exportable narratives of nationhood. I also examine the role of analogy in legal reasoning, where the mobilizing of ideologically and affectively loaded examples shape the outcome of legal decisions. In the final section of this article, I reflect on the effects of the decency clause today.

Governmentality, law and cultural policy

This discussion of *NEA v. Finley* attends to the discourses through which sexual subjectivity is constituted and the institutional mechanisms and practices through which American citizenship is produced. Michel Foucault's (1979, 2008) theory of governmentality — that is, the technologies, tactics, procedures and strategies through which the State's power is maintained by the repetition of practices that structure, order and discipline individuals and populations — is a useful way to understand the production of sexual subjects through the law and cultural policy. Austin Sarat and Kearns' (1998) scholarship about the role of law, especially their insight that the 'production, interpretation, consumption and circulation of legal meaning suggests that law is inseparable from the interests, goals, and understandings that shape or comprise social life' gestures towards the significance of law in determining the domain of culture (p. 6). Both law and cultural policy are not only key technologies through which subjects are formed and constrained, but are also central to the formation of narratives about national identity that are circulated domestically and globally. Critically, Sarat and Kearns (1998) argue that law is constitutive of culture, entering social practices, shaping consciousness and making law's 'concepts and commands seem, if not invisible, then perfectly natural and benign' (p. 6).

Similarly, cultural policy is a technique of governmentality, and a means through which citizenship and national identity is constituted and regulated, and self-governance inculcated. Policies such as the 'decency' clause depend on a series of coercive technologies and practices which ensure that only particular kinds of individuals are understood as embodying norms, thus allowing these individuals to be considered genuine subjects. Toby Miller and George Yúdice (2002) argue that cultural policy is 'bureaucratic rather than creative or organic', and that organizations 'solicit, train, distribute, finance, describe and reject actors and activities that go under the signs of artist or artwork, through the implementation of policies' (p. 1). Cultural policy is instrumental in the formation, development and export of narratives that celebrate national identity. Both cultural policy and law depend on the operation of technologies of the self, which are a series of techniques and practices through which subjects constitute themselves within and through systems of power by regulating their bodies, practices and conduct. Technologies of the self may appear natural but are inextricably linked to governmentality. Government is a contact point through which techniques of domination and technologies of the self interact (Foucault 1980). Graham Burchell (1996) argues that this contact point is where techniques of the self are integrated into structures of coercion. The introduction of the decency clause by Congress in the reauthorization legislation, which the National Endowment for the Arts (NEA) was required to implement, was not just a mode of biopower employed to shape both citizen-subjects and their artistic work, but may also be also located within a history wherein obscenity and indecency have shared murky sociocultural and legal terrain.

The introduction of the 'decency' clause may be understood then, at least in part, as a response to a perceived failure in the arts community of some individuals to effectively self-regulate and embody standard sociocultural norms. The performance art of Karen Finley, John Fleck, Holly Hughes and Tim Miller took to task dominant sociocultural scripts that constructed America as a place of liberty and justice for all citizens.

Obscenity, decency and indecency in American law and culture

Obscenity, decency and indecency are contested and historically contingent terms. While there has been considerable research about obscenity within American law (Friedman 1970, Schauer 1976, Petrie 1997) and to a lesser extent, within American culture more broadly (Kobylka 1991, Saunders 1996, Kerstein 2007), decency and indecency appear to be more nebulous, and less the focus of legal and cultural research (Heins 1993, Lane 2006, Lipschultz 2008). The modern socio-legal approach focused around suppressing sexual expression is a product of the Victorian era (Foucault 1976/1998). Early English common law involving obscenity was focused around sedition, blasphemy or breaching the peace (Boyce 2008). Modern conceptions of obscenity were constructed during nineteenth century social turmoil as an increasingly literate and politically active working class challenged the traditional wielders of power, secular and otherwise. The first reported obscenity decisions in the USA imported the English common law doctrine of obscene libel, and the first federal legislation in 1842 regulating obscenity targeted importing 'all indecent and obscene prints, paintings, lithographs, engravings and transparencies' [(State cases included *Commonwealth v. Sharpless* 1815 and *Commonwealth v. Holmes* 1821) Boyce 2008].[3]

Championed by US Postal Inspector and politician, Anthony Comstock, The Comstock Act (1873) prohibited sending 'obscene, lewd, and/or lascivious' materials through the mail, including contraceptive devices and family planning information. The Comstock Act did not define obscenity but rather covered a wider range of materials than previous legislation, which meant that the federal courts applied the *Hicklin* test (*Regina v. Hicklin* 1868). *Hicklin* understood obscenity by asking whether the tendency of the matter charged was 'to deprave and corrupt those whose minds are open to such immoral influences' and focused on the effect of isolated passages on readers who were deemed 'vulnerable' [children, youth, women and the working and disadvantaged classes (*Regina v. Hicklin*)]. The *Hicklin* test was superseded by the 1957 Supreme Court case, *Roth v. United States*, which adopted a new standard to determine obscenity: 'whether, to the average person, applying contemporary community standards, the dominant theme of the material taken as a whole appeals to the prurient interest'.[4] The community standards test was adopted as a supposedly more liberal, objective and definite alternative to *Hicklin*, but the *Roth* decision marked the 'first time that the Court had placed constitutional limits on the criminalization of sexual speech' (Boyce 2008, p. 317). In a six to three decision written by Justice William J. Brennan Jr., the court held that obscenity was not 'within the area of constitutionally protected speech or press' (*Roth v. United States* 1957). The majority held that such a definition of obscenity gave sufficient fair warning, satisfying the demands of due process.

However, in *Miller v. California* (1973) the US Supreme Court argued that any speech considered obscene was not entitled to protection under the First Amendment. In a five to four decision that changed the test for obscenity established in *Roth*, the court held that obscene materials did not have First Amendment protection. The court defined obscenity as:

1. The average person, applying contemporary community standards, must find that the work, taken as a whole, appeals to the prurient interest;
2. the work must depict or describe, in a patently offensive way, "sexual conduct" as the term is specifically defined by applicable state law; and
3. the work, taken as a whole, must lack serious literary, artistic, political, or scientific value.

(Miller v. California 1973)

Decency is a standard used in the regulation of broadcast media to protect minors, but is not part of the *Miller* test. Most recent discussions and cases argued in the courts — with *NEA v. Finley* as a notable exception — address decency or indecency with regard to regulating media broadcasting and the Internet (Chiu 1995, Petrie 1997). Frederick S. Lane (2006) argues 'the term "indecent" (and by extension "decent") is too vague to offer a realistic and predictable guide for conduct, particularly when the consequences of violating an "indecency" statute include a possible prison sentence' (p. 15). Standard definitions of decency reveal meanings associated with a sense of propriety, virtue and sexual modesty, as well as a description of circumstances or events being 'adequate' or 'appropriate', while indecency is vaguely defined as 'not in keeping with accepted standards of what is right or proper in polite society', or 'offending against sexual mores in conduct or appearance' (Lane 2006, p. 14). Meanings constructed around decency and indecency shift according to the social and political mores and values of a culture and time period, and primarily re-enter public discourse with the introduction of new technologies.

Rapid changes in new technology, and ease of access to new technologies, have frequently contributed to community anxiety about regulating content that can be accessed in public and private spaces. Sara L. Knox (2000) argues that fears about new technology taken up by popular culture frequently eclipse fears about earlier mediums. Socio-political and technological change have often been perceived as a potential challenge to the moral order, with conservatives — and their sometimes unlikely political allies — transforming the language of moral anxiety into bureaucratic regulations and advisory language with varying levels of success. In recent times politicians and their constituents seeking to employ standards of decency to regulate representation have generally targeted speech that contains sex or violence.[5] Such measures are most frequently informed by an anxiety about the changing nature of constructions of national culture and community, and new aspects of popular culture, or cultural forms that have attained unprecedented popularity (as with the regulation of the motion picture industry by the Hays and then the Breen code, both of which were energized by pressures from the National Catholic Legion of Decency).

Recently, debate has taken place about both broadcast and Internet indecency — both of which have been subject to action by federal regulators, the US Congress, and the courts for more than 30 years (Lipschultz 2008). The Federal Communications Commission (FCC), an independent US government agency established by The Communications Act (1934), regulates interstate radio, television, satellite, wire and cable. Sanctions against content perceived as indecent, as opposed to obscene, became possible after the adjudication of the 1978 US Supreme Court Case, *Federal Communications Commission v. Pacifica Foundation* (hereafter referred to as *Pacifica*). Five years earlier, a radio listener had lodged a complaint about Pacifica radio in New York City's broadcast of George Carlin's monologue, 'Filthy Words'. Carlin, like comedian Lenny Bruce more than 10 years earlier, had fallen afoul of New York Penal Code 1140-A, which prohibited the broadcast of indecent material. Ultimately, the 1978 Supreme Court decision of *Pacifica* upheld the position of the FCC, which had in 1976 defined indecent broadcasting, inter alia, to forbid the use of 'any obscene, indecent, or profane language by means of radio communications' (*Federal Communications Commission v. Pacifica Foundation* 1978). The Supreme Court argued that the routine was indecent but not obscene, despite *Pacifica's* argument that it was protected by the constitution. The Court ultimately supported the government's desire to protect children from material considered patently offensive, keeping unwanted speech out of the home environment. In 2011, the FCC further articulated a description of indecency as 'language or material that, in context, depicts or describes, in terms patently offensive as measured by contemporary community standards for the broadcast medium, sexual or excretory organs or activities' (FCC 2011).[6] Like the legal definition of obscenity, indecency is here measured by community standards, wherein the 'community' is assumed to be the opinions and values of the dominant culture. The FCC further state that material deemed indecent may be restricted to avoid its broadcast during times of the day when there is a reasonable risk that children may be in the audience. The FCC has determined, with the approval of the courts, that there is a reasonable risk that children will be in the audience from 6 am to 10 pm, local time. Therefore, the FCC prohibits station licensees from broadcasting indecent material during that period (FCC 2011).[7]

The FCC's regulatory code reveals the ways in which the discourse of decency is constructed, both around maintaining the innocence of children, and also by understanding time according to heteronormative constructions of family wherein the normative scheduling of daily life is governed by an imagined set of children's needs (Halberstam 2005). Such scheduling infantilizes adult citizens, and positions the government in the role of a parental figure, charged with monitoring the sexual knowledge of adults (Berlant 1997, Davies 2008, 2012). The FCC's regulation is focused around the neoliberal technology of risk management, wherein calculations of risk are associated with the threat of litigation and financial penalties.

The use of language considered indecent on television arose again when Fox Television Stations broadcast the 2002 Billboard Music Awards during which musician Cher Sarkissian dismissed her critics, saying, 'fuck "em"'. Then, in 2003, presenter and television personality Nicole Richie made an on-camera quip about her own show: 'Why do they even call it *The Simple Life?* Have you ever tried to get cow shit out of a Prada purse? It's not so fucking simple' (Lipschultz 2008, p. 376). The FCC found that the words 'fuck' and 'shit' corresponded with its indecency policy by describing sexual or excretory activities. The language was also 'patently offensive' under the policy's three-factor balancing test because the words invoked explicit sexual or excretory images, and they were used in front of children. A federal court rendered the FCC's policy invalid in 2007, because it was 'arbitrary' and 'capricious', a decision that the Commission appealed in the Supreme Court. The Supreme Court upheld the FCC regulations in *FCC v. Fox Television Stations* (2009), arguing against the claim of arbitrariness and capriciousness under the Administrative Procedures Act (1946). The debate about indecent language continued in the courts in July 2010 when the Second Circuit found that:

> by prohibiting all "patently offensive" references to sex, sexual organs, and excretion without giving adequate guidance as to what "patently offensive" means, the FCC effectively chills speech because broadcasters have no way of knowing what the FCC will find offensive.
>
> (*Fox Television Stations, Inc. v. FCC* 2010)

The court identified evidence indicating that the FCC had previously applied its regulation inconsistently, arguing that the FCC might apply its indecency policy in a subjective or discriminatory way in the future [*FCC v. Fox Television Stations*, 556 US (2009) at 332–333]. The FCC requested, in August 2010, that the Second Circuit reconsider its decision that struck down its indecency regime as unconstitutionally vague and a threat to free speech. Employing the moral force and dominant discourse around the notion of decency, Austin Schlick, general counsel for the FCC, commented that the:

> three-judge panel's decision in July raised serious concerns about the commission's ability to protect children and families from indecent broadcast programming. The commission remains committed to empowering parents and protecting children, and looks forward to the court of appeals' further consideration of our arguments.
>
> (Frankel 2010)

Schlick employs the rhetoric of family values appealing to parental control and the protection of children's *innocence*, linking these to decency in an effort to uphold the status quo and traditional heteronormative family values.

Congress further aimed to regulate explicit material on the Internet and cable television by passing The Communications Decency Act (CDA 1996) to prohibit the knowing transmission of obscene, indecent or patently offensive material to recipients under 18. The American Civil Liberties Union successfully challenged the act, which was struck down in the Supreme Court in *Reno v. American Civil Liberties Union* for violating the freedom of speech component of the First Amendment [521 US 844 (1997)]. The Court decided that the inherent vagueness of the definition of the terms 'indecent' and 'patently offensive' particularly in 'light of the government's inability to identify the relevant community standards by which the material should be judged' rendered the act in contravention of the First Amendment. The CDA, like the NEA (as we shall see below in relation to the term 'decency'), failed to adequately define the word 'indecency', offering no guidelines as to its parameters. In *Reno v. American Civil Liberties Union*, the court was concerned that the CDA statute had not provided a definition of indecency, which could leave uncertainty amongst Internet users. The vagueness of the statute in relation to its construction of indecency was amplified because the CDA was content based and a criminal statute, which meant that the statue could have a chilling effect on constitutional speech. The court's decision in *Reno v. American Civil Liberties Union* demonstrates an understanding that there is an important interest in protecting minors from potentially harmful material on the Internet without limiting the expression of ideas across this medium to those suitable for children. In addition, this case also demonstrated the significance of First Amendment rights associated with speech transmitted through this medium, and suggests that any limitations need to be carefully tailored so that First Amendment rights are upheld, rather than designing overbroad statutes in response to a moral panic about material suitable for minors.

These examples provide an historical context through which the decision in *NEA v. Finley* might be understood with regard to obscenity and indecency. The socio-political context to performance artists, Finley, Fleck, Hughes and Miller taking legal action to have their NEA grants re-instated, and challenge the NEA's decency clause took place amidst another moral panic during the culture wars around visual artists Andres Serrano and Robert Mapplethorpe.

Context to *NEA v. Finley*

In 1987, the NEA funded the North Carolina based Southeastern Center for Contemporary Art's (SECCA) Awards in the Visual Arts series. SECCA re-granted the funding after selecting Serrano and nine other artists who were competitively selected out of 500 applicants (Koch 1998). Serrano was awarded a fellowship worth $15,000, during which he created a photographic work titled, 'Piss Christ' (Tofte 1998, Bauerlein and Grantham 2008). The image featured a crucifix submerged in the artist's urine – a semiotic comment on the commercialization of religious iconography in contemporary culture. When news of Serrano's fellowship was reported in the media, Senators Alphonse D'Amato and Jesse Helms and their political constituents campaigned against the NEA for having indirectly funded the work. In

1989, Reverend Donald Wildmon, then executive director of the American Family Association, positioned the work as part of an anti-Christian campaign, 'which has dominated television and movies for the past decade or more, [and] has now moved over to the art museums', adding that such bigotry against Christians could be found throughout society, 'especially the media' (Bolton 1992, p. 27). Wildmon also suggested that action should be taken against such work before the 'physical persecution of Christians begins' (Bolton 1992, p. 27). Similarly, nationally syndicated columnist and television commentator, Patrick Buchanan warned that the downhill slide of American culture was gathering momentum: nowhere 'is there any evidence of the achievements of American capitalism or democracy' (Bolton 1992, p. 32). In a debate in the Senate over the NEA, Republican Senators Alfonse D'Amato and Jesse Helms described the shock and horror of their constituents at the work, exclaiming that Serrano 'is not an artist, he is a jerk' (Bolton 1992, p. 30).

Generally, the way in which political representatives and their constituents manage their response (other than through those acts of violence or vandalism sometimes practiced by the latter) is to seek legal regulation, or have the offending works banned from public display. In 1997, when *Piss Christ* was shown at the National Gallery of Victoria in Australia during a Serrano retrospective, Catholic Archbishop of Melbourne, George Pell, had sought an injunction from the Supreme Court of Victoria. The injunction was not granted but soon afterwards a patron tried to remove the work from the gallery, and two adolescents attacked the image with a hammer. The director of the gallery cancelled the show, apparently out of concern for the Rembrandt exhibition also on site. In April 2011, a print of Piss Christ was vandalized at a museum in Avignon, France 'with the help of a hammer and an object like a screwdriver or pickaxe' by Christian protestors (Sage 2011). The museum temporarily closed after the incident, but re-opened days later displaying the damaged works 'so the public can appreciate for themselves the violence of the acts' (Sage 2011). This curatorial decision meant that the violence to the image was inscribed as part of the work, and then became part of the exhibition. Not unlike the circumstances in Melbourne, the bishop of Avignon had earlier demanded that the museum remove the work, which attracted the attention of 800 protestors, and death threats to guards working at the museum. Such instances of violence, vandalism and the demand for legal and other forms of regulation and/or censorship, demonstrate the global significance of artistic work produced during the culture wars and subsequent governmental responses to these acts or requests outside the USA.

The work of photographer, Robert Mapplethorpe, has been similarly dogged by controversy. In 1989, the Corcoran Gallery based in Washington, DC cancelled Mapplethorpe's exhibition, which had already toured in Philadelphia and Chicago without incident. The Corcoran's director cancelled the exhibition because a segment titled the *X Portfolio* contained a few homoerotic images, and images of nude children. In another incident in 1998, a senior undergraduate student studying Mapplethorpe's work at the University of Central England's Birmingham Institute of Art and Design had photographed a few images from a library copy of *Mapplethorpe* (published by Jonathan Cape in 1992), intending to use the images as part of the coursework for her degree. When she dropped the film off to be developed at the local chemist, the shocked proprietor had forwarded the negatives to the West Midlands Police paedophile and pornography unit. In October 1997, the police confiscated the book from the library and referred the case to the Crown Prosecution Service. Two photographs from the book were declared obscene and the police informed the university that the book would have to be destroyed, or the offending pages removed.

These controversies did not go unnoticed by the US Congress, which in 1989, cut the following year's budget to the NEA by $45,000 — the exact amount that had been used to fund the works of Serrano and Mapplethorpe (Zeigler 1994, Tofte 1998). Senator Helms proposed an amendment to the annual appropriation legislation for the NEA (known as the 'Helms Amendment') prohibiting that body from funding work deemed obscene:

> None of the funds authorized to be appropriated for the National Endowment for the Arts or the National Endowment for the Humanities may be used to promote, disseminate, or produce materials which in the judgment of the National Endowment for the Arts or the National Endowment for the Humanities may be considered obscene, including but not limited to, depictions of sadomasochism, homoeroticism, the sexual exploitation of children, or individuals engaged in sex acts and which, when taken as a whole, do not have serious literary, artistic, political, or scientific value.[8]

This legislation marked the first occasion on which Congress enacted content-based restrictions on future NEA grant recipients. Miller and Yúdice (2002, p. 52) argue that the language of the obscenity clause parodied civil-rights legislation and the rhetoric of subject positions around which contemporary social movements wage their struggles. The appropriation of civil-rights discourses by the Right made it more difficult for social movements from the Left to set their agenda through public discourse (Miller and Yúdice 2002). NEA chairperson, John Frohnmayer, inserted the 'loyalty oath' into grant applications, requiring applicants to sign a pledge promising not to create obscene work. Frohnmayer (1993) claimed to have inserted the oath into grant applications to force a lawsuit so that the stipulation could be deemed unconstitutional and struck down.

Some grant recipients pointedly responded, refusing to sign Frohnmayer's 'loyalty oath' and rejecting monies that were to adhere to this stipulation.[9] In 1990, the NEA had awarded a grant for $72,000 to the Bella Lewitzky Dance Foundation — a leading international modern dance company — founded by Lewitzky in 1966 (Zeigler 1994, Tofte 1998). However, the award letter contained a document outlining the new obscenity specifications, with which the Foundation disagreed. The Foundation submitted a request for a partial payment of $15,000, crossing out the 'loyalty oath' – or obscenity specification – before signing the request (Zeigler 1994, Tofte 1998). In response, the NEA released the $15,000, and made the Foundation aware that the terms and conditions were not optional (Zeigler 1994, Tofte 1998). The Bella Lewitzky Foundation segregated the money and challenged the obscenity stipulation, claiming that it violated the Foundation's First and Fifth Amendment rights. In *Bella Lewitzky Dance Foundation v. Frohnmayer* (1991), the US District Court for the Central District of California granted summary judgement for the Foundation, advising that the loyalty oath violated the First Amendment because it had a chilling effect on free expression, and contravened the Fifth Amendment because it was unconstitutionally vague.[10] The success of the Lewitsky Foundation at challenging the 'loyalty oath', or obscenity specification, is the context in which performance artists, Finley, Fleck, Hughes and Miller challenged the 'decency' clause.

Decency in *NEA v. Finley*

The discursive history of decency demonstrates that the exact meanings attached to the term shift and change with the introduction of new technologies; changes in government and subsequent amendments to policy, practice and legal regulation; the occurrence of key historical events and the potential for subsequent moral panics in which particular individuals or groups become 'folk devils', or particular practices are demonized. Within a Western context, decency is constituted through dominant and normative socio-political mores, which are culturally and temporally specific. The hegemonic citizen-subject is produced through white, Christian, heteronormative family values. Decency is largely understood through discourses of sex and violence, which individuals and special interest groups seek to regulate through policy, practice and the law. Notions of decency are further mediated through discourses of nationalism, and narratives of nationhood and citizenship.

Before the enactment of the 'decency clause', performance artists, Finley, Fleck, Hughes and Miller, known in the media as the 'NEA Four', had applied to the NEA for grants to fund future performances.[11] The Performance Artists Program Peer Review Panel, an advisory panel to the NEA, recommended approval of the grants applied for by the performance artists but the National Council on the Arts recommended disapproval of these projects, and the artists were ultimately denied funding (see Finley, 524 US at 577). In 1990, the four performance artists filed suit against the NEA in the US District Court for the Central District of California, arguing that their First Amendment rights had been violated by their applications being rejected on political grounds.[12] The suit contended that the NEA had denied their applications on criteria not stipulated by the legislation, and not following mandated procedures (Davies 2012). After the 'decency' clause was enacted, the National Association of Artists' Organizations joined as a plaintiff and the complaint was amended to challenge the clause for vagueness and a facial violation of the First Amendment (First Amended Complaint, 1 Record, Doc. No. 16, p. 1 [(27 March 1991]). In 1992, The District Court found in favour of the performance artists, and the Ninth Circuit Court of Appeals upheld this ruling (*Finley v. National Endowment for the Arts*, C.D.Cal. 1992; *Finley v. National Endowment for the Arts*, 9th Cir. 1996). The Clinton Administration appealed this decision to the Supreme Court (*NEA v. Finley*), ruling in favour of the NEA in 1998.

In *NEA v. Finley*, meanings around decency were constructed as unstable: lacking in definition, criterion and practical application. The amendment mandated by Congress imposed an obligation on the NEA chairperson to ensure that judgments about artistic merit and excellence take 'into consideration general standards of decency and respect for the diverse beliefs and values of the American public' [20 U.S.C. § 954(d)(1) (1990), the 'decency clause']. While the NEA had not formally interpreted the amendment in this way, reading the decency clause in the context of the 'Helms amendment' or 'loyalty oath' demonstrates that the construction of decency in this discursive moment means white, heteronormative, middle class and Christian.

During his line of questioning, Associate Justice Stephen Breyer confessed to not knowing what 'decency' means, but to having 'a sense of it', a sense he linked to 'great work[s] of art' (Justice Breyer, in *National Endowment for the Arts v. Finely*, oral argument 1998, p. 41). Abandoning critical analysis, he relied instead on his instinct, framed through a discourse of morality. Agreeing with the majority, Breyer stated:

> ...the problem in my mind, for you, is I can easily think of some—some instances of importance in the life of the NEA where it would be obviously appropriate or lawful to take into account even tough standards of decency, and the other problem for you is, I don't know what the word decency means. It—there's certainly a sense of decency, a sense of it, in which no work of art that is good could be indecent. It's very hard for me to think, if I think of that sense, that a great work of art is also an indecent work. I can't think of one.
>
> (Justice Breyer, in *National Endowment for the Arts v. Finley*, oral argument 1998, p. 41)

Breyer collapsed discourses of morality with discourses of cultural value, therefore aligning artistic excellence with artwork that reflects, or perhaps calls, for heightened socio-political moral codes. Breyer's position supersedes the requirement for 'general standards of decency' for 'tough standards of decency' without articulating what this might mean or exactly what criteria might be applied. He does not consider the ways in which decency has been understood or determined, socio-politically, historically, culturally or legally. Nor does he take this opportunity to recall works of art now considered 'good' that were censored in the historical period in which they were produced. He determines that the clause is hard to strike down in the context of a challenge on its face, when it is the meaning and application of decency that is unclear.[13]

During the oral arguments for *NEA v. Finley*, Justice Antonin Scalia questioned the process by which decency was to be ensured at the NEA. What, for instance, guaranteed the moral fitness of the assessors, as evidenced by membership of selection panels?

> **Associate Justice Scalia:** Do they [the NEA], indeed, ensure that they have decent panels? I mean, how do they go about ensuring that?
>
> (Laughter.)
>
> **General Waxman:** They ensure—Justice Scalia, they ensure that they have diverse panels, and—
>
> **Associate Justice Scalia:** But that's just half of it. I mean, it says decency, standards of decency and respect for diverse beliefs and values.
>
> I—it's—I guess it's easy to get diverse—maybe it's easy to get diverse, but how do they ensure decency?
>
> **General Waxman:** Well, the chairperson has the discretion to create [...] the selection procedures any way she or he wants, so long as he is satisfied or ensured that general standards of decency will be taken into account in the process. The NEA thus far has considered that, since—for most people—
>
> **Associate Justice Scalia:** What do you mean, in the process?
>
> **General Waxman:** In the process of—
>
> **Associate Justice Scalia:** In the process of selecting the panel?
>
> **General Waxman:** In the process—
>
> **Associate Justice Scalia**: How do you take into account standards of decency in selecting the panel?
>
> General Waxman: In—no.

Associate Justice Scalia: I don't understand how you do that.
(*NEA v. Finley* oral argument 1998, pp. 7–8)

Justice Scalia's line of questioning demonstrates that he is unclear about the NEA's methodology of ascertaining decency: indeed, the concept of what, and who, is decent regresses infinitely, resistant to definition. It is no wonder, then, that the amendment risks being vague and potentially chilling artistic expression. Noting that the statutory provision already required the chairperson to consider diversity as part of assembling review panels, Justice David Souter (the only judge to dissent from the majority's decision), refined the concept of diversity so that it might not carry the baggage of long decades of social change specifically oriented to securing 'inclusion'.[14] The NEA assured the court that they had 'always carried out the decency provision through the panel review process. Our legislation requires us to have diverse panels (geography, expertise, including a layperson) and by doing so we satisfy the decency provision' [NEA (personal communication, September 29, 2011)].

Diversity has often been aligned with a liberal stance and diversity policies have symbolic value in international markets and are frequently employed to promote consensus or cohesion (Blackmore 2006). Diversity incorporates notions of difference to address inequities – of gender, sexuality, ethnicity, cultural background, ability, religion and so on – however, in practice those individuals and organizations applying diversity policies tend to employ a hierarchy of difference in which sexual orientation is perceived as irrelevant, controversial, or as posing problems not raised by other categories of difference (Robinson and Díaz 2006). Because 'diversity' is more easily accounted for than 'decency', the NEA avoid defining decency by managing this requirement under the rubric of 'diversity' – that is, by the NEA having diverse review panels that represent general community standards. However, managing 'decency' through diverse panels does not account for the likelihood that issues of sexual difference will most likely be relegated to the bottom of hierarchies of difference. The NEA avoided defining decency or establishing a criterion for decency protocols to avoid further litigation.

Notable in *NEA v. Finley* is Associate Justice Breyer's use of a racially violent hypothetical analogy as a strategy for legal argument. If decency is most frequently constituted through discourses or sex and violence, then Breyer's equating of perpetrators of racial vilification and violence with queer citizens collapses discourses of sex with violence: implying that both groups are not only similar but similarly *indecent*. Through his choice of hypothetical in *NEA v. Finley*, Justice Breyer negated the circuits of recognition through which queer citizens might be understood by suggesting that representations of alternative narratives about gender and sexuality were in effect doing the same kind of violence to an audience as that of a work expressing ideologies of racial supremacy:

> Now, is it the case... and I'm only asking these questions to get your response, say, if in fact the NEA wants to give a grant for somebody to produce something that's public work, and suppose what they do is a white supremacist group, and they want to have racial epithets all over the picture, and the NEA says we think that's an inappropriate use of this money, in your opinion is that—and we can imagine the most—imagine the most horrible ones you can possibly think of, all right, and they say, the person gets up there and he says, I'm a member of the Klu Klux Klan, or whatever, and this is my point of view, and is it your view that the Constitution requires the NEA to fund that, that particular applicant?
>
> (*NEA v. Finley* oral argument 1998, p. 46)

With the use of this hypothetical, the Supreme Court erases discussion of homosexuality – this unspeakability reinscribes the act of erasure in representation the government seeks to secure in art it chooses to subsidize. Breyer's example gestures to histories of both Nazism and slavery, but its vagueness erases the particularity of each history of racism and violence. Employing the trope of race – that marker of difference so animating in the USA – negates representations of gender and sexuality. The Supreme Court uses a deliberately controversial and ultimately false analogy, de-historicizing images of racial violence in the name of protecting American citizens. The use of a politically loaded and strategically employed analogy positions queer and non-normative artists as indecent American citizens.

Analogies and hypothetical examples selected by legal practitioners negate the circuits of recognition through which incidents, circumstances and subjects are understood, or recognized (Davies 2008, McInnes 2008, Davies and McInnes 2012). Deconstructing these circuits of recognition – that is, the discursive constructions that provide ideological frameworks through which we might understand ourselves and others – is critical given that subject positions are made possible in and through discourse (Foucault 1976/1998). Legal reasoning proceeds by analogy. The identification of resemblances between factual situations, and the identification of difference is made apparent, so that exclusions can be justified (Anleu 2000, Young 2005). Alison Young (2005, p. 11) points out that '"this" can be can be said to resemble "that", while "X" can be disavowed as "not Y"'. While this mode of reasoning appears perfectly logical and formulaic, so too is it ideologically loaded, frequently reinforcing normative values, practices and beliefs. In this case, such a violent analogy attempts to erase the differences between sexual subjects and perpetrators of racial violence, thus implying that both categories are indecent. Sharyn L. Roach Anleu (2000) suggests that reasoning by analogy involves elasticity, arguing that judges can interpret precedents expansively or narrowly in order to achieve a particular outcome.

In her analysis of late-nineteenth century discourses of race and sexuality, Siobhan B. Somerville (2000) shows that such analogies have a specific history and became mobilized at the turn of the century when formations of heterosexuality and homosexuality emerged in the USA through, and not merely parallel to, 'a discourse saturated with assumptions about the racialization of bodies' (p. 4). Somerville (2000) points out that it is all too often assumed 'that being a person of color is "like" being gay and that sexual orientation is "like" racial identity', however, 'these analogies have a history and perform specific kinds of cultural work, often with contradictory political effects' (p. 7). While the circumstances of the culture wars differ to those of the late nineteenth century, it is apparent that the challenge Somerville identifies (viz., to recognize the instability of multiple categories of difference simultaneously, rather than assume the fixity of one to establish the complexity of the other) still plays out in both socio-legal and cultural texts today.

The long-term effects of the decency clause

Understanding the long-term effects of the 'decency' clause is complicated by the NEA's 1995 restructuring of grant-giving procedures from discipline-based categories into broad-based thematic categories as a result of political and financial pressure. This process started in 1995 under Clinton's second term, continued through both of Bush's two terms, and continues today under Obama's first term.[15] In addition to this restructure being a strategic move to ensure the ongoing viability of the NEA, the move towards government regulation to abate further controversy may be understood through discourses and practices of neoliberalism through which subsidies are redirected towards broad-based provision of key growth areas and infrastructure investment (Davies 2012). Critically, as part of this restructure, grants for individual artists in the performing and visual arts were abolished – a clear response to controversy around the works of visual artists Serrano and Mapplethorpe, and performing artists, Finley, Fleck, Hughes and Miller. The restructure and further changes to the NEA reflect a discursive shift from supporting innovative original work, to supporting art and art education and access, and also mark a shift from a focus on the artist to the arts consumer.

By abolishing individual grants in the visual and performing arts, artists in these disciplines not attached to an institution are unable to access NEA funds, clearly leaving them in a disadvantaged position, especially given that an NEA grant both legitimates an artist's work and attracts funding from other sources. Former NEA chairperson, Dana Gioia (2007), suggests that the NEA 'has a proven ability to initiate and sustain powerful trends' in American cultural life, acknowledging that its grants have a 'powerful multiplying effect for recipients wherein every dollar of a grant they offer typically generates seven to eight times more money by way of grant matching, further donations and earned revenue' (p. vii). Visual and performing artists are required to become self-managing, entrepreneurial neoliberal citizen-subjects who may have to compromise the content and mode of expression of their work to suit the demands of the marketplace and to attract private funds. With the turn to neoliberal policy and increasing regulation, the role of the artist is increasingly precarious and dependent on a capacity for entrepreneurialism. Reflecting on the long-term effects of the decency clause, Svetlana Mintcheva (2010), Director of Arts Advocacy at the National Coalition Against Censorship (NCAC) commented, 'It's perfectly clear that for those who introduced it, the [decency] amendment was supposed to make sure that sexually outspoken and religiously controversial work would not receive the legitimacy that public funding could grant'.

NEA v. Finley is a significant sociocultural and legal text in part because it reveals tensions at play at the intersection of sex and politics during the culture wars, and demonstrates the ways in which legal discourse and cultural policy shape sexual citizenship and American public culture (Davies 2008, 2012). This case is particularly significant given that the Communications Decency Act (1996) was struck down in *Reno v. American Civil Liberties Union* (1997) for violating the First Amendment. While the CDA offered a set of parameters by which decency might be understood, the NEA never formally defined or interpreted decency, allowing them to dodge accusations of viewpoint discrimination. As a result of the NEA's decency clause lacking definition or formal interpretation, its potential was limitless in how, and to whom, it might be applied. Carin Kuoni (2010), Director of The Vera List Center for Art and Politics at The New School in New York, notes ruefully how the decency clause has 'changed how our institutions work, how they function, how they are run, and how they're funded', and that 'it has deeply affected our understanding about notions of decency'.

The continuing privatization of American culture, and the subsequent demise of public funding, raises questions about censorship and the First Amendment – freedom of speech – that do not apply in the private sphere. Companies and organizations located in the private sphere can limit and regulate the use of private funds to artists to reflect their own strategic and financial goals. Gioia (2007, p. v) points out that only 'about 13 percent of arts support in the U.S. [comes] from the government, and only about 9 percent from the federal government, of which less than 1 percent [comes] from the National Endowment for the Arts'. Arts organizations applying for public funding have learned to regulate their speech and the themes and concerns of their work not only to reflect artistic merit and excellence but also to accord with community standards of 'decency' in order to gain NEA funding. An arts organization is more likely to be funded through the NEA's sister organization The National Endowment for the Humanities to, say, preserve documentary footage of controversial art performed during the culture wars, than they are likely to receive grants to subsidize the production of work that might challenge the status quo.[16] This demonstrates the discursive shift in public funding towards preservation of art (including performance art) using digital technologies rather than funding the creation of that work.

A key finding of the panels sponsored by the Vera List Centre and the NCAC was that the NEA is rarely considered to be a funding option for young artists or arts organizations today (Mintcheva 2010). The post-broadcast era means that young and emerging artists and organizations are more likely to employ new media forms such as social media, YouTube, blogging, and the use of virtual worlds to reach a large audience and attempt to avoid censorship. There is a whole new generation committed to accomplishing social change through art that is not dependent on big funding streams, however, the effectiveness and sustainability of arts projects by emerging artists/art organizations under these circumstances given the absence of the legitimacy conferred by government funding is another more complicated question (Mintcheva 2010).

In cultural policy today, 'decency' is still understood through discourses of sex, violence and the demands of the production of normative subjectivity. The events of 9/11 have further impacted configurations of sexuality, race, gender, nation, class and ethnicity, which are realigning in relation to contemporary forces of securitization, counterterrorism and nationalism (Puar 2007). Just as cultural policy, regulation and amendments in the arts continue to shape what creative work can be produced with the support of public funds, so to do artists continue to question hegemonic discourses underpinning decency within a much more public international forum.

Notes

1 *National Endowment for the Arts v. Finley* 524 US 569, 118 S.Ct. 2168 (1998).
2 The decency clause stated: '... artistic excellence and artistic merit are the criteria by which applications are judged, taking into consideration general standards of decency and respect for the diverse beliefs and values of the American public...' 20 U.S.C. § 954(d)(1), the 'decency clause'.
3 The Federal Act of 30 August 1842, ch. 270, 5 Stat. 548, 566. This prohibition was extended in 1857 to include photographs, images, and all other obscene articles in Act of 2 March 1857, ch. 62, 11 Stat 168.
4 Roth's case was combined with *Alberts v. California*, in which a California obscenity law was challenged by Alberts after his similar conviction for selling lewd and obscene books.
5 In the context of the First Amendment, speech also includes verbal, non-verbal, visual and symbolic expression.
6 Federal Communications Commission, Indecent Broadcast Restrictions http://www.fcc.gov/guides/obscenity-indecency-and-profanity, accessed 3 January 2011.

7   In *FCC v. Fox Television Stations* (2012) No. 10–1293 challenged the FCC assessment of regulating speech as unconstitutionally vague. In an 8-0 decision, the Supreme Court ruled that because the regulations at the time did not cover 'fleeting expletives' the fines were invalidated as 'unconstitutionally vague'. The regulations have since been amended to include 'fleeting expletives'.

8   See 135 Cong. Rec. 16, 276 (1989). The amendment was Number 420 to the Department of the Interior and Related Agencies Appropriations, Fiscal Year 1990 Act. H.R. 2788, 101st Cong., first Sess. (1989).

9   Fifteen arts organizations refused grant monies including Joseph Papp's New York Shakespeare festival. Leonard Bernstein and Stephen Sondheim refused National Medal of the Arts commendations awarded by the NEA in protest of the restrictions placed on grant monies.

10 The Lewistky decision also disposed a case with almost identical issues at law – a suit filed by the Newport Harbor Art Museum. See a discussion of the case in the 'NEA's Obscenity Pledge Voided: Law: Arts groups hail ruling in suits by a dance company and a Newport Beach museum seeking federal funds', *Los Angeles Times*: http://articles.latimes.com/1991-01-10/local/me-11211_1_art-museum, accessed 30 March 2012.

11 In November 1990, Congress passed the Williams/Coleman Amendment in Public Law 101-512 sec 103 (b) amending the legislation for the NEA 20 U.S.C. 954 (d).

12 The plaintiffs also claimed that by releasing information from their applications for funding, the NEA had violated the Privacy Act of 1974.

13 My critique of Breyer's logic here is interested in unpacking how discourses of decency are formed and inscribed culturally and legally, rather than to make any accusations of homophobia. Breyer was part of the majority that struck down the sodomy law in Texas, and subsequently 13 others states, making same-sex sexual activity legal across the US in the 2003 *Lawrence v. Texas* decision.

14 *NEA v. Finley*. 524 US 569, 118 S.Ct. 2168 at 2188–2189 (Justice Souter, dissenting).

15 The NEAs first goal is survival, especially given the current fiscal climate, and the continued push for cutting the NEA budget and under-valuing the role of the arts, especially as outlined in conservative rhetoric. See *The Huffington Post* (2012).

16 For example, Franklin Furnace received support from the National Endowment for the Humanities and signed a collaboration agreement with ARTstor 'to digitize and publish on the web documentation of events it presented and produced, with the goal of embedding the value of ephemeral art practice in art and cultural history'. Franklin Furnace, Organizational Overview, accessed 3 January 2011 http://franklinfurnace.org/about/institutional_history/organizational_overview.php

References

Anleu, S. L. R. (2000) *Law and Social Change*, London, Sage Publications Ltd.

Bauerlein, M. & Grantham, E. (eds) (2008) *National Endowment for the Arts: A History 1965–2008*, Washington, DC, National Endowment for the Arts.

Berlant, L. (1997) *The Queen of America Goes to Washington City: Essays on Sex and Citizenship*, Durham, Duke University Press.

Blackmore, J. (2006) 'Deconstructing diversity discourses in the field of educational management and leadership', *Educational Management, Administration and Leadership*, vol. 34, no. 2, pp. 181–199.

Bolton, R. (ed.) (1992) *Culture Wars: Documents from the Recent Controversies in the Arts*, New York, New Press.

Boyce, B. (2008) 'Obscenity and community standards', *Yale Journal of International Law*, vol. 33, pp. 299–368.

Burchell, G. (1996) 'Liberal government and techniques of the self', in *Foucault and Political Reason: Liberalism, Neoliberalism, and Rationalities of Government*, eds A. Barry, T. Osbourne & N. Rose, Chicago, The University of Chicago Press, pp. 19–36.

Chiu, D. W. (1995–1996) 'Obscenity on the Internet: Local community standards for obscenity are unworkable on the information', *Santa Clara Law Review*, vol. 36, pp. 185–218.

Davies, C. (2008) 'Proliferating panic: Regulating representations of sex and gender during the culture wars', *Cultural Studies Review*, vol. 14, no. 2, pp. 83–102.

Davies, C. (2012) 'It's not at all chic to be denied your civil rights': Performing sexual and gendered citizenship in Holly Hughes', *Preaching to the Perverted, Sexualities*, vol. 15, no. 3, pp. 277–296.

Davies, C. & McInnes, D. (2012) 'Speaking violence: Homophobia and the production of injurious speech in schooling cultures', in *Rethinking School Violence: Theory, Gender, Context*, eds S. Saltmarsh, K. Robinson & C. Davies, Palgrave, Macmillan, pp. 131–148.

Federal Communications Commission (FCC) (2011) 'Obscene, indecent and profane broadcasts' [online] Available at: http://www.fcc.gov/cgb/consumerfacts/obscene.html (accessed 24 January 2011).

Foerstel, H. N. (1997) *Free Expression and Censorship in America: An Encyclopedia*, Westport, CT, Greenwood Press.

Foucault, M. (1976/1998) *The History of Sexuality Vol. 1: The Will to Knowledge*, London, Penguin.

Foucault, M. (1979) 'On governmentality', *Ideology & Consciousness*, vol. 6, pp. 5–22.

Foucault, M. (1980) *Truth and Subjectivity*, Berkeley, Mimeo, The Howison Lecture.

Foucault, M. (2008) *The Birth of Biopolitics: Lectures at the College de France 1978–1979*, Basingstoke, Palgrave Macmillan.

Frankel, A. (2010) 'FCC Seeks En Banc Rehearing of 2nd Circuit Ruling on Indecency Policy', [online] Available at: http://www.law.com/jsp/law/LawArticleFriendly.jsp?id=1202471213771&slreturn=20120730202256 (accessed 3 April 2011).

Friedman, L. (1970) *Obscenity: The Complete Oral Arguments Before the Supreme Court in the Major Obscenity Cases*, New York, Chelsea House Publishers.

Frohnmayer, J. (1993) *Leaving Town Alive: Confessions of an Arts Warrior*, Boston, Houghton Mifflin.

Gioia, D. (2007) 'Preface by Dana Gioia', in *National Endowment for the Arts: How the United States Funds the Arts*, National Endowment for the Arts Office of Research & Analysis, Washington, DC, pp. v–viii.

Halberstam, J. (2005) *In a Queer Time and Place: Transgender Bodies, Subcultural Lives*, New York, New York University Press.

Heins, M. (1993) *Sex, Sin, and Blasphemy: A Guide to America's Censorship Wars*, New York, New Press.

Kerstein, M. (2007) *Art and Obscenity*, New York, I.B. Taurus.

Kobylka, J. F. (1991) *The Politics of Obscenity: Group Litigation in a Time of Legal Change*, New York, Greenwood Press.

Koch C. (1998) 'The contest for American culture: A leadership case study on the NEA and NEH funding crisis', *Public Talk: Online Journal of Discourse Leadership*, [online] Available at: http://www.upenn.edu/pnc/ptkoch.html (accessed 24 January 2011).

Knox, S. (2000) 'A world made of glass: Crime, culture and community in an age of hyper-media', *Theory and Event*, vol. 4, no. 4, [online] Available at: http://muse.jhu.edu/login?auth=0&type=summary&url=/journals/theory_and_event/v004/4.4knox.html (accessed 3 April 2011).

Kuoni, C. (2010) 'How Obscene is This', Panel 2, The New School, [online] Available at: http://www.youtube.com/watch?v=tbaOl7JafZA&feature=relmfuaccessed (accessed 15 December 2010).

Lane, F. (2006) *The Decency Wars: The Campaign to Cleanse American Culture*, New York, Prometheus Books.

Lipschultz, J. H. (2008) *Broadcast and Internet Indecency: Defining Free Speech*, New York, Routledge.

Miller, T. & Yúdice, G. (2002) *Cultural Policy*, London, Sage.

Mintcheva, S. (2010) 'How Obscene is This' Panel 2, The New School, [online] Available at: http://www.youtube.com/watch?v=tbaOl7JafZA&feature=relmfuaccessed (accessed 15 December 2010).

McInnes, D. (2008) 'Sissy boy melancholy and the educational possibilities of incoherence', in *Judith Butler in Conversation: Analyzing the Texts and Talk of Everyday Life*, ed. B. Davies, New York, Routledge, pp. 95–116.

Petrie, S. J. (1997) 'Indecent proposals: How each branch of the federal government overstepped its institutional authority in the development of Internet', *Stanford Law Review*, vol. 49, no. 3, pp. 637–665.

Puar, J. (2007) *Terrorist Assemblages: Homonationalism in Queer Times*, Durham, Duke University Press.
Robinson, K. H. & Díaz, J. (2006) *Diversity and Difference in Early Childhood Education: Issues for Theory and Practice*, Maidenhead, Berkshire, Open University Press.
Sage, A. (2011) 'Vandalism and threats greet "Piss Christ" in France', *Reuters*, [online] Available at: http://www.reuters.com/article/2011/04/18/us-france-art-idUSTRE73H4JR20110418 (accessed 25 April 2011).
Sarat, A. & Kearns, T. R. (1998) *Law in the Domains of Culture*, Ann Arbor, University of Michigan Press.
Saunders, K. W. (1996) *Violence as Obscenity: Limiting the Media's First Amendment Protection*, Durham, Duke University Press.
Schauer, F. F. (1976) *The Law of Obscenity*, Washington, Bureau of National Affairs.
Somerville, S. (2000) *Queering the Color Line: Race and the Invention of Homosexuality in American Culture*, Durham, Duke University Press.
The Huffington Post (2012) 'Romney Would Cut Funding for Arts by Half', *The Huffington Post*, 14 August, [online] Available at: http://www.huffington-post.com/2011/11/11/what-romney-would-do-with_n_1088851.html (accessed 14 August 2012).
Tofte, B. L. (1998) 'Baby, It's cold outside: The chilling effect of the decency clause on the arts in the aftermath of National Endowment for the Arts v. Finley', *Hamline Law Review*, vol. 22, no. 1, pp. 303–352.
Young, A. (2005) *Judging the Image: Art, Value, Law*, London, Routledge.
Zeigler, J. W. (1994) *Arts in Crisis: The National Endowment for the Arts Versus America*, Chicago, A Cappella Books.

Cases cited

Bella Lewitsky Dance Foundation v. Frohnmayer, (C.D. Cal. 1991), 754 F. Supp. 774.
Commonwealth v. Holmes, 17 335, Massachusetts (1821).
Commonwealth v. Sharpless, 2 Serg & R. 91 (Sup. Ct. Penn. 1815).
FCC v. Fox Television Stations, 556 US (2009).
FCC v. Fox Television Stations, No. 10-1293 (2012).
Federal Communications Commission v. Pacifica Foundation, 438 US 726 (1978).
Finley v. National Endowment for the Arts 795 F.Supp. 1457 (C.D.Cal. 1992)
Finley v. National Endowment for the Arts 100 F.3d 671 (9th Cir. 1996).
Fox Television Stations, Inc. v. FCC, 613 F.3d 317 (2010).
Justice Breyer, in *National Endowment for the Arts v. Finley*, oral argument, 1998 p.41.
Miller v. California, 413 US 15 (1973).
National Endowment for the Arts v. Finley 524 US 569 (1998).
Regina v. Hicklin (1868), LR 3 QB 360, in English Common Law.
Reno v. American Civil Liberties Union, 521 US 844 (1997).
Roth v. United States, 354 US 476 (1957).

Acts cited

Administrative Procedures Act, Pub.L. 79-404, 60 Stat. 237, enacted June 11, 1946.
Communications Decency Act of 1996. Pub L. 104-104. 1 Feb. 1996. Title V.
Department of the Interior and Related Agencies Appropriations Act, Pub. L. No. 101–121, 304(a), 103 Stat. 701, 741 (1989) codified as amended at 20 USC 954 1994.
The Comstock Act, 17 Stat. 598, enacted March 3, 1873.
The Communications Act, Pub.L. 416, 48 Stat. 1064, ch. 652, enacted 19 June, 1934.

Amended complaint cited

First Amended Complaint (of 20 U.S.C. § 954(d)(1) (1990)), 1 Record, Doc. No. 16, p. 1 (March 27, 1991).

Rana Jaleel

WEAPONS OF SEX, WEAPONS OF WAR

Feminisms, ethnic conflict and the rise of rape and sexual violence in public international law during the 1990s

> *Recent international attention has focused on designations of rape and sexual violence in conflict zones. The most formative debates on this issue centre on the 1990s-era conflicts in the former Yugoslavia and Rwanda, which also involved heated debates amongst feminists over designations of rape as genocide. While the International Criminal Tribunal for Rwanda case, the Prosecutor v. Akayesu, resulted in the first formal charge of wartime rape as genocide within international criminal law, the first case to charge wartime rape as genocidal occurred in US federal court. This project looks for the overarching social and political meaning of the contemporary international legal focus on rape and sexual violence. It examines why, how, and to what extent US and transnational feminist legal academics and activists transmitted and secured their understandings of the relationships between sex, violence and ethno-religious difference within the international legal arena. In doing so, I argue that their participation in the contemporary recognition and narration of sexual injury in a global context both retreads and reconfigures the heated 1980s-era US Sex Wars debates on the workings of gender, sex, race and power.*

Introduction

Over the past decade, wartime sexual violence horror stories have become headline mainstays – particularly in reference to what UNICEF has described as Africa's ongoing 'rape epidemic' (Rape Epidemic in African Conflict Zones 2008). From Rwanda to the Congo, reports of armed militias sexually assaulting women and children as an organized strategy of war have spawned international attention and condemnation. Yet the trouble, the UN suggests, does not only concern armed combatants' use of rape as a weapon. The latest threats involve the 'spread' of rape and sexual violence within civilian populations that have survived – or are currently surviving – armed conflict. In such accounts, rape and sexual violence are intimate outgrowths of rampant social and political instability, thereby presaging – if not already indicating – wholesale social collapse. As UNICEF deputy executive director Hilde Johnson explains, '[w]hen societies collapse there seems to be a license to rape in some of these countries. That's why we call it epidemic proportions—it takes a life of its own' (Rape Epidemic in African Conflict Zones 2008).

The framing of sexual violence as premeditated weapon and social contagion has further mainstreamed a recently popular lexicon of rape, including 'mass rape', 'war-rape' and 'genocidal rape'. Far from trendy or inconsequential shifts in nomenclature, these designations signal slight, yet significant, shifts in the conceptualization of rape and sexual violence. No longer ignored, downplayed or solely portrayed as the essentially private violations of individual victims, rape and sexual violence in and around conflict zones are increasingly characterized as public, collective injuries, mandating nothing short of concerted, global response.

Feminists, NGOs and governments alike have heeded the call, increasingly availing criminal legal responses as the preferred mode of redress. In August 2009, US Secretary of State Hillary Clinton encouraged more frequent international and domestic prosecutions of sexual violence during conflict and announced a US-sponsored $17 million plan that included intensive US-led training for the Congolese army (Gettleman 2009). In 2010, the UN's Population Fund (UNFPA) issued 'The State of World Population' report. In it, UNFPA Executive Director Thoraya Ahmed Obaid, in assessing the generational impact of sexual violence during conflict from Bosnia-Herzegovina to Haiti, calls 'gender-based violence, including rape [. . .] a repugnant and increasingly familiar weapon of war'.

In the early 1990s, however, when the first reports of mass rape in a disintegrating Yugoslavia began to register on the international radar, the International Criminal Court (ICC) did not yet exist, and the status of rape and sexual violence within humanitarian law – the laws of war that include the Geneva Conventions and various other treaties, laws and customary international law – was murky at best. International human rights law was hardly a more welcoming forum. Yet, within a handful of years, rape and sexual violence would be ensconced within the pantheon of human rights and enumerated as war crimes and crimes against humanity within the founding statutes of the ad hoc tribunals for the former Yugoslavia and Rwanda as well as the Rome Statute, which established the ICC. Rape and sexual violence would also be theorized and prosecuted as genocide within these and other legal forums.

Contemporary accounts of, and interest in, wartime rape and sexual violence arise from formative and heated debates involving the 1990s-era armed struggles in the former Yugoslavia and Rwanda, struggles that ignited popular and legal furor over designations of wartime rape and the dearth of institutional mechanisms of redress. But how and why did these conflicts propel rape and sexual violence to this position of relative international legal and cultural prominence? How did the uproar surrounding wartime rape and sexual violence throughout the 1990s contribute to the ascent of feminism that invests in the 'carceral paradigms of social, and in particular gender, justice'? (Bernstein 2010).

As the first major international conflict in a post-cold war era, violence in the Balkans set the prototype for the 'new wars' — conflicts ostensibly galvanized by the ancient feuds of ethnic enclaves (Kaldor 1999). In this context, the apprehension of rape as a weapon of war not only transformed war (understood as ethnic or genocidal conflict) to include rape and sexual violence (understood as violence against women), but also overhauled the scope and sociocultural meaning of rape and sexual violence through an encounter with ethno-religious violence. Accordingly, I examine the feminist genealogies of genocidal rape that helped facilitate the entry of rape and sexual violence into international human rights and humanitarian criminal law — genealogies that reveal disputes between elite legal feminists who formed caucuses and ran NGOs that were party to UN deliberations to determine the scope and content of the tribunal and ICC statutes (Halley 2009) as well as fractures between feminists in the formerly federated Yugoslavia, where ethno-nationalist feminists of different persuasions battled each other and antiwar feminists over the meaning of the newly urgent term (Batinic 2001).

A standard read of international statutory and case law uncovers little trace of these intra-feminist reckonings or the transnational feminist exchanges that produced them. The fraught genealogies of genocidal rape, however, surface in 1990s law journal publications written to promote the inclusion of wartime rape and sexual violence within the statutorily defined jurisdiction of the ad hoc tribunals for the former Yugoslavia and Rwanda (Halley 2009). I argue that the divisive, transnationally mobile feminist theorizations and dialogues represented therein enabled the conflict in the former Yugoslavia to transform human rights discourse by retreading and reconfiguring the heated 1980s and 1990s-era US Sex War debates on the workings of gender, sex, state power, race and violence.[1] Such maneuverings enabled and were sustained by the rise of identity-based conflict as the paradigmatic new face of warfare at the twentieth century's end, decades of global feminist mobilizing to combat 'violence against women', and by representations of war rape by international media and Croatian and Bosnian media and feminists that circulated locally and globally to figure a sexually violent Serbian masculinity and a vulnerable Muslim femininity — a move that in turn pandered to ethno-nationalist elements and encouraged the outlook of ethnically segregated states as the most logical solution to the fighting.

From this vantage, I examine the first two cases to charge wartime rape as a constitutive act of genocide – the 1995 US Second Circuit decision *Kadic v. Karadžić* and the 1998 International Criminal Tribunal for Rwanda (ICTR) case, the *Prosecutor v. Akayesu*. These cases contain the legacies of US feminist fights over the meaning of race, sex, and violence – which enter international law already marked by critiques of universal feminism that emerged through anti-imperialist and women of colour feminism – and demonstrate the consequences of allowing the immediacy of armed conflict to obscure how carceral feminist paradigms understand and distribute gender justice.

The imprint of these encounters between universal feminism and women of colour and anti-imperialist feminisms manifest in the work of elite feminist attorney Catharine MacKinnon – a vocal participant of the Sex Wars and a lead attorney in *Kadic*. MacKinnon, a long-time professor of law, served from 2008 until August 2012 as the first Special Gender Advisor to the Prosecutor of the International Criminal Court, charged with providing strategic advice to the Prosecutor on issues involving sexual and gender violence. MacKinnon's scholarly writings contextualize her role as a prosecutor in *Kadic*, crystallizing the process by which a certain strand of US feminists and fellow travelers carried Sex Wars-era internecine feminist disputes over the relationships between sex, violence and racial/ethnic difference to the realm of international human rights and later, international humanitarian criminal law, gaining purchase through the framing of events in the former Yugoslavia and Rwanda as ethnic conflict.

Yet the following account of the feminist effort to entrench wartime rape and sexual violence within the purview of the international legal system is not a narrative of a 'public campaign at the top' disseminating its 'enlightened' views of gender to a geopolitically disenfranchised people that passively receives them (Amar 2011, p. 304). Rather, this article offers a critical excavation of legal and expert knowledge as contested processes, negotiated by a fractured international legal elite with varying signal commitments and interests, and marked, however imperfectly, by encounters with the multivariate class and national politics of the fracturing Yugoslavia as illustrated by the diverging representations of sexual violence in the conflict by Serbian and Croatian feminists and media outlets.

International human rights and violence against women

Prior to the conflicts in the former Yugoslavia and Rwanda, rapes during conflict were not considered strategic or systemic acts of gendered sexual violence, but portrayed as isolated, individual violations of 'family honour and rights' (1907 Hague Convention), or absorbed under other grave offences

(1949 Geneva Convention) or viewed as 'outrage[s] against personal dignity' (1977 Second Geneva Protocol) (Copelon 2003). Over the 1990s, however, the status of rape and sexual violence within international law underwent profound transformation. At the dawn of the 1990s, no independent, permanent international criminal court existed, yet international consensus demanded that war crimes within the former Yugoslavia and Rwanda — including charges of genocide — be addressed.

On 25 May 1993, the UN Security Council adopted the Statute of the International Tribunal for the Prosecution of Persons Responsible for Serious Violations of International Humanitarian Law Committed in the Territory of the Former Yugoslavia since 1991.[2] In doing so, the UN premiered its first war crimes court and established the first international war crimes tribunal since those at Nuremberg and Tokyo. The formation of a second UN ad hoc tribunal, the ICTR,[3] followed quickly on the heels of first. The tribunals were legal breakthroughs. Their statutes staked the terrain of contemporary international humanitarian criminal law via a reordering and consolidation of several strands of international public law (Halley 2009). Under their charters, rape and sexual violence first attained the status of crimes against humanity and war crimes within international law.

Yet the emergence of rape and sexual violence as cause for redoubled international humanitarian criminal legal concern, much less their definitional scope and application, was no inevitable unfolding of law. As the UN Security Council contemplated, then drafted, the founding charters of the ICTY and the ICTR, feminists from around the world made a global push to secure rape and sexual violence as war crimes subject to the jurisdiction of the tribunals (Copelon 2003, Engle 2005, MacKinnon 2006b, Halley 2009). From pro-nationalist women in the throes of war (including Bosnian and Croatian women's groups *Kareta*, *Tresnjevka*, *Biser*, *Bedem Ljubavi*) to internationalist legal feminist elites (including Rhonda Copelon, Catharine MacKinnon, Valerie Oosterveld and Patricia Viseur Sellers) to feminists in a variety of locations who were suspicious of nationalist predilections (including numerous on-site anti-war feminists such as Djurdja Knezevic, the Zagreb Women's Lobby, Bosnia's *Medica Zenica*, Belgrade's *Žene u crnom* or 'Women in Black' and the US-based NGO MADRE), feminists of many orientations and beliefs railed against sexual violence during the war (Batinic 2001). These efforts were bolstered by transnational activist and professional international feminist networks that had blossomed since the 1970s and the ever expanding responsibilities of NGOs and the proliferation of UN-hosted conferences in the 1990s.[4]

These networks fostered the proliferation of graphic accounts of violence within feminist media that eventually penetrated mainstream conglomerates. Feminist US-based magazines, including *off our backs*, *Spare Rib* and *Ms.*, as well as public letters and publications released by feminist groups immersed in the conflict, offered explicitly feminist, if not necessarily anti-war, conceptual frameworks for addressing war rape and sexual violence (Enloe 1994, Batinic 2001). International reports, with their emphasis on the rapes of Muslim women at the hands of Serbs, also circulated within Croatia throughout the conflict, bringing US feminist and social criticism to bear on the Croatian view of rape in conflict; the Croatian paper, *Vjesnik*, evinces this exchange in an article explicitly crediting feminism for analysing rape as the male domination of women and quoting Black Panther Eldridge Cleaver as portraying rape as a 'dialogue between races' and the "rebellion' of a black man against the white master via the 'desecration of his women'" (Zarkov 2007, p. 137).

At a time when women's rights were far from assured within international human rights agendas, a number of US-based feminist attorneys – including Rhonda Copelon, Celina Romany, Catharine MacKinnon and Jennifer Green – consciously framed rape and sexual violence in conflict zones within ongoing campaigns to help enshrine 'violence against women' (a concept with its own feminist history) within an international human rights framework (Copelon 2003). The phrase 'violence against women' hints at the elasticity of what constitutes abuse – if not necessarily what constitutes 'women' – and suggests evolving feminist strategies on how to best name those violations. Securing the mass rape of women in conflict zones within ongoing attempts to frame women's rights as human rights allowed rape to index other gendered sexual violations occurring both in and out of conflict. While sexual violence in conflict zones might seem like 'unwieldy bureaucratese for "wartime rape"', sexual violence as a legal term references a broad array of crimes, including forced prostitution, forced pregnancy, forced abortion, female infanticide, sexual mutilation and sexual humiliation (Heineman 2008, p. 5).

Perhaps unsurprisingly, the potential breadth of 'violence against women', and the insistence that such violence exceeds declarations of war, led many states to resist feminist attempts to classify violence against women within the scope of international human rights proper (Romany 1993). Relegating rape, marriage practices, abortion and other feminist issues to the realm of the family and sexuality allows states to publicly promote 'women's rights' while nonetheless refusing to intervene or permit external intervention in the personal matters of the private sphere (MacKinnon 2006a). As the rapes in the former Yugoslavia came to be represented as part of Serbian state-coordinated ethnic cleansing of Bosnian Muslims and Croats, the public/private divide became increasingly untenable to those seeking to exclude violence against women from the reach of international human rights law.

With accounts of former friends and neighbours inflicting rapes, sexual humiliation and forced detention on women as part of an organized military operation within the disintegrating Yugoslavia, feminists found paradigmatic examples of a range of sexual and intimate violence against women that exploded the public/private divide. That such violence was popularly considered part of an ethnic conflict in which Muslim women suffered in the crosshairs of both their ethno-religious affiliation and their gender placed violence against women squarely within a human rights frame. The response of international criminal law to rape and sexual violence was thus prompted by a critical discursive move by legal feminists: the gendering of sexual violence within a matrix of ethno-religious difference – for which the conflicts in the former Yugoslavia and Rwanda worked as ideological templates. Longstanding feminist work within international human rights and the international clamour for justice in the midst of violence in the Balkans placed the victims and survivors of war rape squarely at the intersection of humanitarian and human rights law during a transformative moment for both international law and the very concept of warfare. This historic conjunction fostered the uptake of feminist ideals into international institutions, and the resulting revolution in human rights discourse that secured 'women's rights' as human rights fed the call for international criminal prosecution of violations of the laws of war by elevating mass rape and sexual violence to crimes against the very nature of 'the human'. But how did violence against women become a feminist rallying cry?

The US Sex Wars

In the 1960s, US radical feminism emerged as a political movement geared towards upending the class-sex system by rendering gender irrelevant (Echols 1990). For MacKinnon, the class-sex system hinges on sex: 'men may dominate and women must submit and this relation is sexual—in fact, is sex' (MacKinnon 1987, p. 3). MacKinnon's dominance theory offers a version of feminism that is symptomatic of long-standing debates within the movement over the role of sexuality – and its relationship to race, gender, class and violence – in liberation. It is an example of how some strands of the radical feminist analysis of gender could largely constrain liberatory politics to particular practices – namely the need for all women to evaluate their oppression as gender oppression, to parse and privilege gender identity from and against any matrix of racial, sexual, economic or other motivations that might hurt or promote them, and then value this core analytic of gender oppression as the most pressing site for solidarity.

The question of who is the subject of feminism and what one must do to be a proper feminist sparked the internecine disputes that wracked the US feminist movement in the 1970s, setting the stage for the subsequent Sex Wars and the fights over pornography and appropriate sexuality that would later convulse US feminisms and culture. Throughout the 1960s and 1970s, as Civil Rights and counterculture movements gained force, US feminists struggled to find common ground for the movement. Fervor erupted over same-sex sexual desire with some camps equating lesbianism – particularly butch/femme roles – as reproducing masculine sexual oppression, while others advanced lesbianism as the ultimate path to liberation (Echols 1990). Equally loaded debates emerged around issues of race and class in tandem with an increasing tendency for liberal feminists to position anti-rape and battering strategies in alliance with a classist, racially oppressive US criminal justice system (Gottschalk 2006, Gruber 2009).

The current international fixation on 'violence against women' has arisen in part from the self-conscious grappling with questions of difference by western mainstream feminists. In response to critiques of class and racial insularity, some feminists vigorously advanced violence against women as an organizing principle for international feminist action as an expansive gesture – as an earnest, if not always easy, means of moving beyond the narrow politics of self-interest of which they had too often been accused (Echols 1990). As feminist messaging began to coalesce around violence against women, however, the public emphasis on sexual danger came at the expense of a comprehensive press for sexual freedom and economic equality, inadvertently bolstering conservative political frameworks that emphasized sexual danger over sexual pleasure (Vance 1989, p. xviii).

Notwithstanding fractious internal politics and controversies over what exactly constituted 'women's issues', and even the category 'women', US feminists of the 1960s and 1970s mainstreamed the call for freedom from rape and sexual violence as issues of paramount public concern by portraying women and children's lack of protection from male encroachment as part of an escalating 'gender war' (Echols 1990, p. 287, Gottschalk 2006, Bumiller 2008, p. 18). The metaphor of war helped drive a popular sexual panic – of which the fight against pornography was but one front – that conceptually fused women and children together on the basis that both were endangered.

Radical feminists' appeal to women's common stake in prioritizing the end of gender has been widely critiqued from within feminism itself. Notably, the recourse to what US feminist Robin Morgan (1984) terms 'global sisterhood' has sustained heavy criticisms from feminists who insist on reckoning with the fissures racial, sexual and economic difference – not to mention the legacies of colonialism – offer to monolithic accounts of gender and sex. Over time, such critiques have shifted the parameters of what constitutes 'violence against women' away from a presupposed collective interest in combating direct male oppression and domination of women (Kaplan and Grewal 1994). Nevertheless, it is worth considering how radical feminist theorizations of women as a 'global class' suggest legal strategies that might comport with those ideas and ends.

MacKinnon's work illustrates these tensions within current international legal work on rape and sexual violence. In April 2010, at the Nobel Women's Initiative's International Gender Justice dialogue, MacKinnon summarized her take on the direction of international rape law and the concept of gender crime:

> [S]ex crimes are gender based. That means they happen because of the social meaning of sex—being a woman or man in social context [...] Everyone who is raped is harmed individually, but rape itself is an attack on a woman because she is a member of the group women, targeted and defined for this specific violation as such.
>
> (MacKinnon 2010)

MacKinnon presses the case for violence against women as degradations of women's human rights by forging a direct connection to her own domestic path-breaking prior efforts to ensure robust analyses and civil prosecutions of acts of sex discrimination – prejudicial treatment of a person based solely on the person's sex. MacKinnon's sex discrimination casts women globally as a group oppressed by virtue of their sex and conceptualizes violence against women as violations of basic equality guarantees foundational to any understanding of international human rights. Claims of equal citizenship between men and women, she concludes, 'must encompass what women need to be human, including a right not to be sexually violated and silenced' (MacKinnon 2006a, p. 48).

In MacKinnon's account, violence and victim are easily recognizable, transcendent labels: violence is the act of rape; the victim is a woman. Universalizing both women-as-a-category and rape-as-an-act places these terms on a theoretically pristine plane untouched by socio-historical context or competing, interrelated iterations of violence. Critiques of this kind – anchored by an insistence on specific material and historical contexts within which gender and race gain cultural meaning – were not the first levelled at MacKinnon and by the 1990s, the US feminist uproar over pornography had waned considerably (see, e.g. Harris 1990, Duggan and Hunter 1995).

Yet the underlying theorizations of violence, gender and sexuality that drove these debates remain live issues within the international legal arena – particularly in the international criminal circles where global legal responses to rape and sexual violence are currently being forged. This gives lie to the notion that the US Sex Wars decisively exploded the narrow equation of sexuality with violence as well as the notion of a world organized by two transhistorical genders and/or sexes, categories untouched by the vicissitudes of historical and cultural change. While the 1990s saw queer studies make in-roads into universities and other institutions, international criminal humanitarian law on rape and sexual violence did not, by a large, keep pace with those activist commitments.

Genocidal rape

With the splintering of the former Yugoslavia, the 'gender war' motif assumed a new, literalized urgency. As reports of mass rape began to trickle into mainstream media, the notion of a 'war on women' gained traction, as did the notion of gender war crimes. The 1993 World Conference on Human Rights in Vienna – the first such conference since the Cold War's end – was, in Rhonda Copelon's (2003) words, a 'watershed' that capped years of feminist organizing around violence against women. The conference not only located such violence squarely within the international human rights agenda, but also initiated the process of integrating rights to be free of that violence within all strata of the international legal system.

In Copelon's account, objections to the feminist agenda were ultimately vanquished by the participation of women from the disintegrating Yugoslavia. '[T]hat women were being raped systematically in Bosnia—just hours from the site of the Conference—prevailed over objections to incorporating gender violence as a human rights problem' (Copelon 2003, p. 867). Their stories of rape camps and military orders to rape belied the fiction that rape was solely a private matter beyond the scope of international law, overcoming those who did not believe that 'sexual subordination in the home' should be absorbed within the human rights frame (Copelon 2003, p. 867). That those called to testify for suffering sexual violence were primarily Bosnian and Croatian Muslims only strengthened feminist appeals, helping to surmount the 'archly patriarchal and religious', as some feminists termed them, opponents to the establishment of women's rights as human rights: the Holy See and a bloc of countries who follow some iteration of Islamic law (Copelon 2003, Halley 2009).

Some feminists involved in efforts to influence international human rights and humanitarian criminal law (including 'patriotic' women's collectives in Bosnia and Croatia such as *Kerata*, *Trasnjevka*, *Biser* and *Bedem Ljubavi*) also urged consideration of mass rape in the former Yugoslavia not only as war crimes and human rights violations, but as genocidal acts, part and parcel of a concerted Serbian campaign of 'ethnic cleansing' waged against Croatian and Bosnian Muslim people, generally, and Croatian and Bosnian Muslim women, specifically (Allen 1996, p. xiii, Batinic 2001).[5] To insist that rape as a weapon of war could occur on any side, they argued, obscured and trivialized the genocidal nature of these particular rapes. Some feminists, including Catharine MacKinnon and Andrea Dworkin, escalated the political – and legal – import of these mass rapes, viewing them as acts of violence against women that harmed not only Bosnian Muslim and Croatian women, but also women as a global group. By this view, mass rape and sexual violence in the former Yugoslavia were not only genocidal due to the ethno-religious targeting of particular women, but also independently tantamount to 'femicide' or 'gynocide' – a crime against women *en masse* as a globally 'subordinated group' (MacKinnon 2006a, pp. 229–230).

The debates over genocidal rape proved controversial, provoking complex assessments of international legal prohibitions against genocide and the relationship of those prohibitions to gender – a category (unlike religion, race and ethnicity) not explicitly protected by international prohibitions against genocide (Copelon 1994, Engle 2005). While Dworkin and MacKinnon championed the uniqueness of genocidal rape, others, notably feminist attorneys Rhonda Copelon and Hilary Charlesworth, cautioned against distinguishing any iteration of rape as 'worse than or not comparable to other forms of rape in war or peace' (Copelon 1994, p. 199). The notion of genocidal rape was no less contentious on the ground. Within the fracturing Yugoslavia, anti-war feminist collectives – including Belgrade's Women in Black and the Zagreb Women's Lobby – railed against war-mongering appropriations of sexual violence, wherein 'raped women become flags waved by the warring parties' (Zarkov 1995, p. 114).

While designations of genocidal rape aggrieved feminists in the early 1990s, in discussions that prefigured and ultimately resulted in the establishment of the ICC, feminist participants essentially suspended efforts to classify rape itself as a form of genocide (Halley 2009, p. 100). US legal scholar Janet Halley interprets the failure of the Women's Caucus for Gender Justice – a global feminist network seeking the uptake of women's human rights and gender justice within the Rome Treaty – to promote the rape/genocide nexus as evidence of a consolidating feminist alignment with Copelon and Charlesworth's 're-imagin[ing] of conflicts in which rape occurs as continuous not with those conflicts, but with a male war against women going on all the time and everywhere' (Halley 2009, p. 100). Halley terms this coalescing perspective 'feminist universalism', in which 'women are not a particular group of humanity but a universe of their own', wherein 'humanitarian law and international criminal law norms relating to armed conflict could be about women' (Halley 2009, p. 6).

While Halley mentions genocidal rape as a counterpoint to the consensus feminists involved in the Rome Treaty discussion attained, I believe that the genocidal rape debates possess additional significance. When considered within the genealogy of the US Sex Wars, the genocidal rape debates are not a deviation from feminist universalism, but rather re-workings of what universalism could mean in the face of vast differences among women. The underlying view of women as a group united through shared sexual vulnerability is not contravened by the genocidal rape debates, but enhanced by the bare acknowledgement of ethno-religious difference: itself a cipher, in this context, for the undemocratic and oppressed.

Militarized rape and sexual violence as a tactic of ethnic cleansing became the starkest example of the sexual vulnerability of all women in part through a conceptual move that fused ethno-religious sexual targeting with the destruction of women's autonomous reproductive capacity. The association of rape, genocide and forced pregnancy occurred even though the links between forced impregnations and genocide were at best tenuous, their logic depending upon a much critiqued understanding of ethnic identity as following the identity of the Serbian father. The association of rape, genocide and forced pregnancy occurred even though the links between forced impregnations and genocide were at best tenuous, their logic depending upon a much critiqued understanding of ethnic identity as following the identity of the Serbian father (Copelon 1994, Engle 2005, Halley 2009). The emphasis on both female reproduction and forced pregnancy as a war crime, a crime against humanity and a genocidal strategy, helps explain why the sexual abuse of men during the conflict barely rates a mention. The analysis inevitably veers back to the rape of women – and the grouping of women with children – as a systematic component of a policy of ethnic cleansing or other war crime (see Gutman 1993, p. 27, Allen 1996, pp. 67–68).

The increasing acceptance of the word genocidal as a legal descriptor of rapes in Bosnia and Croatia occurred in part for two interrelated reasons. First, the conflicts in the former Yugoslavia and Rwanda were exemplars of what was considered a new model of warfare – ethnic and intrastate conflicts stemming largely from collective identity politics (Kaldor 1999, Münkler 2005). Despite the myopia of framing antagonisms in the former Yugoslavia and Rwanda as solely ethnic, and so downplaying or absenting entirely an accounting of economic and geopolitical factors (Mamdani 2002, Gagnon 2004, Buss 2009, pp. 157–158), the gendered and reproductive aspects of genocidal rape and the purported flare ups of ethnic tension in the late twentieth century proved mutually productive and reinforcing. The uproar around the conflicts in the former Yugoslavia and Rwanda – although not necessarily the gendered, sexual aspects of the violence – are often credited with spurring the formation of the ICC and furthering the international criminal legal system (see, for instance, Gareis and Varwick 2005, p. 171). Secondly, aspirations toward 'global sisterhood' and the legacy of the struggle with racial, sexual and other forms of difference within the US feminist movement motivated radical feminists like MacKinnon to conceive of mass sexual violence in the former Yugoslavia in ways that aimed for specificity in representing the experience of other women. That representation in turn helped justify 'ethnic' as a descriptor of these conflicts.

MacKinnon became one of the first, most vocal supporters of linking wartime rapes to genocide, being retained *pro bono* to represent several women's groups in Croatia and Bosnia-Herzegovina seeking legal redress for mass sexual violence. That redress eventuated in a complex of cases within US federal courts, culminating in *Kadic v. Karadžić* (MacKinnon 2006a, p. 35). After weathering years of criticism for her totalizing view of women, MacKinnon proffered a formulation of rape as genocide that aimed to account for women's group affiliation as both 'ethnic other' and their status as women. For MacKinnon and others, rapes in the former Yugoslavia were 'part of an ethnic war of aggression being misrepresented as a civil war' (see Allen 1996, p. 9) – a situation that left Bosnian Muslim and Croatian women doubly imperiled: at risk of rape in the way that all women were at risk, but also in danger of ethno-religious targeted rape that expressly sought their extermination (Allen 1996, Askin 2003, MacKinnon 2006a, p. 37). To shore up the connection she made between human rights, rape and genocide, MacKinnon compared rape in the Balkans with the Holocaust: '[t]hese rapes are to everyday rape what the Holocaust was to everyday anti-Semitism. Without everyday anti-Semitism a Holocaust is impossible, but anyone who has lived through a pogrom knows the difference' (MacKinnon 1994b, p. 8).

In retaining the notion of a global class of women bound by their mutual susceptibilities to male violence, MacKinnon reiterated an analysis of pornography as the cause of sexual domination, generally, and the perpetration of genocidal sexual violence within the former Yugoslavia, specifically. MacKinnon labelled pornography 'a tool of genocide', arguing that the fall of communism resulted in the country's saturation with sexually explicit, dehumanizing images of women. Sexual war criminals, she argued, 'learned to rape' from the 'motivator and instructional manual' of pornography (MacKinnon 1994a, p. 77). With this, she linked the conscious use of sexually explicit media directly to the alleged uniqueness of the mass sexual violence that occurred in the former Yugoslavia. Pornography became irreducibly coupled to the singularity of the paradigmatic new war: '[i]n the conscious and open use of pornography, in making pornography of atrocities, in the sophisticated use of pornography as war propaganda, this is perhaps the first truly modern war' (MacKinnon 1994b, p. 14).

The formulation of genocidal rape carries with it traces of the US feminist debates that culminated in the Sex Wars. MacKinnon, for example, sidesteps both charges of exclusivity and allegations of speaking for others that had plagued earlier discussions of sexuality and race within feminist circles. She is able to represent her involvement in the conflict as solicited, reflective of the views of women who witnessed the devastation firsthand (MacKinnon 1994a, p. 81). She also presents genocidal rape as foregrounding the differences *between* women, even as their shared susceptibility to male violence knits them in global sisterhood. Thus the plight of US porn star Linda 'Lovelace' Boreman can preface discussions of pornography that ineluctably segue into descriptions of sexual violence in the former Yugoslavia (MacKinnon 1994a, p. 73). In the context of atrocity and armed struggled, questions of consent, pleasure and agency that bedeviled feminists during the Sex Wars could be seen as specious and moot.

Copelon and others, however, condemned popular and legal attempts to champion the uniqueness of genocidal rape at the expense of rapes 'normally' occurring during war or peace. To these feminists, the exaggerated distinctiveness of genocidal rape masked the atrocity of non-genocidal rape and hindered efforts to recognize and address persecutions based on gender both in and out of war (Engle 2005). Copelon instead defines genocidal rape in expansive terms, downplaying fixations on war and specific ethnic/national/religious balances of power in order to emphasize that genocidal rape can occur on all sides, both in and out of war. In doing so, she joins others who critique concepts of ethnicity that tend, regarding the former Yugoslavia, to view all Muslim women as raped women and preclude recognition of women's capacity to be war criminals themselves (Engle 2005).

Other critics – including Bosnian non-nationalist feminists – argued that MacKinnon and Copelon's competing theorizations of genocidal rape both ignored the political histories invoked by the contesting powers within the embattled countries themselves. Within the post-socialist nation, feminists' uptake of genocidal rape impacted not only their approach to the war, but also their political and social viability in the fractured Yugoslavia (Kesic 1994, Batinic 2001). Western feminists who ignored the history of the countries – particularly the historical interplay between socialism and feminism – were arguably doing little more than advancing nationalist projects through their assessment of genocidal rape in the conflict (Kesic 1994, Batinic 2001). Some critics, relying on detailed historical assessments of post-socialist Yugoslavia, also questioned the pivotal role pornography played during the conflict, including the very existence of such media within military campaigns (Kesic 1994, Zarkov 2007).

Despite such trenchant criticisms, MacKinnon's theorizations echo through legal arguments heard by the US Second Circuit Federal Court. *Kadic v. Karadžić* prefigures the debates taken up in the international arena, supplying a template for international jurisprudence of what arguments could find purchase in a reputable domestic court. Questions involving the nature of consent, the limits of state sovereignty in effectively guaranteeing human rights and the notion of sexual assault as a collective versus individual offense first find legal articulation in this suit and do so through ethno-religious-based charges of gendered sexual violence – including rape, forced prostitution and forced impregnation – as genocide and war crimes.

From Kadic to Akayesu

While the 1998 ICTR case, the *Prosecutor v. Akayesu*, resulted in the first formal charge of wartime rape as a constitutive act of genocide within international criminal law, the first case to allege wartime rape as genocidal (as a civil charge) occurred in US federal courts. In the spring of 1993, Catharine MacKinnon was instrumental in bringing a civil action against Radovan Karadžić for his alleged participation in and instigation of a campaign to eliminate non-Serbs in Bosnia Herzegovina (*Kadic v. Karadžić*, 70 F.3d 232 [2d Cir. 1995], *cert denied* 518 U.S. 1005 [1996]). MacKinnon characterized the proceeding as an attempt to seek 'relief specifically for injuries of genocidal sexual atrocities perpetrated as a result of Karadžić's policy of ethnic cleansing in collaboration with Slobodan Milošević's administration in Belgrade, Serbia' (MacKinnon 2006a, p. 205). Other US legal feminists specializing in international human rights law, including Rhonda Copelon and Celina Romany on behalf of the Center for Constitutional Rights, were involved in a separate civil action, *Doe et al. v. Karadžić* (866 F. Supp. 734

[S.D.N.Y. 1994]), seeking damages for people who suffered at the hands of the defendant and his subordinates. When both were collectively dismissed at the district level, the two cases were procedurally consolidated on appeal under the caption *Kadic v. Karadžić* (70 F.3d 232 [2d Cir. 1995], cert denied 518 US 1005 [1996]).

In both initial complaints, plaintiffs alleged that Radavan Karadžić in his capacity as part of a three-man presidency of Srpska, the self-proclaimed Bosnia-Serb republic within Bosnia-Herzegovina, had injured them through planned and systematic human rights abuses carried out by the military forces under his command. The plaintiffs sought relief under the Alien Torts Claims Act (ATCA), a provision of the 1789 Judiciary Act, that human rights attorneys have used since the late 1970s to allow foreign citizens to bring civil actions in US courts for human rights violations committed on foreign soil. Rhonda Copelon and her colleagues at the Center for Constitutional Rights in New York City – all instrumental in the feminist push to influence the development of the tribunals – were well versed in the ATCA case law, having pioneered its use to champion human rights.

On 19 September 1994, the plaintiffs' allegations were dismissed because the district court did not believe that a private individual – not a state or a person acting under the colour of state authority – could violate customary international law and be subject to the workings of a US federal court. The following June, however, the appellate court found that Karadžić's planning and ordering of 'a campaign of murder, rape, forced impregnation, and other forms of torture designed to destroy the religious and ethnic groups of Bosnian Muslims and Bosnian Croats clearly state a violation of the international law norm proscribing genocide, regardless of whether Karadžić acted under the color of law as a private individual' (*Kadic* 1995, p. 242).

The ruling marks a shift in the course of US legal history: the first instance where a federal court explicitly established valid federal jurisdiction for suits alleging torts committed anywhere in the world by states, state actors or *private individuals* against non-US citizens in violation of the laws of nations (Ochoa 2005). The *Kadic* court reached this conclusion given the material facts of the case (extensive allegations of mass rape and murder) within the context of how it understood the conflict in the former Yugoslavia as ethno-religious warfare (warfare premised on identity group aggressions) that by definition predisposed these conflicts to charges of genocide. That genocidal rape and forced impregnation were factual vehicles by which the Second Circuit ruled private individuals able to author international human rights violations speaks to the work of feminists in publicizing the events in the disintegrating Yugoslavia and the court's understanding of the nature of that warfare – even as the naming of rape as genocidal flattened and obscured the contested legacy of sexual violence and difference within US feminisms and those in the former Yugoslavia.

Just three years after *Kadic*, the 1998 ICTR case the *Prosecutor v. Jean-Paul Akayesu* first took up the matrix of rape, sexual violence and genocide within international law, setting the terms for their future treatment in international legal jurisprudence. For his alleged failure to summon assistance or otherwise attempt to quell the violence against the Tutsi population, the ICTR pronounced Akayesu, bourgmestre of the Taba commune, guilty of a numbers of charges, including genocide (with rape specified as an instrument of genocide) and crimes against humanity (with rape a specific allegation). In a move unprecedented within the international legal arena, the ICTR in *Akayesu* explicitly defined rape – solely in conjunction with the charge of a crime against humanity and not as an element of genocide – as 'a physical invasion of a sexual nature, committed on a person under circumstances which are coercive' (*Akayesu* 1998, para. 688). Analogizing rape to torture by assessing rape as the sexualized malicious intent of its perpetrators, the ICTR specified rape to be 'a form of aggression' that defies the standard purely descriptive catalogue of objects and body parts, insisting instead 'that the central elements of rape cannot be captured in a mechanical description' (*Akayesu* 1998, para. 597).

The association of rape with genocide and war transformed the debate around consent and the problem of coercion. *Akayesu* decoupled the traditional linking of coercion and force, stating that '[c]oercive circumstances need not be evidenced by a show of physical force [and can instead] [...] be inherent in circumstances like armed conflict or military presence of threatening forces on an ethnic basis' (*Akayesu* 1998, para. 688). By understanding rape as the default designation of the coercive circumstances inherent in (ethno-religious) wartime conflict, *Kadic* and *Akayesu* provide legal models that effectively dislocate the traditional primacy of individual consent from the definitional heart of rape by focusing on the presence of social coercion rather than the absence of individual consent – an element many domestic courts had previously found to be present without a demonstrable, often physical, show of resistance (MacKinnon 2006b, 940). MacKinnon lauded *Kadic* and *Akayesu*, greeting them as landmark decisions that 'arguably for the first time' accurately recognized the true plight of the rape survivor by defining rape 'in law as what it is in life' (MacKinnon 2006b, 940).

Despite evidence that sexual abuse does not attend every violent conflict (Wood 2006), *Akayesu* advanced a portrait of rape and sexual violence as endemic to the necessarily coercive context of wartime sex, embedding the 'common-sense' notion of cross-ethnic sexual encounters as anomalous (Buss 2009). The emphasis on the material fact of violent war couched as ethnic conflict can segue ineluctably into dominance theory claims on sexuality, activating and reinvigorating the animating logic of the gender war in which women-as-group are perpetually at the mercy of men. This revivifying of the radical feminist 'dangerous (hetero)sex' motif consolidates the project of global sisterhood by reifying, though ultimately subordinating, women's ethno-religious difference through an assertion of women's human rights that serves the trend of seeking international criminal solutions to global sexual problems. As feminists turned violence against women into an international human rights campaign, rape and sexual violence became visible as analogs of ethnic conflict and genocide. Ethno-religious antagonisms – framed as the very mark of difference between women – allowed arguments for women as a globally endangered group to piggyback on analyses of genocide that had already separated women into ethno-religious enclaves.

Conclusion

Since the 1990s heyday of the genocidal rape debates, international humanitarian criminal law on rape and sexual violence has remained in flux, and the intervening case law has complicated *Akayesu* (MacKinnon 2006b, Halley 2009). Read optimistically the rapid changes in the status of rape and sexual violence within international law signal opportunities. Submerged histories and representations of conflicts and violations can resurface if we read simultaneously across and within institutional, legal and cultural accounts of wartime rape and sexual violence. The genealogy of genocidal rape, for instance, is formed through international legal feminist fights among themselves *and* other international law and policy movers and shakers; through local feminist organizing for *and* against nationalist feminisms; and through transnational feminists and organizations that operate across international, national and local scales and include those who might seek recognition of rape and sexual violence as an atrocity that must be addressed while refusing the logic of inevitability that mandates international criminal legal and/or militarized humanitarian response or privileges ethno-nationalist representations of the crisis. Understanding law and feminist activisms as transnational amalgams of negotiated, unstable sites of material and theoretical difference provides crucial insight into the ethno-sexual logics of international governance and legal advocacy that yet retains the possibility of, without prescribing, critical alternatives to the global problem of rape and sexual violence.

Acknowledgements

I thank the Department of Social and Cultural Analysis at New York University and the Center for Gender Excellence at Linköping University for fostering this work.

Notes

1. The US Sex Wars was a series of bitter political and culture battles over issues of sexuality that often touched on the relationship between sex, gender, and violence. Controversies raged within feminist and broader US culture over the regulation of pornography, the scope of legal protections for gay people, the funding of allegedly obscene art, the contents of safe-sex education, and more (Duggan and Hunter 1995, p. 1).
2. UN Doc. S/RES/827 (25 May 1993).
3. UN Doc. S/RES/955 (8 November 1994).
4. For an account of the institutionalization of NGOs within international law and policy, see Buss and Herman (2003).
5. The 1948 UN Convention on the Prevention and Punishment of the Crime of Genocide defines genocide as acts 'committed with intent to destroy, in whole or in part, a national ethnic, racial or religious group'. Genocidal acts as enumerated include 'killing members of the group'; 'causing serious bodily or mental harm to group members'; and 'deliberately inflicting on the group conditions of life calculated to bring about its physical destruction in whole or in part'. The convention also defines genocide as a form of reproductive violence, including acts that 'impos[e] measures intended to prevent births within the group' and the 'forcib[le] transfe[r] of children of the group to another group'.

References

Allen, B. (1996) *Rape Warfare: The Hidden Genocide in Bosnia-Herzegovina and Croatia*, Minneapolis, MN, University of Minnesota Press.
Amar, P. (2011) 'Turning the gendered politics of the security state inside out? Charging the police with sexual harassment in Egypt', *International Feminist Journal of Politics*, vol. 13, no. 3, pp. 299–338.
Askin, K. D. (2003) 'The ICTY at Ten: a critical assessment of the major rulings of the international criminal tribunal over the past decade: reflections on some of the most significant achievements of the ICTY', *New England Law Review*, vol. 37, no. 4, pp. 903–914.
Batinic, J. (2001) 'Feminism, nationalism and war: the Yugoslav case in feminist texts', *Journal of International Women's Studies*, vol. 3, no. 1. Available

at: http://www.bridgew.edu/SoAS/jiws/fall01/index.htm (accessed 8 November 2010).

Bernstein, E. (2010) 'Militarized humanitarianism meets carceral feminism: the politics of sex, rights, and freedom in contemporary anti-trafficking campaigns', *Signs*, vol. 36, no. 1, pp. 45–72.

Bumiller, K. (2008) *In an Abusive State: How Neoliberalism Appropriated the Feminist Movement against Sexual Violence*, Durham, NC, Duke University Press.

Buss, D. E. (2009) 'Rethinking "Rape as a Weapon of War"', *Feminist Legal Studies*, vol. 17, no. 2, pp. 145–163.

Buss, D. & Herman, D. (2003) *Globalizing Family Values: The Christian Right in International Politics*, Minneapolis, MN, University of Minnesota Press.

Copelon, R. (1994) 'Surfacing gender: reconceptualizing crimes against women in time of war', in *Mass Rape: The War Against Women in Bosnia-Herzegovina*, ed. A. Stiglmayer, Lincoln, NE, University of Nebraska Press, pp. 197–218.

Copelon, R. (2003) 'International human rights dimensions of intimate violence: another strand in the dialectic of feminist lawmaking', *American University Journal of Gender, Social Policy and Law*, vol. 11, no. 2, pp. 865–877.

Doe et al v. Karadžić (866 F. Supp. 734 [S.D.N.Y. 1994]).

Duggan, L. & Hunter, N. (1995) *Sex Wars: Sexual Dissent and Political Culture*, Routledge, New York.

Echols, A. (1990) *Daring to Be Bad: Radical Feminism in America, 1967–75*, Minneapolis, MN, University of Minnesota Press.

Engle, K. (2005) 'Feminism and its (Dis)contents: criminalizing wartime rape in Bosnia and Herzegovina', *American Journal of International Law*, vol. 99, no. 4, pp. 778–817.

Enloe, C. (1994) 'Afterword', in *Mass Rape: The War against Women in Bosnia-Herzegovina*, ed. A. Stiglmayer, Lincoln, NE, University of Nebraska Press, pp. 219–230.

Gagnon, V. P., Jr. (2004) *The Myth of Ethnic War: Serbia and Croatia in the 1990s*, Ithaca, NY, Cornell University Press.

Gareis, S. B. & Varwick, J. (2005) *The United Nations: An Introduction*, New York, NY, Palgrave Macmillan.

Gettleman, J. (2009) 'Clinton Presents Plan to Fight Sexual Violence in Congo', *The New York Times*, 11 August, p. A8. Available at: http://www.nytimes.com/2009/08/12/world/africa/12diplo.html (accessed 12 November 2010)

Gottschalk, M. (2006) *The Prison and the Gallows: The Politics of Mass Incarceration in America*, New York, NY, Cambridge University Press.

Gruber, A. (2009) 'Rape, feminism, and the war on crime', *Washington Law Review*, vol. 84, no. 4, pp. 581–660.

Gutman, R. (1993) *A Witness to Genocide*, New York, NY, Macmillan.

Halley, J. (2009) 'Rape at Rome: feminist interventions in the criminalization of sex-related violence in positive international criminal law', *Michigan Journal of International Law*, vol. 30, no. 1, pp. 1–123.

Harris, A. P. (1990) 'Race and essentialism in feminist legal theory', *Stanford Law Review*, vol. 42, no. 3, pp. 581–616.
Heineman, E. (2008) 'The history of sexual violence in conflict zones: conference report', *Radical History Review*, vol. 101, no. 1, pp. 5–21.
Kadic v. Karadžić, 70 F.3d 232 (2d Cir. 1995), cert denied, 518 U.S. 1005 (1996).
Kaldor, M. (1999) *New and Old Wars: Organized Violence in a Global Era*, Stanford, CA, Stanford University Press.
Kaplan, C. & Grewal, I. (eds). (1994) *Scattered Hegemonies: Postmodernity and Transnational Feminist Practices*, Minneapolis, MN, University of Minnesota Press.
Kesic, V. (1994) 'A response to Catharine MacKinnon's article "turning rape into pornography: postmodern genocide"', *Hastings Women's Law Journal*, vol. 5, no. 2, pp. 267–280.
MacKinnon, C. (1987) *Feminism Unmodified: Discourses on Life and Law*, Cambridge, MA, Harvard University Press.
MacKinnon, C. (1994a) 'Turning rape into pornography: postmodern genocide', in *Mass Rape: The War against Women in Bosnia-Herzegovina*, ed. A. Stiglmayer, Lincoln, NE, University of Nebraska Press, pp. 73–81.
MacKinnon, C. (1994b) 'Rape, genocide and human rights', *Harvard Women's Law Journal*, vol. 17, pp. 5–16.
MacKinnon, C. (2006a) *Are Women Human?: And Other International Dialogues*, Cambridge, MA, Harvard University Press.
MacKinnon, C. (2006b) 'Defining rape internationally: a comment on Akayesu', *Columbia Journal of Transnational Law*, vol. 44, no. 3, pp. 940–958.
MacKinnon, C. (2010) 'International gender justice dialogue: professor Catharine A. MacKinnon', Puerto Vallarta, Mexico, video, 20 April. Available at: http://www.nobelwomensinitiative.org/blogs/genderjustice?start=21 (accessed 8 November 2010).
Mamdani, M. (2002) *When Victims Become Killers: Colonialism, Nativism, and the Genocide in Rwanda*, Princeton, NJ, Princeton University Press.
Morgan, R. (1984) *Sisterhood is Global: The International Women's Movement Anthology*, New York, NY, The Feminist Press at the City University of New York.
Münkler, H. (2005) *The New Wars*, Malden, MA, Polity Press.
Ochoa, C. (2005) 'Access to U.S. federal courts as a forum for human rights disputes: pluralism and the alien tort claims act', *Indiana Journal of Global Legal Studies*, vol. 12, no. 2, pp. 631–650.
"'Rape Epidemic'" in African Conflict Zones—UNICEF' (2008) *Reuters*, 12 February. Available at: http://www.reuters.com/article/idUSL12344012 (accessed 12 November 2010).
Romany, C. (1993) 'Women as aliens: a feminist critique of the public/private distinction in international human rights law', *Harvard Human Rights Journal*, vol. 6, pp. 87–125.

The Prosecutor v. Jean Paul Akayesu (1998) Case No. ICTR-96-4-T, Judgment, 3 September. Available at: http://ictr.org (accessed 16 September 2010)

UNFPA: State of World Population Report 2010. Available at: http://www.unfpa.org/swp (accessed 30 November 2010).

Vance, C. (ed.). (1989) *Pleasure and Danger: Exploring Female Sexuality*, London, UK, Pandora Press, an imprint of HarperCollins Publishers.

Wood, E. (2006) 'Variation in sexual violence during war', *Politics & Society*, vol. 34, no. 3, pp. 307–341.

Zarkov, D. (1995) 'Gender, orientalism and the history of ethnic hatred in the former Yugoslavia', in *Crossfires: Nationalism, Racism and Gender in Europe*. eds H. Lutz, A. Phoenix & N. Yuval-Davis, London, UK, Pluto Press, pp. 121–142.

Zarkov, D. (2007) *The Body of War: Media, Ethnicity, and Gender in the Break-up of Yugoslavia*, Durham, NC, Duke University Press.

John Nguyet Erni

LEGITIMATING TRANSPHOBIA

The legal disavowal of transgender rights in prison

> *Transgender persons are strangers to the law; or put more accurately, the legal imagination is so deeply entrenched in normative gender binarism as to effectively render transsexuals a 'freakish' anomaly to law. This essay attempts to offer a reflection on transgenderism, law and sexual crime from a human rights and criminal law perspective. It focuses on one of the most violent types of institution in society — the prison — and asks: what are the legal imagination and practice surrounding transgender prisoners as they are linked to social and cultural transphobia? What 'human' rights can be practiced for a dehumanized class? It first surveys the legal predicament of transgender prisoners in the US prison system in relation to Eighth Amendment rights provided by the US Constitution. The US situation has seen cases that have importantly shed light on other jurisdictions when engaging with the combined questions of prisoners' rights and transgender rights together. The analysis is then taken to the context of Hong Kong prisons in a modest application. In contrast to some other Asian contexts (such as Taiwan, Thailand and Indonesia), critical cultural studies of transgenderism are non-existent in Hong Kong. Meanwhile, human rights studies of the same have only emerged through the work of legal scholar Robyn Emerton. It is hoped that a rights-based approach will emerge in Hong Kong for the protection of transgender inmates from sexual violence in local correctional facilities.*

Understanding 'gender identity' to refer to each person's deeply felt internal and individual experience of gender, which may or may not correspond with the sex assigned at birth, including the personal sense of the body (which may involve, if freely chosen, modification of bodily appearance or function by medical, surgical or other means) and other expressions of gender, including dress, speech and mannerisms.

From the Preamble of the Yogyakarta Principles on the Application of International Human Rights Law in Relation to Sexual Orientation and Gender Identity, November 2006[1]

Introduction

In the legal imagination, transgender or transsexual persons are not subjects; rather, they are an abject class. That transgender rights consistently lag behind gay and lesbian rights in contemporary human rights law stems from an apparent internal hierarchy in queer advocacy practice as well as from immutable law. Gay and lesbian legal activism tends to privilege the politics of sexual autonomy over that of gendered bodily sovereignty, even as it recognizes the complex entanglement of sexuality and gender. The more that national political struggles around the world forge a mainstreaming of gay and lesbian sexual culture in order to gain public representation, the more, it seems, transgenderism is pushed to the political, cultural and legal periphery. But the decimation of the transgender as a representable category of public artifice comes mainly from law. US transgender scholar-activists Currah and Minter (2000) remind us that it is 'not possible to identify any single doctrinal error or logical mistake that will account for—and thus provide a simple means of remedying—the historical exclusion of transgender people from equal protection in the courts' (pp. 37–38). Transgender plaintiffs convey their injuries in a legal system that either does not recognize them at all, or draws a line in such a way as to render them strangers to all of the laws that could protect them. Abby Lloyd (2005) goes so far as to say that:

> '[a]t a systemic level, the law fails to recognize liminal subjects; faced with a transgender person who challenges traditional categories of normalcy, the law makes his or her identity so impossible, invisible, and monstrous as to be outside of the law's protection'
>
> (p. 152).

Palpable here is the hint of legal dehumanization reminiscent of the colonial treatment of racial minorities. Lloyd cites *Ashlie v Chester-Upland School District* (1979), a US court case which held that Jenell Ashlie, a male-to-female (MTF) transsexual schoolteacher, could not seek protection under the privacy doctrine from a state government employer's job discrimination clause. The court supported its judgment with an elaborate analogy:

> It might just as easily be argued that the right of privacy protects a person's decision to be surgically transformed into a donkey. The transformation, by its very happening, would lose the quality of privateness. Certainly, those who had known the donkey as a man would

detect the change, even though those acquainted only with the donkey might never have occasion to remark upon it. In addition, the change from man to beast might be just as devoutly wished, as psychologically imperative, and as medically appropriate as the change from man to woman, but the Constitution, I fear, could not long bear the weight of such an interpretation

(*Ashlie*, pp. 160–161).

Lloyd goes on to demonstrate that beastly analogies abound in the law's delineation of the transsexual's legal personality. In more practical terms, the judicial discourse over the past 40 years, stemming from *Corbett v. Corbett* (1970), has continued to confine transgender persons both for the purpose of marriage and for many other legal purposes to their biological sex as designated at birth, even if they have undergone gender reassignment surgery.

Explicit transphobia in law has receded in more recent times, partly due to the rise of (unstable) legal recognition of same-sex rights in sexual orientation jurisprudence. It has only been very recently that civil law regimes around the world have begun to outline protection for transgender persons, *in so far* as the latter can learn how to 'humanize' themselves by twisting their identities to fit into recognizable domains of law, particularly sex discrimination law, psychiatry-supported disability law, and sexual orientation law. While there is no question about the benefit brought about by advancements in women's rights and same-sex anti-discrimination and equality laws, these advancements are a double-edged sword to transgender people whose very existence defies and repudiates the gender-sexuality system as we know it (see Gordon 2009).

My focus in this essay is expressly limited in scope and context. In asking what the legal imaginations and practices are that construct and impact upon the transgender persons, I focus on relevant laws applied to the treatment of prisoners through a modest legal analysis of transsexuality, law and sexual crime in one of the most violent types of institution in society. In addition, I focus only on US laws, which are generally seen in human rights law as having notable influence on legal thinking in the field of transgender rights (since at least the 1960s; see Spade 2008, see also Lau 2008). Further, given the location where I live and work, my interest in this project has naturally taken me to research on the plight of transsexual prisoners in what I shall discuss later as the sociocultural context of pervasive transphobia in Hong Kong. In contrast to other Asian countries, critical cultural studies of transsexualism in Hong Kong are non-existent. Meanwhile, to date, human rights studies of the same have only been provided through the work of legal scholar Robyn Emerton (2004a, 2004b). This work is inspired by Emerton's pioneering work. Yet the plight of transsexuals in the prison's violent sexual economy goes completely un-researched. It is hoped that this essay will begin to shed some light on an area of human rights law regarding sex and identity that very few have made forays into. But more importantly, this analysis of the human rights crisis regarding the inhumane treatment of transsexual prisoners, it will be argued, helps to crystallize the core ideology of legal transphobia, which is centred on two intertwined cultural authorities: namely the rationalistic authority of clinical science and the epistemological authority derived from the body (in particular the genitalia).

Transgender prisoners in legal discourse

US transgender rights scholars have argued that transgender prisoners are 'doubly imprisoned': first by the pervasive discrimination in the judicial system that continues to fail to give due legal recognition of transgender people's right to dignity and self-identity, and second by the often 'cruel and unusual' mistreatment of them in the prison. The phrase 'cruel and unusual' is used here in explicit reference to US laws, which will be discussed later. My focus in this section is on the question of transgender rights in the specific context of violence in the prison, particularly the violence of sexual harassment and rape visited upon transgender inmates.

Legally speaking, transgender subjects are typically codified with regard to 'transsexualism', since the legal discourse has long been dominated by a psycho-medical view. It is only recently that activists have been able to re-define the term in a more psycho-social and anthropological sense. The advantage of such a re-definition is that it can challenge the courts' tendency to rely on crude physiological markers and conditions of psychiatric disorder (e.g. as defined by DSM-IV) in their determination of a transsexual plaintiff's identity. For example, Justice Souter in *Farmer v Brennan* described Dee Farmer as:

> 'a transsexual, one who has "[a] rare psychiatric disorder [gender dysphoria] in which a person feels persistently uncomfortable about his or her anatomical sex", and who typically seeks medical treatment, including hormonal therapy and surgery, to bring about a permanent sex change'
>
> (*Farmer v Brennan*, 1994, p. 829).

To challenge a reductionist definition of transsexualism, Darren Rosenblum (2000) argues that the word 'transgender' has been used:

> in place of 'transsexual' [which] reflects [a] shift away from the historical primacy of medical treatment, toward a growing awareness of the psychological element of gender identity... 'Transgender' grew into a useful umbrella term, including and not subordinating the proliferation of transgendered people who avoid medical treatment. 'Transsexual' refers to 'sex' rather than 'gender,' a biological emphasis that excludes

> psychological gender identity. 'Transgendered' recognizes the extrabiological nature of gender.
>
> (p. 507)

Nevertheless, courts around the world continue to give prevalence to the psycho-medical labels of 'gender identity disorder' and 'gender dysphoria'. In other words, transgender people yet do not have a liberty interest in defining their own sex; the courts still have not officially held that they had a universal right to self-identify their legal sex.

Within the transgender community, more transgender people are recognizing the right of individuals to define their own gender, regardless of the role of medical procedures. Long-time transgender activist in the US, Kate Bornstein (1994), suggests: 'One answer to the question "Who is a transsexual?" might well be "Anyone who admits it". A more political answer might be, "Anyone whose performance of gender calls into question the construct of gender itself"' (p. 121). Furthermore, due to the significant period of time in transition experienced by transgender persons, they often do not fit neatly into any simple categories at any given point in time. In this way, even convenient categories such as 'pre-operative' and 'post-operative' do not always work, and the transgender community has been prompted to embrace broader, more flexible definitions. Indeed, the prefix 'trans' is a useful reminder of the fluid nature of identities and bodies-in-the-making.

In the context of civil law, the struggle over transgender rights falls into several main areas (see Hunter *et al.* 2004, Sinnot 2004, Rudacille 2005, Currah *et al.* 2006), including:

- Requests for a change of name and sex identification on official documents such as birth certificates (i.e. the right to privacy)
- Seeking the right of legal marriages between transsexuals and non-transsexuals
- Tackling employment discrimination issues
- Assessing whether sex reassignment surgery (SRS) is medically necessary
- Testing transsexuals for athletic competitions
- Seeking asylum for foreign national transsexuals and
- Seeking medical treatment in prison.

In the criminal law context, the problems of hate crime and prison rape stand out as key areas of criminal litigation. This essay focuses on the egregious problem of prison rape, to which many transgender persons are particularly vulnerable.

Prison rape and 'Sexual Terrorism'

'In truth, prison rape is the most tolerated act of terrorism in the United States', states James Robertson (2003, p. 436). Male rape of female, male and transgender inmates is the 'most closely guarded secret activity of America's prisons' (Robertson 2003, p. 435). In a way, the court's sentencing of someone in jail can have a de facto extension of the punishment when prison sexual assaults are allowed to occur. It is difficult to determine with clarity the number of prison rape victims. In 1974 in the US, it was estimated that of the 46 million Americans who would be arrested at some point in their lives, 10 million of them would be raped in prison (Weiss and Friar 1974, p. 61). Between 1980s and 1990s, several authors have put the figure of prison rape victims (or victims of some form of unwanted sexual contact in prisons) at an average of about 15–20 percent of the total male inmate population (see Bell *et al.* 1999, Kupers 2001). The imprecision about the extent of the problem is due to the different ways authors define rape, and the difficulty of pinpointing whether some sexual experiences in prison might be considered consensual or might be framed as consensual in a pervasively coercive atmosphere. Researchers do agree that there is significant under-reporting and that the reported figures indicate a much larger problem. Inmates' fears of reprisals and the demonstrated unwillingness of prison staff to keep reported cases confidential have kept many prison rape victims silent.

Carole Sheffield (1987) defines 'sexual terrorism' as 'the system by which males frighten, and by frightening, dominate and control females' (p. 171). In the eye of the perpetrator, 'femaleness' can be something found in a woman, or a man perceived to be weak, effeminate, or gay, or yet a transgender person. Invariably, the victim of prison rape has been redefined as a submissive 'surrogate woman'. In *Schwenk v Hartford* (2000), for instance, it is observed: 'The victims of these attacks are frequently called female names and terms indicative of gender animus... [such as] "pussy" and "bitch" during the assaults and thereafter' (p. 1203). Worse, in the act of bearing out their 'lost masculinity' in the humiliating prison environment – Gresham Sykes (1958) terms it 'symbolic castration' (p. 70) – sexual aggressors 'take' the 'surrogate woman' in brutal and unprotected sex.[2] Robertson (2003) remarks, 'Widespread unsafe rape turns such sexual contact into "death sentences"' (p. 524). Prison staff appear to condone this aggression, deriding victims as 'weak'. Besides turning a blind eye on sexual violence between inmates, prison staff are themselves implicated as sexual harassers. A 1982 study of correctional officers in a California prison reveals that they strongly support the following propositions, that: 'forced or pressured sexual encounters are very common'; 'homosexual inmates have a more difficult time than heterosexual inmates due to [sexual] pressure' and 'it is a very common occurrence for young, straight boys to be turned out, or forced into being punks' (cited in Robertson, p. 445). Another 1989 study found that 50% of surveyed prison officers in a Texas prison disagreed with the statement that rape was rare, while another 35.5% of them strongly disagreed (Eigenberg 1989, p. 44). Some inmates have complained that prison staff, while acknowledging the prevalence of prison rape, regard it as a legitimate deterrence to crime: 'some staff members...

view prison rape as part of the punishment-risk that lawbreakers take when they commit their crimes. Others see it simply as retribution carried out at an interpersonal level' (Hassine 1999, p. 136). Not surprisingly, the result of placing a transgender person in this environment is humiliation, rape and abuse.

Transgender subjects and prison rape

Gay and MTF transgender inmates have been identified as one of three high-risk groups for prison rape (the other two types being 'snitches', i.e. the whistle blowers, and physically and mentally vulnerable inmates [Robertson 2003, p. 461]). It is explained:

> Gay inmates confront a prison sexual code that defines them as 'fair game.' Expecting little resistance, sexual aggressors will frequently target gays... A transsexual inmate also faces a pervasive risk of sexual assault. The district court in *Star v Gramley* anticipated *Farmer v Brennan* when it observed that 'inmates dressed as females undoubtedly would require heightened protection.' The Supreme Court in Farmer agreed that transsexual inmates should anticipate 'a great deal of sexual pressure'.
> (pp. 464–465)

Placed at the bottom of the masculinity hierarchy in prison, MTF transgender inmates are defined in terms of their femininity. They are called 'punks' for their sexually submissive role, along with other young, heterosexual, less street-wise inmates. More often, they are termed 'queens' for their effeminacy, and are assigned female tasks (such as doing laundry, cleaning the cell, serving drinks). Because they are viewed with contempt by prison staff, queens are routinely denied privileges afforded the other inmates, 'including recreation hall attendance, exercise and fresh air in the yard, library visits, chapel attendance, and hot food' (Peek 2004, pp. 1227–1228). The prison's inhumane treatment of MTF transsexuals begins with a genitalia-based placement policy, and continues with the legal hurdle of denying them the protection from 'cruel and unusual punishment' that is provided by the Eighth Amendment to the US constitution.

Genitalia-based placement policy

Turner v Safley (1987) lays down the criteria for determining whether a prison regulation is reasonable:

> 1) the existence of a valid and rational connection between the regulation and the legitimate interest purportedly advanced by it; 2) the existence of

alternative means for the exercise of the allegedly violated right; 3) the negative consequences to penological interests by the accommodation of the right asserted and 4) the existence of an alternative to the regulation that meets the prisoners' asserted right with minimal cost to penal interests.

(Rosenblum, 2000, pp. 517–518)

However, in considering where best to place transgender inmates, prison officials rarely look for alternatives.[3] The prison system's refusal to accept that there are indeed more than two genders has put transsexuals in grave danger. Pre-sentence reports do not allow for a discussion of the complications that may arise if a transsexual prisoner is placed to a facility based solely on the prisoner's genitalia. For post-operative MTF transsexual inmates, their surgically modified (female) genitalia generally pose no problem for them in their placement to a female cellblock. But pre- and non-operative transsexuals face the most egregious problems when placed according to their birth gender, without due regard for the non-genital physical transformations they may already have undergone (such as breasts, voice change, atrophy of tissue). In *Lucrecia v Samples* (1995), for instance, an MTF transsexual who had received hormonal treatment and castration (the result being that she had a non-functioning penis) was denied a request for special treatment because 'her pre-sentence report identified her as a 32-year-old Caucasian male' (p. 2). The policy that says 'an inmate with a penis is considered male; one with a vagina is considered female. It doesn't matter whether nature or a surgeon provided the part', undermines the complexity of gender identity that is not genitally based.

This unreflexive and inflexible placement policy lies in the more general problem of discrimination in civil law cases involving transgender rights. The transgender persons' subjective or self-proclaimed gender identities are routinely denied legal recognition in the civil law context, most clearly so in requests for legal marriage. Cases like *In re Estate of Gardiner* (2002) and *Littleton v Prange* (1999) see the courts turn down transgender litigants' request for subjective identification of their own preferred genders. As a result, '[j]ust as the courts have professed deference to the legislature in transgender marriage cases, they have shown deference to the executive branch where prison placement policies are concerned' (Peek 2004, p. 1239). While more humane options do exist, such as the segregation of transgender inmates, creating transgender-only facilities, or the placement of MTF transsexuals in female cells, these alternatives are not without problems. Segregation and transgender-only cells often turn out to be another stratum of stigmatization of transgender inmates, and MTF persons placed in female facilities may face prejudice and rejection by other non-transgender female inmates (see Peek 2004, pp. 1239–1244). It is at any rate clear that the 'hands-off approach' of the courts has constituted the basis for possible Eighth Amendment violations.

The Eighth Amendment

Since the 1960s, the judiciary in the US has maintained a 'hands-off approach' towards any issue of cruel or unusual punishment that might arise from conditions of confinement in the context of corrections. The low intervention approach was justified on the basis that the judiciary ought not to encroach upon the functioning of the executive branch. Likewise, federal courts were reluctant to encroach upon state sovereignty by interfering with state prison policies. By the mid-1970s, the Supreme Court departed from the hands-off doctrine by recognizing that certain prison conditions could violate the Eighth Amendment's prohibition on cruel and unusual punishment.

The Eighth Amendment of the US Constitution guarantees that '(e)xcessive bail shall not be required, nor excessive fines imposed, nor cruel and unusual punishments inflicted' upon the incarcerated. The original interpretation of the Amendment by the Supreme Court was to proscribe punishments involving torturous and barbarous treatment. In *Weems v United States* (1910), the Supreme Court reviewed a sentence of 15 years at hard labour for the crime of falsifying a 'public and official document', and found that a sentence of this nature for such a crime is 'repugnant' to the Constitution (p. 380). A proportionality standard was thus introduced into Eight Amendment jurisprudence. In *Estelle v Gamble* (1976), the Supreme Court further expanded the Cruel and Unusual Punishments clause to include punishments incompatible with 'the evolving standards of decency that mark the progress of a maturing society' (p. 102). Punishments involving the 'unnecessary and wanton infliction of pain' or are 'grossly out of proportion to the severity of the crime', were considered excessive and thus unconstitutional. It was also in *Estelle v Gamble* that the Court first articulated the concept of 'deliberate indifference'. This deliberate indifference test would prove detrimental to transgender litigants who were raped in prison, since the test sets an extremely high threshold for proving prison officials' conscious recklessness.

Farmer v Brennan and the deliberate indifference test

Estelle v Gamble involves the question of Eighth Amendment violation in the area of medical care of prisoners. Justice Marshall held that medical negligence alone did not establish a constitutional violation. He stated that 'a prisoner must allege acts or omissions sufficiently harmful to evidence deliberate indifference' (*Estelle v Gamble* 1976, p. 105). He also indicated that deliberate indifference entailed 'wanton infliction of unnecessary pain', but stopped short of explaining the meaning of 'wanton'. Nonetheless, the test paved the way for inclusion of a mental element on the part of prison officials as proof as to whether they had violated prisoners' Eighth Amendment rights.

It was Justice Scalia's opinion in *Wilson v Seiter* (1991) that brought clarity to the deliberate indifference test. Inmate Wilson alleged that the combined effect of overcrowding, insufficient space, inadequate temperature control and ventilation, noise and unsanitary restrooms and dining facilities (among other things) created cruel and unusual conditions of confinement. Justice Scalia ruled that prison conditions, however adverse, could not inflict cruel and unusual punishment unless the defendant prison officer acted with 'a sufficiently culpable state of mind' (p. 2326).

A two-prong test of deliberate indifference was thus introduced by the Court. As Stacey Cozad (1995) explains:

> First, the deprivation must objectively be sufficiently serious to deprive the prisoner of the minimal necessities of life, including food, clothing, shelter, medical treatment, and reasonable safety. As a second component, where the pain inflicted is not a formal part of the punishment set forth by statute or by the sentencing judge, the inmate must be able to show the inflicting officer acted with a 'sufficiently culpable state of mind.'
>
> (p. 186)

Ultimately, it was *Farmer v Brennan* (1994) that cemented this subjective logic as a necessary ground for proving a constitutional violation.

Dee Farmer, a pre-operative transsexual, was sentenced to the Federal Correctional Institute in Oxford, Wisconsin in 1986, for credit card fraud. Still biologically male, Farmer had had estrogen therapy and breast implantation, but the procedure to have his testicles removed had been unsuccessful. He wore women's clothing prior to and during the trial. In prison, he claimed to be continuing hormone therapy. Three years after conviction, Farmer was transferred to a higher security prison in the United States Penitentiary at Terre Haute, Indiana. Although initially placed in administrative segregation, Farmer was eventually integrated into the general prison population – but placed in a male prison because of her pre-operative genitalia identification. Within two weeks of her transfer, Farmer was sexually assaulted by an inmate in her cell. Held down by a knife, Farmer had her clothes torn off and was forcibly raped. She commenced a Bivens complaint (one directed at the prison officials), alleging that despite knowledge of a violent environment and knowledge of her transsexuality, prison officials had placed her in a male cell, making her extremely vulnerable to sexual assault.

The District Court granted summary judgment in favour of the prison officials. The prison officials were not held to be deliberately indifferent because they lacked the criminal recklessness required for an Eighth Amendment violation. Farmer appealed, but the Seventh Circuit Court of

Appeals affirmed the District Court's decision without opinion. The Court reasoned that not 'every injury suffered by one prisoner at the hands of another translates into constitutional liability for prison officials responsible for the victim's safety' (*Farmer v Brennan*, p. 834). The Court framed the issue as a choice between criminal and civil recklessness definitions of deliberate indifference. It 'described the civil law standard of recklessness as a failure to act despite "an unjustifiably high risk of harm that is either known or so obvious that it should be known"'. In contrast, under a criminal law standard, the prison official is only liable if he 'disregards a risk of harm of which he is aware' (Park 2001, p. 428).

The Farmer Court did soften the effect of this harsher standard by allowing plaintiffs to prove through circumstantial evidence that officials subjectively knew a substantial risk existed, including the fact that the risk was obvious to a reasonable person. Justice Souter stated that if the plaintiff can show a risk 'longstanding, pervasive, well-documented, or expressly noted by prison officials in the past, and circumstances suggest that the defendant-official being sued had been exposed to information concerning the risk'. The plaintiff might then use this evidence as proof that the official had actual subjective knowledge (*Farmer v Brennan*, pp. 1981–1982). The Court also stated that officials could not escape liability simply by failing to verify facts that were strongly suspected to be true, or by declining to confirm inferences strongly suspected to exist. However, the Court quickly warned that even when actual subjective knowledge may be shown by evidence that the risk was so pervasive as to be obvious, 'it is not enough merely to find that a reasonable person would have known, or that the defendant should have known' (*Farmer*, 1982, no. 8). Moreover, Justice Souter stated that a prison official with actual subjective knowledge of a risk would not be liable for harm to prisoners if he responds 'reasonably'. Here, the Court echoed *Helling v McKinney* (1993) and *Washington v Harper* (1990), cases that held up the 'reasonable safety' and 'reasonable measures' standard as the prison officials' duty to provide to inmates.

In his concurring opinion, Justice Thomas reasoned that that there was a clear distinction between prison conditions and punishments. He argued that the former, however degenerative, should not be considered as part of the latter. Punishment was interpreted strictly as that handed down by the judge. Justice Thomas found that '[c]onditions of confinement are not punishment in any recognized sense of the term, unless imposed as part of a sentence' (*Farmer*, p. 1990). The opinion, therefore, proposed that Farmer's predicament was 'unfortunate' but not 'punishment' subject to Eighth Amendment scrutiny.

The Farmer decision supported the prison staff's claim that they had no knowledge of the facts underlying the risk of harm, and that even if they had knowledge, they had responded reasonably to the risk, even if they could not avert the harm in the end. As a potential challenge to this trend, Christine Peek (2004) suggests that class action suits alleging a systematically over-sexualized prison environment could be useful, since they (1) present prison rape not as isolated occurrences and (2) attack policies and procedures rather than individuals (p. 1235). But Peek warns, 'class action suits may not be a viable option for transgender prisoners if the attack were an isolated incident or not enough plaintiffs existed to certify a class' (p. 1245). Unfortunately, the Farmer case has set forth a constitutional framework whereby the burden of proof of abuse is placed upon transgender litigants who, with this decision, are doubly victimized. In the first place, how would the plaintiff be able to write a formal complaint when doing so would label them 'snitch' and put their life at risk? In addition, how will they obtain evidence indicating prison officials' actual subjective knowledge of facts underlying a substantial risk, when such evidence may not be within their reach or may be already destroyed? Peek adds:

> The fact that plaintiffs bear this burden creates an incentive for guards to ignore problems. If guards do not know specific details, incidents of sexual assault and exploitation cannot be documented. If they are not documented, guards and higher prison authorities have a stronger argument that they were unaware of the risk. Even if a guard could be held liable for failure to investigate facts underlying a substantial risk, as Justice Souter seems to suggest, higher prison officials would still be insulated on the ground that they had no knowledge of the omission. Because the deliberate indifference analysis focuses on the defendant's state of mind, higher-level officials can argue that they lacked first-hand knowledge of the underlying facts.
>
> (p. 1224–5)

In the end, the deliberate indifference test has severely limited prison rape victims from Eighth Amendment protection.

Assessing the legal protection of transgender inmates from sexual assault in Hong Kong's prisons

Robyn Emerton's (2004a, 2004b) groundbreaking two-part study of transgender rights in Hong Kong represents the first (and to date, the only known) comprehensive analysis of transgender persons' human rights in the territory. Her study focuses on transgender rights in the civil law context, but its findings raise issues about transgender rights in the criminal law context, as in the case of prison rape. This essay aims to address the problem of physical violence against transsexuals in prisons — an area not covered by Emerton. The inadequacies of human rights protection for transsexuals in the civil law context that Emerton identifies also bodes poorly for transsexuals in a criminal law context.

We may recall that the genitalia-based placement policy practiced in the prison system in the US, robs transgender prisoners of the right to a choice of prison placement; their subjective identification of their sex — whether in pre-, post- or non-operative states — is denied and given way to the authority of the genitalia. This denial of rights stems from the refusal of courts to grant legal recognition of transgender status in the civil law context: a form of discrimination thus lays the ground for the transgender inmates' subjugation to sexual terrorism in the prison.

Hong Kong has a small number of transgender people, as recorded in the public health service providing SRS. By the end of the 1990s, less than 100 persons had been assessed by the Gender Identity Team; 48 of those had gone on to have surgery and 7 were still under evaluation (see Cheung 2010). Emerton (2004a) states that of the stable number of persons being managed by the Gender Identity Team over the years, 'roughly 70 per cent of those being diagnosed as transsexuals, and around 50 per cent of those initially referred going on to have gender reassignment surgery' (p. 250). Meanwhile, members of Transgender Equality and Acceptance Movement (TEAM), a local transgender rights NGO, estimate that there are far more transgender persons in Hong Kong than the number reported by the clinic — up to about 3,000, with about 10 percent of those suitable for or having undergone surgery (cited in Shamdasani 2004, p. 4; see also Winter 2009b). Before we discuss the relevant prison laws and codes in Hong Kong and the human rights abuses engendered by them, it is important to place such legal problems in a wider cultural context.

Transphobia in Hong Kong

In Hong Kong, two primary terms commonly call forth the transgender person in public discourse: *bin tai* (or *biantai* in Putonghua) and *yan yiu* (or *renyau* in Putonghua). The term *bin tai* is a common lexicon referring to all real or imagined perversions designated as deviation or subversion of reproductive heterosexual family-centred norms of the body, gender and sexuality. Yet the term's basic meaning is rather innocuous: *bin* refers to change, whereas *tai* means a state of affairs, a condition or a position. But when transposed into an insult to the cross-dresser, the pedophile, the polygamist, the same-sex lover, the masculine woman, the sissy boy and the transgender person, *bin tai* exposes its epistemological foundation in reproductive heterosexual family-centred normativity. As such, it achieves cultural ubiquity in a conservative society like Hong Kong.

Arguably, diverse forms of symbolic and anatomical gender and sexual boundary-crossings have enacted a sweeping 'trans' cultural sensibility in Chinese contexts. This is evidenced by a long history of exquisite queer performativity in the Chinese popular imagination, a tradition that makes it very difficult to distinguish among homosociality, *tongxinlian*, cross-dressing and bodily alterations (see, e.g. Li 2003, Martin 2003, Lim 2006). *Yiu* (or *yau* in Putonghua) is possibly the unifying term that refers to the 'transifying' gender and sexual economy, something that the term 'queer' has always tried to approximate in more global contexts. Seen in this way, *yan yiu* (literally translated as human ghost, human monster or freak) is a term that arguably exceeds a narrow reference to transgender people. Like the term 'queer', *yan yiu* seems to gesture towards a larger economy of liminal socio-sexual practices: all queerly sexed subjects are members of the '*yan yiu* family'. However, in Hong Kong, neither 'queer' nor *yan yiu* has achieved social or linguistic *jouissance*; no cultural celebration or political positivity is in store for queerly sexed subjects like transgender people.

Terms like *bin tai* and *yan yiu* do not usually carry with them a direct indictment of biomedical or religious pathologization. They do not need to. Rather, they command a kind of cultural ubiquity that produces a sensation of shame and humiliation strong enough to induce self-policing. Put differently, they are a language that pierces through the body, gender, and sexuality to perform a deeper social degradation of one's 'personal character'. This explains why *bin tai* and *yan yiu* can mortify an individual into withdrawal from sociality. In Josephine Ho's (2007) ethnographic study of transgender persons in Taiwan, she delineates how transgender people are trapped between two difficult choices: to endlessly craft a self-narrative that will hopefully yield social acceptance, or to withdraw into aloofness so as to preemptively block other people's urge for conversation. Ho suggests that this acute project of daily self-management is an attempt to defend one's personal character in the face of a Taiwanese social atmosphere steeped in 'gender policing' as well as a general erosion of social trust (p. 348–349).

Much of Ho's essay can apply to the context of Hong Kong. Despite the fact that the government of Hong Kong has been providing counselling and SRS since the mid-1980s, and despite the existence of a growing transgender rights movement since the early 2000s (Emerton 2006), transgender people are almost entirely obscured from social existence in Hong Kong. However, as is the case in Taiwan and many other countries, transgender visibility typically arrives as a shock after the (sensationalized) death of a transgender person. In 2004, this happened in Hong Kong when, within a single week, two transgender women – Louise Chan and Sasha Moon – committed suicide. The circumstances of their deaths rehearse the cultural and political tragedy of a city plagued with routine social disregard and degradation, as well as institutional dismissal of transgender people in employment, education, housing, prison and the media (see Winter *et al.* 2008, Winter 2009a). Before her suicide, Louise Chan had been stalked and outed as a transsexual by the local press, costing her job as a hairdresser. And when Sasha Moon leaped from her high-rise apartment to her death, her plunge was captured in a morbid sequence of photographs published in the following morning's local newspapers. 'The media used to treat us like a freak show. Today, we're seen as a genuinely good story', laments a friend of Sasha Moon and a member of TEAM (cited in Watkins 2004, p. 20).

Rampant transphobia in Hong Kong has also been recorded by Mark King (2003) in his small-scale study of secondary schoolteachers. His study confirms a significant level of fear and pathologization of transgender people among schoolteachers:

> '[a]mong the 183 teachers, 54% thought that TG's are mentally ill and need treatment, 16% thought that TG's are promiscuous, also 54% thought that TG's are likely to have diseases requiring treatment. Of the sample teachers, 45% would not be happy leaving their own children alone with a GID/TG individual, 16% thought that they should not be allowed around any children'.

Besides attributing such biases to a general lack of sex knowledge among the populace, King goes further to indicate that transphobia in Hong Kong is in fact mixed with racial phobia, which produces a belief that transgenderism must be rare among ethnic Chinese. King writes:

> The local conceptualization of transgender may also have been conflated with images and ideas of transgender from neighboring Southeast Asian nations, particularly Thailand, Malaysia, and Singapore (and to some degree, the Philippines, Korea, Indonesia, and India). Hong Kong people may also hold ethnocentric views about the possibility of transgendered people within the Chinese race. Numerous informants, although familiar with the linguistic conceptualization in Chinese, declared disbelief about transgendered people of Chinese origin.
>
> (see also King *et al.* 2009).

It should be noted that transgender people in Hong Kong are not totally without any legal rights in the civil law domain. In Emerton's (2004a) study of transgender rights in Hong Kong, she discusses the administrative concessions that the Hong Kong Special Administrative Region (HKSAR) government offers to transgender persons in an attempt to comply with international legal trends. The concessions include the ability for a transgender person to change the name and sex identification on their identity card, driver's license, passport and education certificates once they have provided adequate evidence of their successful transition. The re-issuance of identity card is important, since Hong Kong residents are required to produce their identity card at all times, even though the card does not establish a person's sex for legal purposes. The latter can only be established by one's birth certificate. Unfortunately, current laws in Hong Kong do not allow for the alteration of the birth certificate for post-operative transgender persons, a legal restriction that impacts the right to marriage, custody of children, use of public spaces (e.g. public toilet or changing facility) and on many other legal rights concerns for the transgendered.

The curious case of the (missing) transgender inmate

In my research, I have not been able to find any transgendered prisoners in Hong Kong's correctional services. Neither is there any reported case of, or litigation involving, a transgender inmate being sexually assaulted in Hong Kong's prisons. This zero-case phenomenon, however, begs the question about how prepared Hong Kong's prisons are in handling the legal rights of transgender people, including their need of placement to a prison appropriate to and safe for their chosen sex, of administration of medical treatment in prison and of not being subjected to 'cruel and unusual punishments'.

Male-to-male prison rape, after all, cannot be treated as a hypothetical occurrence in Hong Kong's prison, even though rape and other disorderly criminal conduct in prison have seldom been reported, if at all, by the Hong Kong Correctional Services Department. A study conducted by the Asian Human Rights Commission on the prison conditions and the complaint mechanisms available to prisoners in Hong Kong, includes the following experience by the researcher:

> Although the prison conditions in Hong Kong are not very bad, the Correctional Services Department (CSD) and prison officers are very careful with providing information about the prison system and the actual life in prison. This can be illustrated by the fact that prison guards ordered one of the interviewed prisoners not to talk about the prison conditions and only to talk about himself. In addition, during the visit, a guard was present at all time within sight and sound of the conversation. This resulted in a stressful interview and the prisoner suggested to try to continue the interview in writing. Another prisoner was informed that the officers read the letter, written by the author, with the explanation about the research and the question to be put on the list of allowed visitors. Also to him, they said that they would keep a close eye on him during the visit.

In addition, with an expressly stated goal of rehabilitation, the Department's public record/image tends to focus on prisoners' good conduct, rather than bad. Yet the persistent problem of overcrowding in Hong Kong's prisons has not led to any investigation of the correlation between overcrowding, escalated conflict, and disorderly conduct among the inmates (many of them have backgrounds in the triads). Overcrowding has meant putting two prisoners in a cell built for one, and placing Category C prisoners (those with lower sentence) in maximum security prisons such as Stanley and Shek Pik Prison, thereby subjecting prisoners to the high security rules of the maximum security prison (cited in Asian Human Rights Commission report). In addition, there has been record overcrowding in female prisons as a result of the police's continued effort to crackdown on sex work. In 1994, for the first time, an arrest of a large number of foreign sex workers forced the transfer of these women to a men's detention centre on Lantau Island's Sha Tsui (Thomas 1994, p. 3). Renovations, however, were made to strictly segregate the sexes because under the Prisons Ordinance, male and female inmates must be accommodated separately.

Indeed, section 8 of the Prisons Ordinance in Hong Kong, which stipulates that 'separate buildings or parts of a building shall be used for the men and for the women respectively so as to prevent the one from seeing or communicating with the other', makes no provision for considering the situation of transgender inmates at all, especially those who have not completed, or choose not to complete, SRS at the time of their imprisonment. Despite Emerton's note that '[p]olice and prison practice . . . demonstrate a general willingness on the part of the authorities to recognise the chosen gender of post-operative transsexual persons, and to accommodate those currently completing the "real life test" or undergoing surgery', she does warn that these concessions 'do not extend to all transgender persons, even if they have permanently adopted their chosen gender' (Emerton 2004b, p. 550). In addition, prison rules that ignore transgender inmates' rights of placement also ignore their rights in other prison procedures. For instance, prison rule 10 on 'Provisions as to Female Prisoners' states:

'No prisoner shall be searched other than by an officer of the same sex. In other respects the same course shall be pursued in reference to the admission or discharge of a female prisoner as in the case of a male prisoner'.

In placement as in search procedures, there may be a *prima facie* case of violation of Article 6 of the Bill of Rights Ordinance (BORO). Article 6, which deals with the rights of persons deprived of their liberty, stipulates that '[a]ll persons deprived of their liberty shall be treated with humanity and with respect for the inherent dignity of the human person' (Art. 6.1). The Article also makes special provisions for appropriate segregation of juvenile offenders from adult prisoners, and accused persons from convicted persons. Yet the current judicial refusal to grant legal recognition to transgender persons in the civil law context has not prompted reform of prison rules to bring it into conformity to Article 6.1 of BORO with respect to the dignity of transgender inmates. Nor there has been effort to seek protection of transgender inmates by observation of the Disability Discrimination Ordinance (DDO). Emerton has briefly made such an appeal: 'there is a very strong legal argument that the DDO would prohibit discrimination and harassment against transgender persons. This is because the DDO defines "disability" very broadly, to include "disorders that affect a person's thought processes and emotions"' (p. 272); 'persons who have undergone gender reassignment surgery have incurred the partial or total loss of a part of their body, which is also included under the definition of disability in the DDO' (p. 273). Yet Emerton also warns of stigma by associating transgenderism with disability; besides the Hong Kong courts have yet to confirm whether discrimination of transgender people does indeed fall within the DDO. She concludes, 'There is therefore no legally binding precedent to date which can be relied upon by transgender persons for protection in this field' (p. 275).

In the civil law context in Hong Kong an MTF transgender person cannot in theory be a victim of rape because male-on-male rape is unrecognized by the law, leaving the rape of MTF transsexuals similarly invisible to the law. Perversely, this may explain the zero record of prison rape in Hong Kong's prisons. Unless the HKSAR considers the adoption of something like the Gender Recognition Act of the UK (which Emerton advocates as 'the most attractive model' [2004b, p. 550] for Hong Kong to adopt) the transgender community of Hong Kong will continue to be denied legal rights and responsibilities appropriate to their acquired gender (see Gender Recognition Panel Tribunals Services 2007).

The impact brought about by the lack of protection of transgender rights in the civil law context cannot be underestimated. While the Eighth Amendment of the US Constitution prohibits cruel and unusual punishments of prisoners, neither the Basic Law, nor the BORO, nor the Prisons Ordinance of Hong Kong contain expressed language of similar prohibitions. Prisoners' rights, as such, have not much entered into human rights law locally, let alone human rights litigation. As Peter Wesley-Smith (1998) states:

> '[t]he paucity of cases in Hong Kong where judges have been asked to review decisions made under the Prison rules may reflect the lack of a rights consciousness amongst prisoners, ignorance of the legal possibilities amongst legal advisors, or, on the other hand, a fair and efficient regime of prisons administration giving rise to few complaints'
>
> (p. 315).

Today, the possibility of sexual assault of transgender prisoners in the overcrowded and typically hostile prison environment continues to go unnoticed and unreported, as authorities in Hong Kong's prisons appear to be determined to keep and project a positive image of prison management. It's time we paid attention to the extent of prison violence, including sexual assault, in Hong Kong's prisons, and to the rights and dignity of transgender persons in both the civil law and criminal law contexts.

Conclusion

Pervasive transphobia has led to the disproportionate ostracization of transgender persons from mainstream culture, with this burden falling much heavier upon MTF transgender persons than upon female-to-male (FTM) transgender persons. Existing anti-discrimination laws have been blind to the plight of the transgender subjects. Disempowered and degraded, transgendered persons (mainly MTFs) are often forced into criminalized economies, most prominently sex work and drug economies. Josephine Ho (2007) relates to this in the context of Taiwan:

> Within [a] social context where gender non-conformity is looked upon with suspicion and body transformation procedures are both hard to come by and expensive to acquire, quite a number of trans subjects are forced to resort to various forms of entertainment work or sex-related work as their only viable source of income and the only site where their chosen embodiments and identities are at least applauded or appreciated as spectacles
>
> (p. 351).

Yet, such a space of survival is often a criminalized space. The result is that transgender persons are disproportionately likely to be arrested, convicted and sentenced to prison. While incarceration is a brutal experience for any prisoners, the hyper-gendered prison experience is especially terrorizing for transgender individuals.

A 2006 study of US prisons regarding their management of transgender prisoners finds that of the 44 states surveyed, only 7 have relevant written policies. Of the majority of states without any written policies, 26 have corrections personnel unwilling or unable to speculate as to how a transgender inmate would be treated in their facilities (Tarzwell 2006, p. 190). In the absence of policy, prison staff have unfettered discretion. Some prison staff resort to humiliating 'gender-check' strip searches in order to categorize inmates, while others leverage their control over the goods and services available to prisoners to coerce female as well as transgender prisoners into sexual bartering (Tarzwell, p. 178). In Hong Kong there is an absence of written policies regarding the humane treatment of transgender prisoners. Neglect breeds neglect, and this should compel us to re-assess the zero-case scenario. A bottom-line for a basic human rights protection of transgender persons in Hong Kong would comprise an anti-discrimination bill valuing life narratives over clinical psychological classifications and criminalizing accounts, a bill confirming the reconstructions of somatic reality over an epistemology premised on genitalia. The reason why it is important to consider the case of transgender prisoners is that their dehumanizing experience presents to us a paradigmatic view of existing and ongoing risk to transgenderism at large.

This risk that is visited upon transgender persons emanates from a spiralling *transphobic structure*, which begins with gender and sexual essentialism, moves through a system of social and economic discrimination, then through legal condemnation, and ends with sexual terrorism as a direct result of those preceding problems. This transphobic structure assigns *imprisonment* (in conceptual, social, economic and legal senses of the term) to transgender persons as their paradigmatic destiny. Against this structure, how should we develop a moral-juridical culture based upon life narratives of the *pastiche* and bodily comportment of transgender persons? Sadly there is a 'Catch-22' situation, where on the one hand, the conventional legal narratives of binaristic gender roles and bodily classification potentially hold the key to a legal recognition, but on the other hand, twisting one's identity to fit within one of the recognized legal narratives – sex discrimination, disability discrimination, etc. – might mean enacting a conceptual imprisonment to a transgender person's sense of self and bodily sovereignty.

Notes

1   The full text of the Yogyakarta Principles is available at: http://yogyakartaprinciples.org/principles_en.htm (accessed 13 March 2011).
2   As a side note, there has not been much research done on the needs of FTM transgender prisoners. A noted exception is Howell's (2010) study in which she cited an interview she conducted in 2006 of an FTM transgender who had been incarcerated in New York's Bedford Hills Correctional Facility for women. Howell writes that the FTM inmate 'related that even though he and other FTM inmates that he met while at Bedford Hills wanted to be housed in a men's prison, they would have had to be housed in a special unit for safety. This is because the average FTM is of slight build (like the average genetic woman) and those FTMs would be unable to protect themselves from predatory male inmates who pose a danger to slightly built genetic male inmates. He acknowledged that FTMs, if not housed in a special unit, would have to align themselves with stronger male inmates as their "bitches" for protection' (189).
3   To address and respect the complex relationship among gender identity, expression and body diversity, flexible self-identification remains the ideal prison cell classification policy (see Faithful 2009). Mann (2006) has suggested that several non-US jurisdictions had adopted some form of this policy. New South Wales, Australia, for example, presumes that: 'inmates have a right to be placed in the facility of their "gender identification" unless it is determined, on a case-by-case basis, that they should be placed elsewhere' (105). Within such a system, default classification falls on gender identity, not genitalia.

References

Asian Human Rights Commission. *Case studies of Hong Kong, Thailand and Malaysia with regard to prison conditions and the complaint mechanisms for prisoners*, [online] Available at: http://www.hrschool.org/doc/mainfile.php/lesson31/51/ (accessed 22 March 2011).

Bell, C., et al. (1999) 'Rape and sexual misconduct in the prison system: vanalyzing America's most "open" secret', *Yale Law & Policy Review*, vol. 18, pp. 195–233.

Bornstein, K. (1994) *Gender Outlaw: On Men, Women, and the Rest of Us*, New York, Routledge.

Cheung, P. K. E. (2010) 'GID in Hong Kong: a critical overview of medical treatments for transexual patients', in *As Normal as Possible: Negotiating sexuality and gender in mainland China and Hong Kong*, ed. Yau Ching, Hong Kong, Hong Kong University Press, pp. 75–85.

Cozad, S. L. (1995) 'Cruel but not unusual: *Farmer v Brennan* and the devolving standards of decency', *Pepperdine Law Review*, vol. 23, pp. 175–203.

Currah, P. & Minter, S. (2000) 'Unprincipled exclusions: the struggle to achieve judicial and legislative equality for transgender people', *William & Mary Journal of Women & Law*, vol. 7, no. 1, pp. 37–60.

Currah, P., Juang, R. & Minter, S. (eds), (2006), *Transgender Rights*, Minneapolis: University of Minnesota Press.

Eigenberg, H. (1989) 'Male rape: an empirical examination of correctional officers' attitudes toward rape in prison', *Prison Journal*, vol. 69, no. 2, pp. 39–56.

Emerton, R. (2004a) 'Neither here nor there: the current status of transsexual and other transgender persons under Hong Kong law', *Hong Kong Law Journal*, vol. 34, no. 2, pp. 245–277.

Emerton, R. (2004b) 'Time for change: a call for the legal recognition of transsexual and other transgender persons in Hong Kong', *Hong Kong Law Journal*, vol. 34, no. 3, pp. 515–555.

Emerton, R. (2006) 'Find a voice, fighting for rights: the emergence of the transgender movement in Hong Kong', *Inter-Asia Cultural Studies*, vol. 7, no. 2, pp. 247–277.

Faithful, R. (2009) 'Transitioning our prisons toward affirmative law: examining the impact of gender classifications on US transgender prisoners', *The Modern American*, vol. 5, no. 1, pp. 3–8.

Gender Recognition Panel Tribunals Services (UK) (2007) *Gender Recognition Act 2004: A Guide for Users*, [online] Available at: http://www.grp.gov.uk/documents/guidance/ExplanatoryLeaflet.pdf (accessed 22 March 2011).

Gordon, D. (2009) 'Transgender legal advocacy: what do feminist legal theories have to offer?', *California Law Review*, vol. 97, pp. 1719–1762.

Hassine, V. (1999) *Life Without Parole: Living in Prison Today*, 2nd edn, Los Angeles, Roxbury Publishing Company.

Ho, J. (2007) 'Embodying gender: transgender body/subject formations in Taiwan', in *The Inter-Asia Cultural Studies Reader*, eds. Kuan-Hsing Chen & Chua Beng Huat, London & New York, Routledge, pp. 347–363.

Howell, A. W. (2010) 'A comparison of the treatment of transgender persons in the criminal justice systems of Ontario, Canada, New York, and California', *Buffalo Public Interest Law Journal*, vol. 28, pp. 133–205.

Hunter, N., Joslin, C. & McGowan, S. (2004) *The Rights of Lesbians, Gay Men, Bisexuals, and Transgender people: The Authoritative ACLU Guide to a Lesbian, Gay, Bisexual, or Transgender Person's Rights*, 4th edn, Carbondale, IL, Southern Illinois University Press.

King, M. (2003) *Research and Discussion Paper: Perceptions of MTF Transgendered Persons and Their Sexual Partners in Hong Kong: A Study of Social, Emotional, and Cognitive Sources of Biases*, [online] Available at: http://web.hku.hk/~sjwinter/TransgenderASIA/paper_perceptions_of_mtf.htm (accessed 8 March 2011).

King, M., Winter, S. & Webster, B. (2009) 'Contact reduces transprejudice: a study on attitudes towards transgenderism and transgender civil rights in Hong Kong', *International Journal of Sexual Health*, vol. 21, pp. 17–34.

Kupers, T. A. (2001) 'Rape and the prison code', in *Prison Masculinities*, eds. Don Sabo, Terry A. Kupers & Willie London, Philadelphia, PA, Temple University Press, pp. 111–115.

Lau, H. (2008) 'Sexual orientation and gender identity: American law in light of East Asian developments', *Harvard Journal of Law & Gender*, vol. 31, pp. 67–100.

Li, S. L. (2003) *Cross-dressing in Chinese Opera*, Hong Kong, Hong Kong University Press.

Lim, S. H. (2006) *Celluloid Comrades: Representations of Male Homosexuality in Contemporary Chinese Cinemas*, Honolulu, University of Hawai'i Press.

Lloyd, A. (2005) 'Are transgender people strangers to the law?', *Berkeley Journal of Gender Law & Justice*, vol. 20, pp. 150–195.

Mann, R. (2006) 'The treatment of transgender prisoners, not just an American problem—a comparative analysis of American, Australian, and Canadian prison policies concerning the treatment of transgender prisoners and a "universal" recommendation to improve treatment', *Law and Sexuality*, vol. 15, pp. 91–133.

Martin, F. (2003) *Situating Sexualities: Queer Representation in Taiwanese Fiction, Film and Public Culture*, Hong Kong, Hong Kong University Press.

Park, J. J. (2001) 'Redefining Eighth Amendment punishments: A new standard for determining the liability of prison officials for failing to protect inmates from serious harm', *Quinnipiac Law Review*, vol. 20, pp. 407–466.

Peek, C. (2004) 'Breaking out of the prison hierarchy: transgender prisoners, rape, and the Eighth Amendment', *Santa Clara Law Review*, vol. 44, pp. 1211–1248.

Robertson, J. (2003) 'A clean heart and an empty head: The Supreme Court and sexual terrorism in prison', *North Carolina Law Review*, vol. 81, pp. 433–481.

Rosenblum, D. (2000) '"Trapped" in Sing Sing: transgendered prisoners caught in the gender binarism', *Michigan Journal of Gender & Law*, vol. 6, pp. 499–571.

Rudacille, D. (2005) *The Riddle of Gender: Science, Activism, and Transgender Rights*, New York, Pantheon Books.

Shamdasani, R. (2004) 'Victory of woman in sex bias dispute', *South China Morning Post*, 14 October, p. 4.

Sheffield, C. (1987) 'Sexual Terrorism: the social control of women', *Analyzing Gender*, eds M. M. Ferree & B. B. Hess, Newbury Park, CA, Sage, pp. 171–189.

Sinnot, M. (2004) *Toms and Dees: Transgender Identity and Female Same-sex Relationships in Thailand*, Honolulu, University of Hawai'i Press.

Spade, D. (2008) 'Documenting gender', *Hastings Law Journal*, vol. 59, pp. 731–832.

Sykes, G. M. (1958) *The Society of Captives*, Princeton, NJ, Princeton University Press.

Tarzwell, S. (2006) 'The gender lines are marked with razor wire: addressing state prison policies and practices for the management of transgender prisoners', *Columbia Human Rights Law Review*, vol. 38, pp. 167–219.

Thomas, H. (1994) 'Prostitutes sent to men's jails due to overcrowding', *South China Morning Post*, 8 September, p. 3.

Weiss, C. & Friar, D. J. (1974) *Terror in the Prisons: Homosexual Rape and Why Society Condones It*, Indianapolis, Bobbs-Merrill.

Wesley-Smith, P. (1998) 'Judicial review and the prison rules', *Hong Kong Law Journal*, vol. 28, pp. 315–329.

Winter, S. (2009a) *Country Report: Hong Kong: Social and Cultural Issues*, [online] Available at: http://web.hku.hk/~sjwinter/TransgenderASIA/country_report_hk_social.htm (accessed 20 March 2011).

Winter, S. (2009b) 'Lost in transition: transpeople, transprejudice and pathology in Asia', *International Journal of Human Rights*, vol. 13, no. 2/3, pp. 357–382.

Winter, S., Webster, B. & Cheung, P. K. E. (2008) 'Measuring Hong Kong undergraduate students' attitudes towards transpeople', *Sex Roles*, vol. 59, no. 9/10, pp. 670–683.

Cases cited

Ashlie v Chester-Upland School District, no. CIV78-4037, U.S. Dist. (1979).
Corbett v Corbett [1970] 2 All ER 33.
Estelle v Gamble, 429 U.S. 97, 102 (1976).

Farmer v Brennan, 511 U.S. 825 (1994).
Helling v McKinney, 113 S. Ct. 2475 (1993).
In re Estate of Gardiner, 42 P.3d 120 (Kan. 2002).
Littleton v Prange, 9 S.W.3d 223 (Tex. App. 1999).
Lucrecia v Samples, No. C-93-3651, 1995 WL630016.
Schwenk v Hartford, 204 F. 3d 1187 (9th Cir. 2000).
Turner v Safley, 482 U.S. 79 (1987).
Washington v Harper, 494 U.S. 210 (1990).
Weems v United States, 217 U.S. 349, 380 (1910).
Wilson v Seiter, 111 S. Ct. 2321, 2326 (1991).

Index

'24' (television drama) 15–21, 23–4, 25, 54–5, 63

Abu Ghraib 73, 76; and the image of torture 59, 62–7
accountability 19–20, 22, 76, 86, 88
Afghanistan 57, 58, 59, 63; Bagram Air Base 63–4, 73; CIA secret prison/black site *see* Salt Pit: torture and death of Gul Rahman
Agamben, G. 50, 77, 78
Akayesu 118, 128, 130, 131
Alien Torts Claims Act 129
Allen, B. 124, 126
Althusser, L. 32
Amar, P. 118
American Civil Liberties Union 98–9
Améry, J. 58, 59
analogy in legal reasoning 93, 105–7, 130, 137–8
Anleu, S.L.R. 106
Aquinas, St Thomas 13
Arendt, H. 65
Aristotle 20
artists *see* decency
Asian Human Rights Commission 151, 152
Asimow, M. 31, 40
Askin, K.D. 126
Australia 100, 155n3

Bagaric, M. 16
Baheer, Ghairat 76
Balkin, J. 19
Batinic, J. 117, 119, 120, 124, 128
Batman 19
Bauerlein, M. 99
Bell, C. 141

Bella Lewitszky Dance Foundation v. Frohnmayer 101–2
Belley, J.G. 15
Berkowitz, R. 13, 21
Berlant, L. 97
Bernstein, E. 117
Bin Attash, Mr 81
bio-politics 50, 59, 61, 78, 81
biopower 81, 85, 94
black sites *see* Salt Pit: torture and death of Gul Rahman
Blackmore, J. 105
Blair, Tony 22
blogging 109
body building 58
Bolton, R. 100
Bornstein, K. 140
Bosnia-Herzegovina 116, 124, 126, 129
Boyce, B. 95
Bradbury, S. 61–2, 65, 86
Bruzzi, S. 31, 33, 34, 36, 42
Buchanan, Patrick 100
Bumiller, K. 122
Burchell, G. 94
Bush, George 16, 21–2, 55, 67, 74, 107
Buss, D.E. 126, 130
Bybee, J. 51–5, 73, 74–5, 79, 82, 83, 84–5

Caldwell, Melissa 15
Carlin, George 97
Chan, Louise 149
Charlesworth, H. 125
Chase, A. 3
Cheney, Dick 16, 21, 22, 61, 65
Chertoff, Michael 84
Cheung, P.K.E. 148
China *see* Hong Kong: transgender prisoners
Chiu, D.W. 96

INDEX

Christ-centred model of justice 20–1, 22
CIA 54, 60, 61–2, 65, 66; secret prison/black site *see* Salt Pit: torture and death of Gul Rahman
Clanchy, M. 24
class 40, 121, 122
class action suits 146–7
Cleaver, Eldridge 120
Clinton, Bill 103, 107
Clinton, Hillary 116
Cochran, Robert 17, 54
colonialism 14–15, 73, 77, 122
Communication Act (1934) 97
Comstock Act (1873) 95
confessions, false 60, 61
Congo 115, 116
Constitution (US): First Amendment 98–9, 102, 108; Fifth Amendment 61, 102; Eighth Amendment 142, 144–7; Fourteenth Amendment 61
constitutionalism, redemptive 43–4
Convention against Torture (CAT) 51, 63, 65
Coombe, R. 3
Copelon, R. 119, 120, 124, 125, 126, 127, 128–9
Cornell, D. 42–3
Cover, R. 12, 14, 18, 43
Cozad, S.L. 145
crimes against humanity 116, 119, 126, 130
Critical Legal Studies (CLS) 2, 3
Croatia 119, 120, 124, 126
CSI franchise 23
cultures wars (1980s–1990s in US) *see* decency
Currah, P. 137, 140

D'Amato, Alphonse 99, 100
dance 101–2
David, G. 20
Davies, C. 93, 97, 103, 106, 107, 108
De Grazia, S. 23
decency 92–3; context to *NEA v. Finley* 99–102; Federal Communications Commission (FCC) 96–8; freedom of speech 98–9, 102, 108; governmentality, law and cultural policy 93–4; long-term effects of decency clause 107–9; in *NEA v. Finley* 102–7; new technologies 96, 102; obscenity, decency and indecency in American law and culture 94–9
Derrida, J. 16, 18, 19, 20

Dershowitz, A. 16
Dilawar, Mr 63–4
disability discrimination 152–3, 155
discrimination 98, 108; disability 152–3, 155; racism *see separate entry*; sex 123, 138, 155; sexual orientation 138; transgender persons 138, 139, 140, 143, 148, 152–3, 154, 155
Dollahite, D. 44
Duggan, L. 123
Dworkin, A. 124, 125

Echols, A. 121, 122
Eco, U. 19
Egypt 75
Ehrlich, E. 14
Eigenberg, H. 141
Elias, N. 24
Emerton, R. 138, 147, 148, 149, 150, 152–3
England, L. 59, 63
Engle, K. 119, 125, 126, 127
Enloe, C. 120
entertaining torture, embodying law 49–50; Abu Ghraib and the image of torture 59, 62–7; Bybee torture memo 51–5; *First Blood* 55–9, 64; from tortured to torturer 59–62
ethno-religious difference *see* rape and sexual violence in conflict zones

Faludi, S. 16, 19
Fanon, F. 78
Farmer v Brennan 139; and the deliberate indifference test 144–7
fatherhood and law in *To Kill a Mockingbird* 30–3, 42–4; coloured balcony 41–2; disobedient children/non-compliant jurors 37–41; 'what kind of man are you?' 34–7
FBI interrogators 60–1
feminists/feminism 116, 117, 118, 119–23, 124–5, 126–9, 130–1
film 24–5, 50, 65; *Batman* 19; *First Blood* 55–9, 64; regulation 96; *Rocky* 59; *To Kill a Mockingbird* 30–44; *V for Vendetta* 19; Wild West 19–20
Finlay, Karen *see National Endowment for the Arts v. Finley*
Finnegan, Patrick 55
First Blood 55–9, 64
Fitzpatrick, P. 2, 13, 14
Fleck, John *see National Endowment for the Arts v. Finley*

INDEX

Foerstel, H.N. 93
folk music 24–5
Foucault, M. 50, 78, 81, 93, 94, 95, 106
France 100
Frank, J. 32
Frankel, A. 98
Freedman, M.H. 31
freedom of speech 98–9, 102, 108
Freud, S. 32
Friedman, L. 94
Frohnmayer, John 101
future called into being *see* fatherhood and law in *To Kill a Mockingbird*

Gagnon, V.P., Jr 126
Garber, M. 31
Gareis, S.B. 126
gender 31, 59, 105–6, 117, 118, 121, 122–5, 127; transgender prisoners *see separate entry*
Geneva Conventions 63, 65, 74, 116, 118–19
genocidal rape 116, 117, 123–31
Gettleman, J. 116
Ghul, Hassan 86–7
Gibbs, B. 22
Gioia, D. 107, 108
Goldberg, D.T. 2
Golden, T. 63–4
Goldman, A. 76–7, 84
Gonzales, Alberto R. 74
Goodrich, P. 32
Gordon, D. 138
Gottschalk, M. 122
governmentality, law and cultural policy 93–4
Govier, T. 22
Grant, G. 24
grants to artists *see* decency
gratuitous and instrumental violence *see* Salt Pit: torture and death of Gul Rahman
Green, A. 55
Green, J. 120
Greenberg, K.J. 16, 74
Griffiths, J. 14
Gruber, A. 122
Guantànamo Bay 57, 58, 63, 73; Emergency Response Force (ERF) interventions 65
Gutman, R. 126

Hague Convention (1907) 118
Haiti 116

Halberstam, J. 97
Halley, J. 117, 119, 124, 125, 126
Hambali, Mr 81
Harris, A.P. 123
Hart, H.L.A. 14
Hartman, G. 32
Haslem, W. 19
Hassine, V. 142
Heineman, E. 120
Heins, M. 95
Helms, Jesse 99, 100, 101
Hersh, S.M. 65, 66
Ho, J. 149, 154
Hobbes, T. 13
Holcomb, M. 31, 33, 40
Holy See 124
homoeroticism 58–9
homosexuality 105–7, 121–2, 137, 141, 142
Hong Kong: transgender prisoners 138, 147–8, 154–5; curious case of the (missing) transgender inmate 151–3; transphobia 148–51
Horwitz 13
Hughes, Holly *see National Endowment for the Arts v. Finley*
Hunter, N. 140
Hutchings, P.J. 50

Illich, I. 24
indecency *see* decency
indigenous societies 24; legal orders 14–15
instrumental and gratuitous violence *see* Salt Pit: torture and death of Gul Rahman
International Committee of the Red Cross (ICRC) 79, 80–1
International Criminal Court for Former Yugoslavia 119
International Criminal Court (ICC) 116, 117, 118, 125, 126
International Criminal Tribunal for Rwanda (ICTR) 116, 118, 119, 128, 130, 131
international human rights law 116, 117, 118, 118–21, 124, 129
international humanitarian law 116, 117, 118, 119, 123, 124, 131
Internet 96, 98–9, 109
Iraq 57, 58, 59; Abu Ghraib and the image of torture 59, 62–7
Islamic law 124

INDEX

Jacob, R. 20
Johnson, Hilde 116
judges 18, 20–1
The Judgment of Cambyses (David, 1498) 20

Kadic v. Karadžić 118, 126, 128–9, 130
Kahn, P.W. 2
Kaldor, M. 117, 126
Kaplan, C. 122
Kaufman, M.T. 50
Kesic, V. 128
King, M. 150
King, Martin Luther 58
Kleinman, S. 61
Knezevic, D. 119
Knox, S.L. 96
Kobylka, J.F. 95
Koch, C. 99
Korean War 60
Kuoni, C. 108
Kupers, T.A. 141
Kurtz, H. 65

Lane, F.S. 95, 96
Lau, H. 138
legal positivism 13
lesbianism 121–2, 137
Levinas, E. 19
Li, S.L. 149
Lim, S.H. 149
Lippens, R. 20
Lipschultz, J.H. 95, 96, 98
Lloyd, A. 137, 138
Luban, D. 73
Lubet, S. 19, 30–1

Macauley, S. 3
McCain, John 60–1
McCoy, A.W. 82
McInnes, D. 106
MacKinnon, C. 118, 119, 120, 121, 122–3, 124, 125, 126–7, 128, 130, 131
MacNeil, W.P. 3, 12
Mahoney, M.E. 83, 85
Malinowski, B. 1
Mamdani, M. 126
Manderson, D. 19, 54
Mann, J. 65
Mapplethorpe, Robert 100–1, 107
market economy 13
Martin, F. 149
Mayer, J. 15, 16, 17, 54–5, 59–60, 61
medical personnel 79–81, 85

medieval and early modern Europe 20, 24
Melissaris, E. 14, 15
Melzer, A. 23
memory and echo 11–12, 25; active constitution of law 15–18; continuities: cultural representations as sites of recollection and resistance 12–15; contradictions: cultural representations and problems of modernity 21–5; longue durée of memory and tradition 18–21; paradox of technology 23–5; trust 21–3
Merry, S.E. 15
Meyer, L. 32
Miller, Tim *see National Endowment for the Arts v. Finley*
Miller, Toby 94, 101
Mintcheva, S. 108, 109
Mitchell, James 60, 61
Mohammed, Khaled Shaik 80
Mohr, R. 20–1
Moon, Sasha 149–50
Moore, S.F. 15
Moran, L. 12
Morgan, R. 122
Morocco 75
Morrell, D. 57–8, 59
Moses 33
Münkler, H. 126
music 24–5

National Catholic League of Decency 96
National Endowment for the Arts v. Finley 92–3; context to 99–102; decency in 102–7; governmentality, law and cultural policy 93–4; legal reasoning by analogy 106; long-term effects of decency clause 107–9; obscenity, decency and indecency in American law and culture 94–9
National Endowment for the Humanities 108
Native Americans 77
neoliberalism 3, 97, 107, 108
Nietzsche, F. 18–19
non-governmental organizations (NGOs) 116, 117, 119, 148
North Korea 60

Obaid, Thoraya Ahmed 116
Obama, Barack 107
obscenity *see* decency
Ochoa, C. 129
Ong, W. 24

INDEX

Oosterveld, V. 119
Osborn, J.J. 31, 34

Paglen, T. 87, 88
Papke, D.R. 33
paradox of technology 23–5
Parents' Television Council 15
Park, J.J. 146
paternalism 33
Peek, C. 142, 143, 146–7
Pell, George 100
performance artists *see* National Endowment for the Arts v. Finley
peroneal strike 63–4
Petrie, S.J. 94, 96
Phelps, T.G. 31
Phillips, J.E.S. 82
'Piss Christ' (Serrano) 99–100
pluralism, legal 14–15, 23
Poland 75
Popsopil, L. 15
pornography 121, 122, 123, 127, 128; *see also* decency
Post, R. 2
pre-sentence reports 143
prisoners: torture *see separate entry*; transgender *see separate entry*
privacy 137–8, 140
proportionality 144
prospective power of law *see* temporal horizons: law and fatherhood in *To Kill a Mockingbird*
Puar, J. 6, 109
Pugliese, J. 3, 5, 66, 73, 74, 76, 78

race and feminism 121, 122, 123, 126, 127
race and rape 120
race and transphobia 150
racism 73, 77, 105–7; temporal horizons: law and fatherhood in *To Kill a Mockingbird see separate entry*
Rahman, Gul *see* Salt Pit: torture and death of Gul Rahman
Rahman, Habib 75, 87
rape: rape and sexual violence in conflict zones *see separate entry*; transgender prisoners *see separate entry*
rape and sexual violence in conflict zones 115–18, 131; from *Kadic* to *Akayesu* 128–31; genocidal rape 116, 117, 123–31; international human rights and violence against women 118–21; US sex wars 121–3, 127
redactions 66, 73, 82–3, 86–8

redemptive constitutionalism 43–4
Redhead, S. 2
Rejali, D. 82
religious and ethnic difference *see* rape and sexual violence in conflict zones
Reno v. American Civil Liberties Union 99, 108
responsibility 19, 20, 22
Richie, Nicole 97–8
Rizzo, J.A. 79–80
Robertson, J. 140, 141, 142
Robinson, K.H. 105
Rocky films 59
Romany, C. 120, 128–9
Rosenblum, D. 139–40, 142–3
Rudacille, D. 140
Rumsfeld, D. 49, 65, 66, 67
Russia 60
Rwanda 115, 116, 117, 118, 119, 121, 126; *Akayesu* 118, 128, 130, 131

Sage, A. 100
Salt Pit: torture and death of Gul Rahman 72–3; advance pardons 83–5; beyond US jurisdiction: the Salt Pit 75–6; captive flesh 76–9; instrumental and gratuitous violence 73, 81–3, 85; laboratories of torture 79–81; redactions 73, 82–3, 86–8; torture law 74–5
Santner, E.L. 50
Sarat, A. 2, 3, 8, 12, 31, 93, 94
Sarkissian, Cher 97
Saunders, D. 2
Saunders, K.W. 95
Scarry, E. 18, 50, 51, 66, 67, 78
Schauer, F.F. 94
Schlag, P. 31
Schlesinger, J. 57, 64
Schlick, Austin 98
science 23
Sebald, W.G. 62
securitization 109
Sellers, P.V. 119
SERE (Survival, Evasion, Resistance, Escape) training 58, 59–62, 63, 65
Serrano, Andres 99–100, 101, 107
sex discrimination 123, 138, 155
Sex Wars, US 121–3, 127
sex work 154
sexual abuses at Abu Ghraib 64–5
sexual violence: rape and sexual violence in conflict zones *see separate entry*;

INDEX

transgender prisoners *see separate entry*
sexuality 121, 126, 127; sexual orientation 105–7, 121–2, 138; transgender prisoners *see separate entry*
Shaffer, T. 41, 44
Shamdasani, R. 148
Sheffield, C. 141
Sifton, J. 83–4, 86–7
Silbey, S.S. 3
Silverman, K. 33
Sinnot, M. 140
social media 109
social movements 101
Somerville, S.B. 106–7
Sontag, S. 66–7
de Sousa Santos, B. 1, 14, 15
sovereignty 13; *First Blood* 56, 59; torture and abuse 64, 65–7
Soviet Union 60
Spade, D. 138
Spillers, H.J. 77, 78, 79
Stallone, S. 57, 58
strip searches 154
subsidies to artists *see* decency
Sugarman, D. 15
Superman 19
Surnow, Joel 54–5
Sykes, G.M. 141

Taiwan 149, 154
Tamanaha, B. 20
Tarzwell, S. 154
teaching 22
technology, paradox of 23–5
television 25, 50, 65; '24' 15–21, 23–4, 25, 54–5, 63; *CSI* franchise 23; trust 21
temporal horizons: law and fatherhood in *To Kill a Mockingbird* 30–3, 42–4; coloured balcony 41–2; disobedient children/non-compliant jurors 37–41; 'what kind of man are you?' 34–7
Thailand 75
Thomas, H. 152
Thompson, E.P. 13–14, 15, 21, 23–4
time: 24/7 23–4
To Kill a Mockingbird 30–3, 42–4; coloured balcony 41–2; disobedient children/non-compliant jurors 37–41; 'what kind of man are you?' 34–7
Tofte, B.L. 99, 101
torture; '24' (television drama) 15–18, 54–5, 63; Bybee torture memo 51–5, 73, 74–5, 79, 82, 83, 84–5; CIA secret prison/black site *see* Salt Pit: torture and death of Gul Rahman; Convention against Torture (CAT) 51, 63; efficacy 16, 18, 61; entertaining torture, embodying law *see separate entry*; exceptionalism 16, 18, 54, 55; guilt 16, 17; medical personnel 79–81, 85; Office of Professional Responsibility (OPR) 73, 84; urgency 16, 17, 18, 50, 54, 55
transgender prisoners 136–9; burden of proof 147; civil law 140, 143, 148, 150–1, 153; Eighth Amendment 142, 144–7; *Farmer v Brennan* and deliberate indifference test 144–7; genitalia-based placement policy 142–3; Hong Kong 138, 147–55; in legal discourse 139–40; prison rape and 'sexual terrorism' 140–2; prison rape and transgender subjects 142
transsexualism 139–40
trust 21–3; social 149
Twain, M. 13–14
'24' (television drama) 15–21, 23–4, 25, 54–5, 63

United Kingdom 100–1, 153
United Nations (UN) 115–16, 117; Security Council 119
US Constitution: First Amendment 98–9, 102, 108; Fifth Amendment 61, 102; Eighth Amendment 142, 144–7; Fourteenth Amendment 61

V for Vendetta 19
Vance, C. 122
vandalism 100
video games 25
Vietnam War 57–8
visual artists *see* decency

Walzer, M. 33
war crimes 116, 119, 126
'war on terror' 16, 21–2, 56, 60, 65
Watkins 150
Weiss, C. 141
Wesley-Smith, P. 153
Wild West 19–20
Wildmon, Donald 100
Winter, S. 148, 149
Wolff, T. 22
Wood, E. 130
Woodward, B. 21–2
Wright, W. 19
writing 12, 24

INDEX

Young, A. 106
YouTube 109
Yugoslavia, former 116, 117, 118, 119, 120–1, 123–5, 126–9

Zarkov, D. 120, 125, 128

Zeigler, J.W. 101, 102
Zizek, S. 25

www.routledge.com/9780415826334

Related titles from Routledge

Legal Pluralism and Shari'a Law
Edited by Adam Possamai, James T. Richardson and Bryan S. Turner

Legal pluralism has often been associated with post-colonial legal developments especially where common law survived alongside tribal and customary laws. Focusing on *Shari'a*, this book examines the legal policies and experiences of various societies with different traditions of citizenship, secularism and common law. Where large diasporic communities of migrants develop, there will be some demand for the institutionalization of *Shari'a* at least in the resolution of domestic disputes. This book tests the limits of multiculturalism by exploring the issue that any recognition of cultural differences might imply similar recognition of legal differences. It also explores the debate about post-secular societies specifically to the presentation and justification of beliefs and institutions by both religious and secular citizens.

This book was published as a special issue of *Democracy and Security*.

July 2013: 246 x 174: 110pp
Hb: 978-0-415-82633-4
£85 / $145

For more information and to order a copy visit
www.routledge.com/9780415826334

Available from all good bookshops